7.50

RECOVERING POLITICAL PHILOSOPHY

SERIES EDITORS: THOMAS L. PANGLE AND TIMOTHY W. BURNS

PUBLISHED BY PALGRAVE MACMILLAN:

Lucretius as Theorist of Political Life
By John Colman

Shakespeare's Political Wisdom
By Timothy W. Burns

Political Philosophy Cross-Examined: Perennial Challenges to the Philosophic Life (forthcoming)
Edited by Thomas L. Pangle and J. Harvey Lomax

Also by Timothy W. Burns

After History? Francis Fukuyama and His Critics (editor)
Recovering Reason: Essays in Honor of Thomas L. Pangle (editor)
Political Philosophy: An Introduction (co-author, with Thomas L. Pangle)
Brill's *Companion to Leo Strauss' Writings on Classical Political Thought*
    (editor, forthcoming)
*Philosophy, History, and Tyranny: Re-examining the Debate Between Leo Strauss
    and Alexandre Kojève* (co-editor, with Bryan-Paul Frost, forthcoming)

SHAKESPEARE'S POLITICAL WISDOM

Timothy W. Burns

SHAKESPEARE'S POLITICAL WISDOM

Copyright © Timothy W. Burns, 2013.

First published in 2013 by
PALGRAVE MACMILLAN®
in the United States—a division of St. Martin's Press LLC,
175 Fifth Avenue, New York, NY 10010.

Where this book is distributed in the UK, Europe and the rest of the world,
this is by Palgrave Macmillan, a division of Macmillan Publishers Limited,
registered in England, company number 785998, of Houndmills,
Basingstoke, Hampshire RG21 6XS.

Palgrave Macmillan is the global academic imprint of the above companies
and has companies and representatives throughout the world.

Palgrave® and Macmillan® are registered trademarks in the United States,
the United Kingdom, Europe and other countries.

ISBN: 978–1–137–32085–8

A portion of Chapter One of this volume was published in *Shakespeare and
the Body Politic*, edited by Bernard J. Dobski and Dustin A. Gish (Lanham,
MD: Lexington Books, 2012). It is reproduced by the kind permission of
the Rowman & Littlefield Publishing Group.

Library of Congress Cataloging-in-Publication Data

Burns, Timothy, 1958–
        Shakespeare's political wisdom / by Timothy Burns.
            pages cm.—(Recovering Political Philosophy)
        Includes index.
        ISBN 978–1–137–32085–8 (alk. paper)
            1. Shakespeare, William, 1564–1616—Political and social views.
        2. Justice in literature. 3. Nobility in literature. I. Title.

PR3017.B87 2013
822.3'3—dc23   2012041570

A catalogue record of the book is available from the British Library.

Design by Newgen Imaging Systems (P) Ltd., Chennai, India.

First edition: April 2013

10 9 8 7 6 5 4 3 2 1

To Ilsa

CONTENTS

NOTE FROM THE SERIES EDITORS

Palgrave's *Recovering Political Philosophy* series was founded with an eye to postmodernism's challenge to the possibility of a rational foundation for and guidance of our political lives. This invigorating challenge has provoked a searching reexamination of classic texts, not only of political philosophers, but of poets, artists, theologians, scientists, and other thinkers who may not be regarded conventionally as political theorists. The series publishes studies that endeavor to take up this reexamination and thereby help to recover the classical grounding for civic reason, as well as studies that clarify the strengths and the weaknesses of modern philosophic rationalism. The interpretative studies in the series are particularly attentive to historical context and language, and to the ways in which both censorial persecution and didactic concerns have impelled prudent thinkers, in widely diverse cultural conditions, to employ manifold strategies of writing—strategies that allowed them to aim at different audiences with various degrees of openness to unconventional thinking. The series offers close readings of ancient, medieval, early modern, and late modern works that illuminate the human condition by attempting to answer its deepest, enduring questions, and that have (in the modern periods) laid the foundations for contemporary political, social, and economic life.

This study of five of Shakespeare's plays, while grounded in an implicit wide familiarity with Shakespeare scholarship, contemporary and traditional, speaks with unusual directness to students and teachers—of politics, philosophy, psychology, and religion, along with the Shakespeare-loving general public. The plays are interpreted with a subtlety and erudition and philosophic sophistication that will instruct and challenge literary scholars; but the approach is not academic or even quite "literary." Instead, the dramas are viewed afresh, from the perspective of a thoughtful reader encountering them, if not for the very first time, then with a newcomer's thirst to learn, arising from a candid but unsophisticated fascination with the moving depth and humanity of the dramas. The introduction affords a broad historical, philosophic, psychological, and religious context; then each of the chapters shows Shakespeare grappling with broad and deep existential questions, whose roots stretch back to classical antiquity and whose implications are timeless. Shakespeare's wisdom, this study contends, consists in truly revelatory analyses of agonizing tensions that pervade civic and religious and erotic and familial life—tensions that still underlie our lives but that have in some measure become obscured by the shallow distractions with which our contemporary society tempts us (and yes, by the abstractions that becloud much academic writing). This study of Shakespeare is thus an essay in civic-cultural retrieval that is, as such, simultaneously a penetrating and constructive critique of our contemporary civic culture.

INTRODUCTION

This book offers interpretations of five Shakespearean plays, with a view to the enduring guidance those plays can provide to human, political life. The subject matter of the plays I have selected for study is *political*. That is, the plays portray not only social but public activity, and hence go beyond the merely private or interior life—especially of love affairs—so favored by modern novelists. The plays have been chosen for their relentless attention to the questions that once were and may someday again become, or at least be recognized as, the heart and soul of politics: Who should rule? What is justice? What is nobility? What are the virtues that make one worthy of ruling, and the vices that make one unworthy of ruling? What virtues belong to a citizen or to a subject? What is the relation of these virtues and vices to human happiness? Do these virtues have the support of reason? Do they stem from a coherent understanding of human life? Does justice or any other virtue have divine or cosmic support?

That Shakespeare's plays should address these questions in a manner that rewards careful study should not be surprising. We are, as Nietzsche puts it, "the beast with red cheeks" (*Zarathustra*, Second Part, "On the Pitying"), feeling shame or guilt when we fail to live in accord with our opinions of what is just or noble or high—that is, in accord with our moral opinions. And political life was once the forum in which human beings argued and acted on those opinions. Prior to the emergence of modern political philosophy, political life was, more than in our day, a stage on which virtues and vices were made manifest, where office would show the man. Specifically human capacities that can develop fully only in the bright, moral light of public opinion could develop there, and be exercised as the spiritual core of one's being. And Shakespeare made human beings who lived that full political life the subject of many of his plays. For this reason his plays were able to shape the taste and prudence of generations of statesmen and citizens. Political men and women found in them vivid examples of political greatness, sound and flawed. Marlborough, for example, tells us that he formed his understanding of English history from Shakespeare alone, and Lincoln found *Macbeth* to be the perfect illustration of tyranny and murder.

If Shakespeare's plays are no longer a major part of the education of political men and women, we are arguably the worse for it. We are even likely to sense, as we read the plays, that political life in our time, even at its best, lacks the richness and the elevation of reflection that we meet on their every page. We who live in an age that we sense to be politically impoverished may thus stand, and become aware that we stand, in greater need of Shakespeare's plays than did citizens of past generations. They provide us with something that we are not likely to witness in our daily lives: moving and comprehensive pictures of the fate of tyrants, comprehensive portrayals of the character of good rulers and good regimes, of the relations of friends, and of the duties of citizens and subjects. The situations, customs, and beliefs of the characters we confront in the plays are, to be sure, particular: Brutus is Roman, Macbeth a Scot. Yet the wisdom that Shakespeare conveys through the characters' speeches and deeds is permanent and universal. His characters wrestle with some of the deepest moral and political problems that any serious human being is likely to confront. And as our minds are gradually opened by the plays, we come to realize that those problems remain with us, if in sometimes degraded contemporary forms; they are permanent problems. As we become engaged with the plays—as we are moved by them—we are compelled to reflect on those problems. A full awareness of them, such as Shakespeare provides, can then begin to assist us in understanding our own political and moral lives.

But to take advantage of the opportunity that Shakespeare thus affords us to better understand ourselves and our political life requires something unusual of us. We need to refrain from imposing contemporary thought on the plays; we must try to understand his characters as they understood themselves. And this is no easy thing. Like human beings anywhere, we are deeply shaped by the political regime in which we live, and so we have to make great efforts if we wish to be free of its particular limitations. As it happens, our political regime is to a remarkable degree formed by both modern political philosophy and contemporary social science. These two forces inhabit and form our opinions and thoughts. We often use words such as "ego," "identity," "culture," "rights," "self," "dysfunctional," "role model," and so on, without realizing their modern provenance, or questioning their adequacy to the phenomena they are meant to describe. While this can be the source of good things, it can impede us when we approach the works of a thinker like Shakespeare. Instead of becoming a guide for us, his plays can become trapped and bound by our own vocabulary and jargon, or confidently rejected by our conviction that we live in an enlightened era, one ready to condemn quickly any apparent lapse into the thought of the past. I have therefore attempted to approach his plays *naively*, without the sophistication that is lent to our thinking by contemporary social science and by modern political philosophy, as well as by contemporary literary criticism, which is so deeply shaped by postmodern philosophic thought. When it seemed appropriate, I have brought to bear on my interpretation ancient and medieval texts with which Shakespeare appears to have been familiar. To state this somewhat differently, modern political-philosophic doctrines have put a divide between us and these plays, and we need to set aside or bracket those doctrines if we are to understand the plays. I have in mind, for example, the doctrine of individual rights or claims that we have against one another; of human beings as seekers of something called "power"; of government being instituted by means of a social contract or the consent of the governed in order to secure those rights; of institutions that deliberately check and balance one another; and of technology that is fostered as a means for conquering an allegedly chaotic nature so that the resulting material plenty can be consumed and human misery and labor lessened. While all of these doctrines have had doubtless salutary effects on the lives of men and women in liberal democracies, the way of life that used to be called political is distinct from them, and Shakespeare can help us recover that life.

Political life proper is, as we see in *Julius Caesar*, something very close to what Aristotle describes in his *Politics*: it is distinguished not by obedience to the commands of a king, nor by a subrational attachment to one's country or fatherland, nor by an individualist concern to protect and advance one's rights. It is distinguished, rather, by common deliberation about what is good and bad, just and unjust, noble and base—by the exercise of our moral judgment about morally serious matters, and by the common, confirmatory honoring of what is considered worthy of our admiration and devotion, and dishonoring of what is considered base or contemptuous. Political life proper involves, then, careful cultivation by citizens of certain virtues, not as means to some other end, but as ends in themselves, and the selection or support of those who possess such virtues to lead or rule the community. It involves prudence, deliberation, rhetoric, and soul craft. And its central question, made abundantly clear in *Julius Caesar* though also in other plays, such as the opening ship-of-state scene of the *Tempest*, or in the exchange of Malcolm and Macduff in *Macbeth*, is: Who should rule? Who deserves to rule? What are those virtues that would qualify a human being to exercise leadership over others, and what are those vices that would disqualify one from such leadership and perhaps even disqualify one from life itself? Who can best guide us in common to our end as citizens, and hence who is everyone else morally obligated to obey?

Students of political philosophy are very familiar with the ways in which modern political philosophy has moved political life, and with it, the lenses that interpreters of Shakespeare train upon the plays, away from these questions. But the general reader may find the following brief sketch of the most salient features of this development helpful.

★   ★   ★

The question "who should rule?" disappears from political life, and with it the larger question of worth or desert, or distributive justice, with the emergence of the modern doctrine of prepolitical, inalienable natural rights. Thomas Hobbes, the author of that doctrine, lets us know that this is its intended effect by declaring that "the question 'who is the better man,' has no place in the condition of mere Nature." All human beings are by nature, Hobbes argues, in all politically significant respects, equal. "Or," he adds, significantly enough, "if Nature have made men unequal, yet...such equality must be *acknowledged*."[1] And the reason for this pretense of equality, he makes clear, is to end the warfare to which all titles to rule usually lead. Titles to rule are to be understood as "vainglorious," not articulations of any true worthiness but instead expressions of mere vanity—of that uniquely human but irrational joy that we take in what is eminent.[2] To replace all such claims, and found a way of life that does not permit them, Hobbes gives us his novel doctrine of natural rights, which limits the end or purpose of "government," and thereby brings into being something altogether new.

To grasp the significance of the new doctrine for political life, it is crucial to observe how Hobbes grounds the doctrine of natural rights, and the kind of society that adherence to those rights calls into being. Among the many and arbitrary passions that move us, Hobbes argues, is a fear of violent death. Since it is a compelling fear, we cannot help but be moved by it to secure ourselves. And if we cannot help but have and act on this fear, then we cannot be blamed for doing so. For justice does not ask the impossible of us. We have then a *right*, by nature and before entering civil society, to all things that we do in accord with this fear of violent death.[3] We each, that is, have a selfish but justified claim to all things. And in our effort to escape the sorry state in which each of us acts upon that unlimited right, we enter civil society. We agree to relinquish the natural right to all things in order safely to obtain some things that we all need, free of the threat of other human beings. We settle for those "rights," or claims, that we can all secure peacefully.

Establishing civil society on this basis—the securing of inalienable rights—means that we do not understand ourselves to set up a "ruler." We instead contract to set up a sovereign, who will represent us to ourselves, someone who will remind us of our fear of violent death and the need to avoid death by acting peacefully rather than vaingloriously. The person or group of people whom we set up to do so may have unlimited power but is radically limited in aim or intention: protecting rights and thereby securing peace, or ensuring the comfortable self-preservation of citizens. The sovereign *governs*; he does not *rule*. He acts as does a governor on a car or truck, not directing it toward an end but merely keeping our individual, subjective, arbitrary, passionate pursuits in line. We are left free (*liber*) to do in fact whatever the law does not forbid; the law does not and cannot legitimately command us to devote ourselves to an alleged common good, or to the cultivation of virtue or excellence. As Richard Kraut puts it, the purpose of individual rights is to protect us from the demands of others, or "carve out a zone in which one is relieved of the task of having to contribute to the common good."[4] The compelling fear is understood to grant to its possessor an unblamable claim universally valid and unlimited in the state of nature, and limitable only by the conclusions, the laws, that a fear-induced, calculative reason posits. Hobbes intends what he calls the law of man, *do not* do unto others, to replace the law of the gospels, *do* unto others. Devotion to the good of others as part of a whole to which one belongs is to give way to indifference to them.

That arena in which we are left by the powerful but indifferent sovereign to pursue our various desires comes to be called "society." There one may with equal dignity pursue the occupation one wishes, for there is no true or intrinsic worth to any activity or calling. "Worth" is rather determined in society by the selfishly driven forces of commercial markets. As Hobbes wryly puts it, in wartime generals are at a premium, but in peacetime, judges.[5] Worth or desert is determined, then, by what an aggregate of unfathomable others desire and happen to believe. The ordering principle of the liberal regimes is official indifference to the question of worth or desert, to titles to rule; they reject the pretense to know what is best for human beings and the need or authority to direct citizens in accordance with it. The unencumbered or autonomous self, as he has come to be called, who creates his own meaning as it suits him,[6] is the latest and by no means unintended result of the modern doctrine of "natural rights." That self and his overriding concerns is not found in Shakespeare's plays.

To approach Shakespeare's plays naively means above all to approach them without taking for granted the truth of these modern doctrines— with which, in however modified a form, we have all grown up—and with a conscious effort to avoid imposing them and their corollaries on the plays. It requires an openness to the plays as they present themselves to us, with all of their bracing challenges to our own presuppositions and assumptions about political life.

★ ★ ★

Few are likely to question the inclusion of *Julius Caesar, King Lear,* or *Macbeth* in a book devoted to Shakespeare's political wisdom. But *The Merchant of*

Venice and *The Tempest* may seem odd choices. Why not examine instead the history plays, since the history of England clearly supplies material that is political in the sense that I have indicated—presenting a protracted plot that turns upon successive changeover among those who exercised political authority, and thus one that turns upon the political question, "who should rule?" Do those plays not confront us with scenes in which opposed conceptions of authority, and of what constitutes the human good and hence of what the right order of society is, are contending for rule? This question is a serious one, and one to which I am compelled to provide at least the outline of a response.

The history plays allow Shakespeare to present his understanding of the ways in which Christianity transformed the natural political life of the British Isles, and how various spirited human beings attempted to wrest themselves free of Christian political theology. But for the same reason they present to us political life not in its full, natural, and robust form, but as it is in varying degrees suppressed or distorted by Christianity. This begins to become clear—one might say that it is even announced—in the first play of the second tetralogy, *Richard II.* Examining its opening scenes, one is struck by their strangely antique character: we see a king performing his duties, and we hear professions of love and allegiance to him; we see preparations for a joust, for a trial by combat replete with formulaic statements by the king's marshal and herald, and similarly formulaic chivalrous professions by the contestants. The scenes are extraordinarily conventional, like a medieval tapestry hung on a wall, and the overwhelming sense they convey is of static conventionality. What we witness in them is the England that in the nineteenth century became the object of romantic longing, the England that had in the fifteenth century given rise to Thomas Malory's retelling of the Arthurian legends. It is the England that Monty Python is so good at sending up, an England that is already antique to Shakespeare's contemporaries. The audience is made to witness the beginning of the end of medieval England—we see, for example, the very last domestic trial by combat that will ever take place in England.

But the opening scenes are strange in another way as well: a trial is called for by King Richard and is to take place. Bullingbrook, a nobleman, has accused Mowbray, another nobleman, of treason. And then? *Nothing* happens. Strong accusations of treasonous conduct against the king are proffered by both parties, but there is, amazingly, no trial at all, no sifting of evidence, no prosecution, no defense or rebuttal. If we compare this abortive trial with, say, the trial in *The Merchant of Venice*, or the equivalent of a trial held after Caesar is killed in *Julius Caesar*, with Brutus and Antony contending in their speeches for the hearts and minds of the citizens of Rome, we are struck by the complete *absence* here of any political deliberation.

Having heard the hot accusations of his subjects, King Richard simply asks the two parties, quite preposterously, to *reconcile*, something that the mutual attacks of their respective good names cannot possibly brook. And so Richard is compelled to agree to preside instead over a trial by combat: a joust, in which the winner will be declared in the right, and the loser in the wrong. That is, just as in trial by ordeal, not human reasoning but divine intervention—the intervention of the just, omnipotent, Christian God—is to demonstrate who is in the right. A similar trial takes place, to be sure, in the final act of *King Lear*. But it at least *takes place*, with a result that had to be explained politically. When the scheduled trial by combat is about to occur in *Richard II*, by contrast—in scene three—it is halted at the last minute, and Richard instead banishes both men from his realm, with no rational account of his action except the expressed need for the peace of the realm. We are thus left with the overwhelming impression of an amazing *absence* of any political action proper. That absence cannot help us, obviously, understand political life, and it arguably cannot even be seen for what it is without the account of political life that we receive in the plays that we examine here.

Political life proper is banished from England, moreover, not only in the opening scenes of *Richard II* but throughout the play, as human deliberation is usurped by the will of the divine. When threatened by Bullingbrook, Richard hopes that God and the angels in God's pay will come to his aid as the divinely anointed king, and then, when they fail to appear, he despairs of having anything in this world at all, and is prepared to die a monk with an unmarked grave. He is either God's anointed king, or he is nothing. There is no in-between. And the in-between is precisely the place of the political, of political action, just or noble action, action taken on behalf of a common good. Neither can Richard's antagonist, Bullingbrook, fully abandon the doctrine of divine right, despite the fact that it never stopped him from dethroning and finally requesting the murder of Richard. Bullingbrook is wracked by guilt: he never fully gets over having committed the sin of Cain, as he calls it, as much as he always wanted the outcome of that sin, that is, the throne. He vows to make a hard crusade to the Holy Land to atone for his sin—to abandon his kingship. At the same time, he cannot successfully appropriate the doctrine of divine right, as he must. (For in a Christian England the throne can be publicly usurped, Shakespeare suggests, but the sanctity of the throne cannot.) And so the deposing of Richard II, of God's king, rends the social fabric as much as it rends Bullingbrook's soul; the moral authority of the monarchy has suffered terrible harm, precisely because of Bullingbrook's ambition. Already at the end of *Richard II* we see the precariousness of Bullingbrook's authority, as news of a violent rebellion in Gloucestershire reaches the new king.

That Christianity is the cause of the suppression of political life in *Richard II* is made especially clear in the words and deeds of John of Gaunt, who will not avenge the murder of his brother Woodstock because he will not lift a hand against God's anointed king. Richard's title to rule clearly rests on this doctrine, and John of Gaunt's words are explicitly echoed by York, by the bishop of Carlisle, and of course by Richard himself: the king rules by God's will and must be obeyed, unquestioningly. Because of the doctrine of divine right, the central question of political life—who deserves to rule?—has become a nonquestion or a merely technical question (handled through lineage charts). It is a matter settled by God, not by men.

I have suggested that the relative dearth of political life in the history plays has its source in Christianity. The belief in the king having his title by a divine gift, and hence of the inviolability of that title, emerges out of Christianity—we may say in the briefest possible compass—for the following reasons. There is very little political or even legal teaching in the Christian scriptures. Jesus famously tells an inquirer to render under Caesar the things that are Caesar's and unto God the things that are God's, tells Pilate that his kingdom is not of this world, and tells his disciples that they cannot serve both God and mammon. St. Paul, who brought Jesus's teaching to the Gentiles, in Chapter 13 of the *Letter to the Romans*, tells his readers—who were, let us remember, living under the tyrant Nero—that they are obliged to obey their rulers. And the reason he does so, as Christian theologians like St. Augustine were compelled to spell out (see, e.g., *Letter* 138), is that the Christian good news or evangel tells us that this world is merely a pilgrimage to another and potentially better one, that the earthly city in which we live is a vale of tears, a testing ground for the heavenly city—that the merely apparent goods of this world are rightly given up or sacrificed for the sake of the heavenly city of God. Hence Augustine suggests that the moral virtues spoken of by Greek and Roman thinkers and statesmen are not genuine virtues at all but splendid vices, serving the end of personal honor and glory rather than the glory of God. Not proud pagan magnanimity but rather humility, he and other Christian theologians and divines argue, is the right disposition for human beings. Christians are counseled to follow Jesus's injunction to turn the left cheek when the right is struck, or to bear injustices patiently, in order lovingly to show their oppressors how little value there is in the worldly goods that they seek by their injustices to obtain, as compared with the true good of an upright soul and the heavenly reward of which it will make them worthy. They are told through the Sermon on the Mount that the poor in spirit, the sorrowing, the pure of heart, the meek, and those who hunger and thirst for holiness, are blessed—that their reward in heaven shall be great. Worldly rule comes therefore to be understood to have as its end not noble deeds, nor the common cultivation of pagan moral virtues, but the keeping of peace and the cultivation of heavenly or divine virtues; one can even be the best of Christians by living a life apart, in a monastery or even alone in the desert. Political life proper, the life of noble action, comes to be seen as a life of mere vanity. Whomever God has decided to put on the throne for his purposes belongs on the throne, and while that person ought to perform his or her duties as a good Christian, political office per se can have no intrinsic dignity to it apart from being given by the divine will.

A second effect of such Christian beliefs is that the attempt to abjure natural political judgment and sentiments in the name of adherence to Christian teachings turns decent men into mere neutrals, or neuters, as York calls himself in *Richard II*. (The would-be neutral in *King Lear*, Albany, by contrast never goes nearly so far.) Neutrals like York end up taking a position that is utterly impossible for politics, since others, who take up the cause of the oppressed, must necessarily cry out against them: why aren't you helping us?

A third effect is the elevation of women, who come to offer as it were a more natural reaction to events—one based on natural affection and senti-ments—than do the pious, ruling men. But in the history plays the women are led through these sentiments to utter despair. The Duchess of York cries out for mercy for her son over and against her husband's fanatic devotion to the new, divinely anointed king, to no avail. The Duchess of Gloucester, similarly, cries out for vengeance, but is led by the lack of any spirited, manly human action to die of despair: Richard's sins are the sins of God's vicar on earth, Gaunt tells her, so she should go and take up her complaint with God. "Yes, I'll do that," she bitterly responds, and *dies*. Thoughtful, politically inclined women cannot simply accept or endure the consequences of the prayer "thy will be done." In a world in which God demands patient endur-ance of wrong, and is moreover to receive all the glory for himself, death rather than life becomes desirable for such women.

In the subsequent history plays, moreover, Christianity continues to induce a suppression of the political and an attention to the question of how the political might be restored; it does not show us the political on its own, but investigates its fate in the face of Christian theology. Bullingbrook's heirs fail to wrest themselves free of that theology. We receive a foretaste of this in Act V of *Richard II*, when it is reported that Bullingbrook's son Hal, who will become King Henry V, has agreed to come to the jousting match at Oxford bedecked with the glove of a whore and ready to vanquish any-one, a defiance of courtly custom that clearly rankles Bullingbrook. For as King Henry IV, Bullingbrook attempts, unsuccessfully, to restore Christian custom and ceremony. As Henry V his son Hal attempts, on the other hand,

to eschew and overthrow ceremony, to solve his father's problem of legitimacy by enhancing his own personal prestige rather than by enhancing the
prestige of the monarchy. He creates through his deeds the astonishing spectacle of an apparent n'er-do-well turned into a man of great manly virtue;
he kills his rival Hotspur and thereby takes over all Hotspur's glory; finally,
he invades France, uniting nobles, clergy, and commoners in the glory of
conquest, and so grants himself title to rule through what he presents as the
miraculous victory of his band of brothers, the happy few, at the battle of
Agincourt. Henry V achieves even this, however, only through granting his
famous victory to *God* rather than to himself. For while he declares to his
soldiers, in his St. Crispin's Day oration, that if it be a sin to covet honor,
he is the most sinful man alive, he instructs his men after their great victory
to sing "Te Deum" and "Non Nobis Domine." We see, that is, a return of
the old problem: is it divine grace, or Henry's own merit, that is responsible
for this splendid victory? Is he a Caesar, as the people call him, prepared
to accept honor, or a David, who must be humble before God? We see in
him some political greatness, but ever accompanied by the doubting of the
proud love of honor that the Christian conscience must induce. It comes
as no surprise that Henry's more deeply pious son, Henry VI, loses France
and the civil peace. The successful break with Christian political theology,
and perhaps the beginning thereby of the end of Christian England, comes
only with Henry VIII, who not only overcomes the authority of the papacy
but goes down the path rejected by Henry V, taxing the clergy and creating thereby his own standing army of nobles. We are compelled to note,
however, that each attempt to break free of Christian theology comes at the
expense of justice and the public good. Bullingbrook's seizure of the throne
is imitated in the thievery of men like Falstaff, and Henry V's aggressive
war against France further unleashes acquisitiveness and competition for
rule at home: the War of the Roses, and Richard III's murderous would-be
Machiavellian tyranny. The influence of Christianity as a problem for the
political life of England, a cause of the diminution of that life, is an over-
arching theme of the history plays.

★   ★   ★

I have neglected the history plays, then, because they show us not so much
political life as its diminution and distortion. The effect of Christian theology is so very dominant in them, in its restriction of the political, that they
cannot afford us the access we need to premodern political life in all of its
richness and in its own problematic character. I have not, however, neglected
the political phenomena that Christianity brings into being. All of the effects
of the Christian political theology of divine right and humble submission

are, as it seems to me, captured sufficiently in *Macbeth*. The pious Macduff, for example, is deferential to the rule of the pious, consecrated king; he does little against injustice, being too "gospelled" (see *Macbeth* III.1.87) to seek vengeance and too reliant on "heaven" to save his family. In his absence Lady Macduff trusts that her innocence of wrongdoing will protect her, but realizes, too late, that this defense is woefully insufficient in this world. And it is only with the restoration of the non-Christian Malcolm that political life is restored to Scotland. But we see also in *Macbeth* the effect of Christian politics on a politically ambitious couple who stand as it were between Christian piety and the ancient, natural desire for rule. We see, that is, not the death of political life but its mutation into a new form: the tyrannical rule of bad Christians.

By demoting political life, Christianity and its emphasis on the next life can also have the effect of elevating private life, and hence of making possible a Christian commercial republic—through a corruption of Christian teachings. Christians who pursue wealth rather than the kingdom of God—as the gospels forbid them to do—can tell themselves that they do not love lucre but are instead intent on its acquisition for the sake of other good and even pious things. The Christian commercial republic of Venice is a perfect example of the outcome, and becomes thereby the setting for Shakespeare's play about a nominally Christian merchant, Antonio. His best friend Bassanio praises him, though not as a Christian but for having the noble heart of a *Roman*—of an Antony—and Shakespeare thereby signals that the play continues to examine political life proper. Antonio's understanding of the virtue he practices toward his friends resembles pagan munificence more than Christian charity. And Portia, Antonio's rival for Bassanio's love, though careful to keep up the appearance and traditions of her pious Christian father and his wishes, also displays virtues more appropriate to her Roman namesake. She too represents a revival of the ancient Roman soul, but in a woman who finds herself now so elevated, in a Christian world, that with a certain outward deference to its beliefs and a certain amount of deception, she can exercise the kind of political prudence that had been common among the men of Rome—though for a private end. Unlike the women of the history plays, Portia straddles two worlds, allowing us to see the political judgment of a Roman woman at work in a Christian world. And in her attempt to curb what she considers to be the troubling profligacy of her Christian husband's affection, she has more in common with the pre-Christian Shylock than with her beloved Bassanio. Her deft exploitation of Antonio's plight permits her to subordinate Antonio, and his affection for her husband, to her own marital bliss, and it is her "pagan" understanding of virtue and of law, here as in her actions with her many suitors, that directs her actions and permits her to succeed.

In the drama between her and Antonio we see Shakespeare's transposing of Roman virtue to the context of a Christian, cosmopolitan world, where it is able to secure the private happiness of a couple against the threats that that world poses to it. Political life, in its problematic character, stays alive here, if in a subdued or partially privatized manner, and in some ways becomes more revealing.

While the belief that a king has a sacred and inviolable title to rule by a divine gift belongs, as I argued earlier, to Christianity, it is not unique to Christianity; it is found, for example, in the Koran and in the Hebrew Scriptures. It is a grave mistake, moreover, to think that Christianity is unique in claiming that there is a divine law, or in claiming that there is divine support for human justice, for law, or for lawful rulers. That claim is common to virtually all premodern political life; one sees it in what the Melians say to the Athenians, for example, in Book V of Thucydides's history (5.105ff.). Shakespeare shows it to us even in *Julius Caesar* when he presents Casca's interpretation of the unusual weather in Rome as a divine omen. And in *King Lear* he presents to us a pagan king's disappointed faith that providential gods punish sinners and reward the just. *King Lear* presents us with the attempt of a thoughtful and remarkably resilient former king whose experiences drive him to an active doubt of divine law and move him, through the "tempest" of his mind, toward an understanding of "unaccommodated" man, man as he is by nature and without any of the artful conventions that support the belief in providential gods. Though Lear considers this path "madness," and while it does tax his wits beyond what they can bear, it leads him to what might have been a more serene life of acceptance of nature's necessities but for the murder of his beloved daughter. Edgar, whose youthful, supple soul enables him to benefit from an observation of Lear's hard experiences, is the better able to endure suffering himself and to provide a salutary, hopeful, pious version of the truth about human life to his father—and then to his future subjects.

In *The Tempest*, to which we turn in the conclusion of this study, Shakespeare presents us with the educational project of Prospero, who lost his rule of Milan through his philosophic study of the liberal arts and who endeavors, on behalf of his daughter and himself, to educate poetically— through their imaginations—those who come under his rule, in the manner that Edgar educates his father. Prospero attempts to teach Alonzo, Sebastian, and Antonio the existence of divine providence, through the magical apparition of a feast and of a harpy announcing delayed, fateful vengeance upon them for their crimes. He educates Ferdinand and Miranda through similar apparitions. And the education he provides them is informed by a hard-won awareness of the true place of human beings in an indifferent universe that must vanish as completely as do his poetic apparitions. I have thus chosen *The Tempest* to conclude this study for its attention to both the question of divine justice and the related, central question of political life, of who should rule. If Lear was ultimately unable to quiet the tempest in his mind, Prospero proved able to do so. And so too did Shakespeare, whose own educational "project" is, as the epilogue to this remarkable play suggests, indistinguishable from that of Prospero.

Divine justice is the deepest question explored in these five plays, and the one on which Shakespeare invites us most often to reflect. Does the universe care at all about human beings? Is there (are there) a God (or gods) and, if so, what does He (or they) ask of us? If not, does it make sense to be just? Does it make sense to treat certain deeds, like child-killing, as inherently evil or abhorrent, hence never to be countenanced? Does it make sense to pursue noble ends strictly and exclusively through noble means? To keep our hands clean and not think, like Pilate, that one can wash away guilt like dirt? Is there, in short, some genuine cosmic support for justice? Or is it rather the task of men like Edgar (in *King Lear*), Prospero (in *The Tempest*), and perhaps Shakespeare himself to foster the illusion that there is indeed the support for justice that our deepest hopes and longings would have there be, while at the same time realizing its problematic character? The question of divine justice and its demands is explored in *The Tempest* with a view not only to the primary question of who should rule but also—perhaps in response to that question—with a view to the poet's role in educating citizens. Bringing together in this way the major themes of all the plays, *The Tempest* offers a comprehensive and hence appropriate conclusion for this study.

★ ★ ★

I am indebted for my approach to Shakespeare's works to the ground-breaking work of Allan Bloom[7] and the outstanding and magisterial work of John Alvis.[8] Among other excellent studies with the same approach to Shakespeare's texts are those of Paul Cantor,[9] Mary Nichols,[10] David Lowenthal,[11] Leon Craig,[12] Jan H. Blits,[13] Nasser Behnegar,[14] and—most recently—Dustin A. Gish and Bernard J. Dobski.[15] In my effort to approach the plays naively, I have for the most part examined these thinkers' interpretation of plays other than those that are the object of this study, and so the reader will find very few references to their writings. Their guidance in my approach to the plays has, however, been considerable; whatever insights I might provide have been assisted by their direction, for which I am most grateful. I would also like to thank Fred Baumann, Devin Stauffer, Robert Bartlett, Wayne Ambler, Lorraine Pangle, and above all Stuart Witt, for their very helpful comments on earlier versions of these essays. Finally, I wish to thank Tom and Lorraine Pangle, with whom I have for the past several summers made a trip to the Shakespeare Festival in Stratford, Ontario, to see first-rate performances of these and other plays of Shakespeare. The Pangles' insights and provocative questions have been a great boon to my reflection on Shakespeare's political wisdom. Any mistakes are, of course, my own.

CHAPTER 1

JULIUS CAESAR: THE PROBLEM OF CLASSICAL REPUBLICANISM

Julius Caesar is Shakespeare's masterpiece. In it he brings all of his gifts to bear on the problem that Aristotle presents as confronting political life at its peak—the problem of the outstandingly virtuous individual, and the dilemma that his rule poses to the life of virtue.[1] In artfully presenting the drama of this problem as it confronted and was faced by noble Romans, Shakespeare affords his readers the means to reflect seriously on an issue that contemporary politics—the politics of indirect governance of allegedly sovereign individuals—veils from us. Our particular historical circumstances make the play's probing drama more vital than ever to our understanding of the human condition.

★   ★   ★

We are confronted with the elements of the problem in the opening scene, in the actions and words of Flavius and Murellus, tribunes who prove in their relation to the commoners to represent two sides of the republican principle. Shakespeare's use of them is daring inasmuch as they will never be seen again, their disappearance only remarked upon darkly in a subsequent scene. They are upset with the commoners for being idle and well-dressed on what is not a holy day but a laboring day. But when Murellus questions one of the commoners about his activities, he is unable even to understand him, despite the commoner's effort to speak as Murellus would speak. The distinction between classes, and especially between the common people and all others, is prominent, and so then is the question of what Rome's leaders have done and should do with and for the people, the many, in the republic. Caesar, we will learn, has been executing a plan for the commoners.

The cobbler, leader of the parade of commoners, has however his own plan. Through a series of puns we learn that he is a "mender of soles," who leads the crowd into activities that cause their soles/souls to be in need of mending. Were the setting a Christian nation and the man a priest, we would have here a biting forerunner of Nietzsche's presentation of the Christian priest as one who makes the souls of his flock sick in order to tend them. But this is pre-Christian Rome, and a priest is not yet the chief leader of the commoners. Another person is, and he seems by some to be now considered a god; the holiday (in fact, the Lupercal) is being celebrated to honor him. In the cobbler's comic banter we get a whiff, in other words, of the Christian leadership to come, or a brief look at the shore to which Shakespeare bids adieu as he heads back to pagan Rome, where we find leaders of quite a different stamp—not proclaiming human guilt and a need to confess sins, nor counseling humility and meekness but instead pride and strength, bent themselves on achieving honor as a confirmation of their worth.

As we are immediately made to see, however, the mature and robust political life that characterizes leadership in the Roman republic is problematical. Murellus delivers (at 1.1.32–55) a harangue of the commoners in which he upbraids them for infidelity to, or loss of enduring gratitude for, Pompey. He bids them be gone, to run to pray that the gods might intermit a plague to punish their ingratitude. His warning of divine punishment seems as heartfelt as it is harsh. Flavius, on the other hand, is poetic rather than pious in his brief address to the commoners. And his poetic appeals are of a worldly but noble sort: he invites his "good countrymen" to weep into the Tiber their lowest stream of tears, so that it will end up "kissing the exalted shores [of Rome]." When he then asks Murellus for a disrobing of the images (1.1.65), Murellus shows that he fears any such impious act. Flavius insists, however, that the disrobing is a political matter, and that the vulgar must be driven from the streets. The reason he then gives for *his* objection to Caesar's popularity differs strikingly from Murellus's reason. Its basis is a noble pride: he does not wish to live in "servile fearfulness," as he would were republican rule of equals to be lost. He says nothing of Pompey—whose rule would, of course, be as objectionable as Caesar's in soaring too high.

We see from the start, then, a principled division in the political class, even among members of the tribunate. The two tribunes embody each a different principle of republican rule. On one hand the pious Murellus objects not to the imperial rule of Pompey but to Caesar's ascent, precisely because it came at the cost of Pompey and his sons, to whose preeminence he shows no aversion and for whose just deeds on behalf of Romans he demands enduring gratitude from the people—a demand supported, in his mind, by divine justice. He demands that Romans accord the virtuous their just deserts, and since Pompey was most virtuous, honoring his successful opponent is unjust.[2] Flavius, on the other hand, wishes to take action against Caesar on opposite grounds. When he looks up it is not to another human being nor to gods, but to *Rome*, the exalted city, whose members are equal. He would pluck the feathers from Caesar's wings lest Caesar soar above the view of man and keep "us," all others, in servile fearfulness. Flavius would rather die than submit to the rule of another man, be it of Pompey, Caesar, or any other. However beneficent their rule, he implies, it would render him and every other Roman a kept man, and destroy the legal equality on which depends the freedom that characterizes republican political life.

While Murellus stands, then, for just desert and hence for the rule of the most deserving, Flavius stands for freedom grounded in a rough equality of virtuous men—though a freedom, as is here manifest, that depends on those men not exploiting the desires of the commoners in order to gain authority over other virtuous men. These two principles of justice, honoring the most virtuous and equality in virtue, which guide republican Rome, sit together uneasily. Their tension drives the action of the play, disclosing a problem within justice that rises to the surface when political life produces an outstandingly virtuous human being.[3]

⋆ ⋆ ⋆

Having thus introduced the central problem to which the play is addressed, Shakespeare gives us, in scene two, our first of only three scenes in which Julius Caesar appears. The paucity of Caesar's lines compels us to examine them closely if we are to understand the title character. But we must first pause and puzzle over the fact of this paucity. Most of the play involves not Caesar's actions and words but a failed conspiracy and its aftermath, a conspiracy to eliminate him and thereby restore the republic that his rule threatens. Caesar is killed, but others take his place and defeat the conspirators. He lives on, as it were, in Antony and (eventually) in Octavius, or "Augustus Caesar." And of course he lives on much longer, in the titles of subsequent Roman emperors (made permanent in Rome by Vespasian) and rulers elsewhere who aspired to his greatness: Czar, Kaiser, Qaisar-e-Rūm, and so on. "We have no king but Caesar," shouts the crowd of an outlying province to Pontius Pilate, 74 years after Julius Caesar's death. Subsequent political life and perhaps all political life seems haunted by, or in some way to point to, Caesar as its peak and culmination; it points to the virtuous ruler who, being without peer, deserves to rule alone, and to an ambition to emulate his rule. Yet if he rules alone, he destroys political life properly speaking; he casts a shadow over the virtuous activities of others, who are

unable to rule or to have their chance, their place in the sun, their opportunity to manifest virtue and thereby fulfill themselves through service to
their city or country. Can it really be just, then, that such a one rule? We
thus see a possible reason for the play's title: Caesar is as much a central,
problematic phenomenon of political life as he is a historical character or
actual person, and as such deserves our attention.

The first word out of the mouth of the man Caesar is a call to his wife:
"Calpurnia!" But the call is not an indication of any primary concern for
his private life. On the contrary, it is a summons; Caesar's verbs are all in
the imperative. Wanting an heir, he summons his wife to enact a superstitious fertility ritual connected with the chariot race he is observing. As we
will learn later, his apparent superstitious proclivity is a recent development,
corresponding to his rise in public esteem. In his subsequent lines (1.2.13f.)
Caesar gives more orders and refers to himself (when speaking to soothsayers) twice in the third person. His self-presentation is that of a man who
is himself bigger than human, or who is aware and wishes that his public
deeds hold at least highly unusual significance for their observers. And those
around him appear in their remarkable deference to accept this, though the
broader context (of the play and of the Roman plays collectively) makes
this deference somewhat suspicious. We see and hear Antony, who appears
utterly subservient, hearing and obeying, slavishly—yet this man will himself
rule half the world, to be pulled away from that rule only by the beautiful
Cleopatra. We see likewise Casca, who appears as another acolyte of Caesar
but who is in fact ready to join a conspiracy against him, and who is known
by at least one shrewd observer to adopt a simple or even a rustic simpleton's
demeanor in order to maintain an inner freedom.

And we immediately learn, from a private conversation that takes place
while the public actions of Caesar continue in the background (1.2.25–50),
that a deep discontent among Rome's foremost citizens has set afoot the
tentative beginnings of a conspiracy against Caesar. Cassius for some time
has wanted to approach Brutus, but has been held back by Brutus's behavior. He has found Brutus stubborn and strange to his "friend that loves
him." He suspects, we gather, that Brutus suspects him. (Caesar for his part,
as we'll see, does suspect Cassius.) But Cassius seems to have been mistaken
about Brutus, who has been out of sorts indeed but for a different if related
reason:

> Vexed I am
> Of late with passions of some difference,
> Conceptions only proper to myself,
> Which give some soil, perhaps, to my behaviors;
> But let not therefore my good friends be griev'd

(Among which number, Cassius, be you one),
Nor construe any further my neglect,
Than that poor Brutus, with himself at war,
Forgets the shows of love to other men. (1.2.39–47)

Brutus is torn by some contradiction, which he doesn't state but which Shakespeare gradually unfolds for us in Act I.

Reassured, Cassius begins his attempt to win Brutus over. Why he must do so becomes clear from the adjectives he uses to describe his friend: "Gentle Brutus...noble Brutus." Cassius offers to be a mirror for Brutus's soul, to supply him with self-knowledge, to show him his hidden worthiness. He fulfills the offer by first telling Brutus how highly others think of him and of how they, groaning under this age's yoke, have wished that noble Brutus had the eyes to see the reflection of himself in them or in their longing for a savior. Brutus is the savior of suffering Romans. Can he not see this? Sensing what Cassius has in mind, Brutus warns him: it is not in me, and it is dangerous. Cassius must therefore establish his trustworthiness: he is not fickle or false when he declares his love or friendship, but is true. Brutus makes no reply.

For at this point the first shouts of the crowd are heard, and Cassius uses them in his efforts. "I do fear," Brutus remarks, "the people choose Caesar for their king." Cassius replies: "Ay, do you fear it? / Then must I think you would not have it so" (1.2.80–82). Here, then, is the first disclosure of the contradiction that has been troubling Brutus. He loves Caesar, which bespeaks Caesar's worthiness of devotion, yet he would not have him king. This trouble reflects another in himself:

But wherefore do you hold me here so long?
What is it that you would impart to me?
If it be aught toward the general good,
Set honor in one eye and death i' th' other
And I will look on both indifferently;
For let the gods so speed me as I love
The name of honor more than I fear death. (1.2.83–89)

If Cassius's plan with respect to Caesar is for the general good, the common good, Brutus will be indifferent to death or honor. Or rather, as he restates it, to death; he loves the name of honor *more* than he fears death. The tension between the first and second statements is not insignificant. It reflects a great difficulty for a noble man: he must be prepared, as virtue demands, to sacrifice even his life for the common good, yet would such a one be willing to sacrifice his *honor*, his virtue, for the common good? Can the honor that confirms the nobility of sacrificing oneself for the common good—can that common good—demand that he give up his virtue, that he become vicious? How could that be an honorable thing? And if it is, can a noble person do it? Or is his honor and virtue not emphatically *his* virtue, which he will not give up? But then is not the noble person really self-concerned, after all? Is there a genuine common good? Or does the city instead simply afford men the opportunity to obtain honor by manifesting their virtue? Surely in standing ready to serve what he holds to be the common good, Brutus is moved by the most just motive there is. His devotion to it, as he senses, makes him trustworthy, worthy of rule and of the people's affection. But if his fundamental concern is with his own virtue and the honor that confirms it, then the deep devotion he believes himself to have, and to make him worthy of honor, is something he does not actually possess. (Cf. Aristotle, *N. Ethics* 1123b16ff.) His position would be similar to that of a lover who professes devotion to his beloved's happiness but who would in truth be disappointed to learn that his beloved is quite happy when on holiday with others, since the lover wishes to be *himself* the source of that happiness. With such a dilemma besetting the moral life, it is little wonder that the noble Brutus is troubled.

Cassius attempts to win over the troubled Brutus by persuading him that Caesar is not worthy of ruling as he does. The attempt brings to light another aspect of the dilemma that besets both citizens. Cassius argues first against awe or reverence of Caesar, who is merely human. Freedom, self-rule, having a share in rule, requires a recognition of a fundamental equality. Caesar eats, and so on, like all humans, does he not? Both Brutus and Cassius can endure cold "as well as he," no? If Caesar is a god, on the other hand, that makes Cassius a slave, a "wretched creature," created as it were by Caesar; he'd be no more than what *Caesar* wants. Honor must be roughly equal, in other words, if there is to be freedom.

Yet Cassius's examples immediately and as it were inevitably move from showing Caesar's *equality* in virtue to revealing his *deficiency* in virtue. The claim against Caesar's outstanding superiority leads to examples of Caesar's comparative deficiency: I, Cassius, went into the Tiber and bid Caesar follow, and ended up saving him when he cried for help, carrying him on my shoulder like Aeneas. Cassius beautifully employs a Virgilian metaphor to make himself, over and against Caesar, appear to be the true emulator of the epic founder of Rome (1.2.112).[4] Caesar is by contrast a feeble man, less worthy than Cassius. He is even a coward, crying like a girl when sick. And this wimp, Cassius protests, is being called a god? An immortal? Cassius expresses astonishment in the end not that *a* man should "bear the palm alone," but that *such* a man should do so. He thinks, in other words, that a human being of superior virtue would indeed deserve to do so—that perhaps he himself deserves it—but Caesar is certainly not such a one. The movement of his argument indicates that as a title to rule, virtue points inevitably not to *equality* in rule among the virtuous but to the rule of the most virtuous simply, the virtuous *without equal*, the virtuous par excellence.

Yet another shout suggests that more honors are being heaped on Caesar, and they visibly trouble Brutus. Cassius is reminded by the shouting to turn back to his initial republican appeal to a rough *equality* in virtue, and he makes the appeal directly to Brutus. How can it be just that *one man* rule?

> Why, man, he doth bestride the narrow world
> Like a Colossus, and we petty men
> Walk under his huge legs, and peep about
> To find ourselves dishonorable graves.
> Men at some time are masters of their fates;
> The fault, dear Brutus, is not in our stars,
> But in ourselves, that we are underlings.
> Brutus and Caesar: what should be in that "Caesar"?
> Why should that name be sounded more than yours?
> [...]
> When went there by an age since the great flood
> But it was fam'd with more than with one man?
> When could they say, till now, that talk'd of Rome,
> That her wide walks encompass'd but one man?
> Now it is Rome indeed and room enough,
> When there is in it but one only man. (1.2.135–143, 152–157)

Not the rule of an *unworthy* man, but monarchy per se is a disgrace to the rest of the Roman citizenry. Surely there is more than one virtuous man in Rome, republican Rome. Cassius completes his case with an appeal to Brutus's namesake, who drove out the Tarquin monarch. And now, finally, Brutus says that he trusts Cassius loves him, while indicating that he nevertheless has other thoughts about this matter that he will relate later. He concludes his response with his own echo of an epic line, comparing himself implicitly to Achilles—who would rather be a peasant ("villager") than be a king ("a son of Rome") in Hades ("under these hard conditions"). He bids Cassius chew on this; he won't yet be moved further.

The echo is well worth chewing on. It suggests that Rome under Caesar is a hell, but the echo's power comes from the fact that the life of a peasant on earth was utterly unattractive to the live Achilles—that he was one who wished to be a *king* on earth. And so it forms an appropriately ambiguous end to an exchange that has brought out more clearly the dilemma that Brutus and indeed each and every noble Roman confronts. Cassius's two appeals to the (quite different) republican principles of justice have had some effect, but when thought through they bring out the fundamental dilemma. His initial and final appeals are to the principle of freedom based upon a rough equality of worth or virtue: all have sufficient virtue or capacity to deserve self-rule, or are worthy to belong. But if all are equal, why not let the commoners rule too? If they are *not* worthy of rule, if instead only the *virtuous* should be honored with rule, then should not the *most* virtuous rule most, or "bear the palm alone?" Does not the most virtuous most deserve to rule? Yet that rule would necessarily deprive others of their share of the noble, their opportunity to shine. It would reduce them to dwarves under the feet of a Colossus. It would therefore be opposed *necessarily, inevitably*, to the common good. Not tyranny but *monarchy*, the rule of the one most virtuous, is at odds in this way with justice. Two parts of justice seem to be at odds, then, with themselves, and their contradiction points, as it had in the speech of Brutus, to the self-concern even of the noble lovers of freedom and virtue.

★   ★   ★

As Caesar and his cohort return to the stage, we see that all has not gone well for them, though we do not quite know why. According to Brutus Caesar is angry; the rest look scolded or reproved. Calphernia is pale; Cicero, fiery. In this situation Caesar notices Cassius, and calls Antony's attention to his "lean and hungry look." Cassius, Caesar implies, thinks too much; Caesar wants fatter, satisfied men. When Antony counsels Caesar not to fear noble Cassius, Caesar offers additional astute observations on Cassius's perpetual dissatisfaction, attributing it to his being a-music, to being filled with ambition and unable to look up to any man. Caesar at the same time implies that he himself is a man, not a god. Yet he ends his remarks with another third-person reference to himself, emphatically using his name, Caesar, to as it were personally elevate or crown his public self: "Always I am Caesar. I don't fear; I rather tell what is to be feared." That he himself is not moved by fear seems preposterous, a too brave show or boastful in its claim to a divine or quasi-divine soul. Yet Caesar shows simultaneously that he is quite aware of at least his human, physical infirmities: he is deaf in one ear. Is it possible that he knows full well what he is doing in acting the part of a superhuman, either for his own sake or that of Rome, or both? Is it possible that he wishes to overcome the problem we have indicated by turning himself into a god?

★   ★   ★

When Casca speaks, reluctantly, with Brutus and Cassius, it is in the guise of a country bumpkin, with cockney idioms, comically vulgar references, and a boast of his capacity to see shrewdly through attempts to pull the wool over his and the people's eyes. Ceasar, Casca claims, wanted the crown, but swooned in a seizure. It's all theater to Casca; while the crowd swallowed whole Caesar's "I am at your mercy" boilerplate, he for his part didn't believe a word of it. Brutus remarks that Caesar came away sad from the scene, and we learn Casca's view that the refined Cicero was actually amused by it. We learn too of the death of Murellus and Flavius, who have been "put to silence," somehow, in what was a dark, official act. In a final piece of vulgarity, Casca insults Cassius while accepting his invitation to dinner, and Brutus, after Casca's departure, remarks on Casca's decline from a refined man to a rube. Cassius, who sees through Casca's guise, reassures Brutus that it is all a veil, designed to hide Casca's superiority and the truth of his judgments. Caesar was right: Cassius is indeed a careful observer of men, a great reader of them. But what does this say of Brutus? While not altogether naive, he does seem to have more of the simplicity that goes with nobility. Suspiciousness would be as beneath him as would a lack of frankness. But such virtue clearly comes at a price, and he must in any event now stoop to conspiracy, before it is too late.

Cassius concludes the scene with a soliloquy that reveals his attempt to seduce Brutus precisely by appeals to his nobility. He will work the "honorable mettle" from that to which it is already disposed. He will use Brutus's devotion to honor to turn him into a conspirator—with false letters from Romans pleading for him to act. Cassius stoops to a deception to which Brutus never would, exploiting thereby Brutus's virtue. He rightly calculates that when Brutus believes he is called not only by Cassius but by many Romans to become their savior, he will act.

★ ★ ★

As the conspiracy proceeds in the act's final scene, we see the true Casca, in exchanges with Cicero, Cassius, and Cinna, about the gods and alleged portents or omens. The first is most remarkable. As Shakespeare well knew, Cicero was not only an outstanding statesman but also a philosopher, and Cicero's brief appearance provides us with a standard against which to assess Brutus and Cassius, each of whom claims later to be a member of a philosophic sect. In his exchange with Cicero we see Casca's speech change from cockney to poetry, and he appears quite pious. The storm raging overhead is, he suggests to Cicero, from the gods, who send punishment for hubris. Cicero's reaction to this claim is a polite rebuke: "Why, saw you anything more wonderful?" Undeterred, Casca describes a series of prodigies and upbraids Cicero, who would call the occurrences "natural" (1.3.30). They are, Casca insists, portents or signs. Cicero agrees that the times are strangely disposed, but retorts that the weather has nothing to do with that. He gently suggests that Casca's pious interpretation of the weather is traceable to his desires and fears rather than to anything in the things themselves. He does, however, learn from Casca that Caesar will be coming to the capitol tomorrow. Gently amused by claims about portents, Cicero is keen to know the particulars of Roman political life.

When Casca meets Cassius, we see another attitude toward the storm and hence toward the gods. Cassius bares his breast to the storm, daringly, and reinterprets its meaning for Casca as a warning to brave men about Caesar. He in this way begins to bring Casca into the conspiracy, and adds a significant teaching about suicide: "Cassius from bondage will deliver Cassius. / Therein, ye gods, you make the weak most strong; / Therein, ye gods, you tyrants do defeat" (1.3.90–92). This is why some are, he suggests, fit to be slaves: they submit to tyrants rather than kill themselves, disclosing their cravenness. So it is now with the Romans, who have become sheep and thereby made Caesar a wolf. The gods, it seems, wish men to display their manliness, which they can always do. This is all Casca needs to hear. Declaring that he is not a slave or a snitch, he proposes that they kill Caesar, and thus joins the conspiracy. And like Cassius, he sees the importance for the enterprise of winning over Brutus, to whose house Cinna is about to bring letters written by Cassius:

> O, he sits high in all the people's hearts;
> And that which would appear offense in us,
> His countenance, like richest alchymy,
> Will change to virtue and to worthiness. (1.3.157–160)

The honorable Brutus is not only trustworthy but, being gentle rather than harshly spirited or contemptuous, he stands high in the opinion of the people, who now have a great hand in the destiny of Rome. For Caesar has brought them, as we've seen, from the side of Pompey over to his side. Brutus's place among the conspirators will assure that the conspirators' deed appears to the people public-spirited. There would be no need for such an appearance, of course, if the deed were manifestly public-spirited. That it is not—that Caesar is arguably deserving of rule rather than of death—is precisely what is keeping Brutus from joining the conspiracy. The success of the conspiracy will depend entirely on him and therefore on the success of his resolution of the dilemma that Caesar represents.

Act II

Brutus's attempt to think his way through to the resolve to kill Caesar, in his "It must be by his death" soliloquy, begins with the observation that he has no personal cause to attack Caesar but, again, would act "for the general" cause or good. That cause would seem to be determined simply by the fact that Caesar "would be crown'd." For his crowning would deprive others, as we have seen Cassius argue, of their share of the noble. Yet Brutus does *not* address that problem. He turns instead to the more limited question of how Caesar being crowned "might change his nature." Let Caesar become king and he may become, like an adder, dangerous, abusing his greatness. He may "disjoin remorse from power," that is, become unjust or (to use a later term) lose his conscience. Caesar would have to change from what he is, that is, for him to become a tyrant. As Brutus admits, "to speak truth of Caesar, / I have not known when his affections sway'd / More than his reason" (2.1.19–21). Caesar as Brutus knows him is fair or impartial, uncorrupt. Why, then, kill him? But it commonly happens, he notes, that those who ascend are corrupted. So it *may* happen in Caesar's case, and "lest it may, prevent."

Yet Brutus knows that this case for a preemptive strike isn't sound. "The quarrel / Will bear no color for the thing he is." Caesar is a human being, and an honorable one. "Therefore, fashion it thus …" Call him a serpent in an egg; color it in this way. But this again demonstrates that Caesar is not what he would have to be for the argument to be convincing, and even why it cannot be convincing. We may well kill serpents in the egg, if we have reason to fear them. We don't kill human beings who just *may* do bad things to us, for the same reason that we don't praise and blame serpents. Human dignity or worth rests on the recognized human capacity to choose good from bad and just from unjust. A presumption of a moral freedom stands under our praise and blame of human actions. To act against Caesar at this point, with a view to his future evil deeds, would be to deny human freedom; it would require that Caesar be seen as compelled, like a serpent, to act viciously. It would be to punish Caesar before he commits any crime, and also to call those crimes innocent. Brutus, in other words, by changing Caesar in speech or imagination into a serpent in an egg instead of waiting to see if Caesar will "change his nature" when crowned, does the latter himself before hand, lest Caesar be crowned. Rather than change his understanding of virtue, Brutus would magically change the nature of Caesar.

Brutus will thus not permit the office to show the man. Caesar, who by Brutus's own admission most deserves honor in Rome, is to be killed, on the ground that the political power that he would acquire would make him *potentially* dangerous. Caesar might, for example, begin doing things like killing good people whom he in fact merely fears or suspects may do wrong. He may begin treating people like …serpents. The problem with Brutus's reasoning is too obvious to miss. The preemptive strike he would launch could never be just, since it violates the very heart of justice by substituting necessity for human freedom.[5]

That Brutus is aware of this great difficulty—that his self-conscious attempt to "color" the matter and change the fact of Caesar's humanity has not really persuaded him—is made clear as the play proceeds. In Act IV, for example, in his dispute with Cassius over whether to overlook their soldiers' small injustices in wartime, Brutus's position turns on the important and indisputable point that for their war to make any moral sense and to be therefore worthwhile, they must themselves remain just—that noble ends require noble means. And in the course of making this case, Brutus bids Cassius

> [r]emember March, the ides of March remember:
> Did not great Julius bleed for justice' sake?
> What villain touch'd his body, that did stab,
> And not for justice?" (4.3.18–21)

Brutus's argument at this point assumes that Caesar had *already* committed injustices before being stabbed. And when about to expire at his own hand in Act V, Brutus bids Caesar or his spirit "be still: / I kill'd not thee with half so good a will." Brutus has never convinced himself of the justice of a preemptive strike.

But even had Brutus been able to do so, the great difficulty that lies behind his trouble would not have been overcome. We may even say that his extended reasoning about the need for a preemptive strike is no more than an effort to avoid that true difficulty. For that difficulty is *not* that Caesar might turn from a monarch into a tyrant. The true difficulty is that monarchy, a *virtuous* Caesar's rule, would still be at odds with the common good. Brutus's turn to the narrow or special problem of the likelihood of Caesar becoming unjust in his rule—becoming tyrannical or unconscientious—is a desperate attempt to avoid this larger or true difficulty. Brutus permits himself to address a problem that includes a consideration of both Caesar's (present) virtue and the possible oppression of the Romans through his rule—a problem, that is, that contains the two essential elements of the real problem, and to this extent can pose, in his mind, as the real problem, of which he is aware but which he does not wish to face. Shakespeare points to this true problem and Brutus's dodging of it by surrounding the soliloquy with instances of Brutus ordering around his slave, Lucius, who hasn't even the normal human privilege of sleep. Lucius's master is awake, so must he be, to take orders, one of which is contradicted by the next, as Brutus's own perceived needs change. Brutus needs Lucius for his leisure, if he himself is to engage in an honorable political life, but this means that Brutus needs more than virtue. He needs "equipment." Yet the equipment is and must be another human being, whose good is not by any means clearly served by taking orders from his lord. Brutus is, of course, not without concern for Lucius's good, but that good is clearly subordinate to his own. Lucius stands to Brutus as all Romans would stand to Caesar's rule. Yet Brutus accepts his own monarchic rule over Lucius as just. He even understands the human mind's rule over the body, or "mortal instruments," to be absolutely monarchical, that is, to be rule by order or decree: when the body and mind are "in council," he states, it is like an "insurrection" in "a little kingdom" (2.1.61–69, and cf. 4.3.30–34). Brutus is not in principle opposed to monarchy, then; he even considers it, in some sense, the best form of rule. Still, perhaps the justice of political or public life, of "Rome," is quite different from that of the private life of an individual or household. When reading one of the letters tossed into his room—the only one whose contents we hear—Brutus does suggest as much, addressing as he does the grave matter of Caesar being a monarch and Rome standing "in awe of one man." He addresses it, however, only by remembering his ancestors' noble overthrow of the Tarquin, "when he was called a king." He provides no other reason to oppose monarchy, no any reason why his ancestors' actions shouldn't have been called an "insurrection." We could say that Brutus implicitly agrees with Cassius that a monarch would deprive all others of rule and hence of the opportunity for virtue, but the implicit character of this agreement allows him to avoid the fact that one aspect of justice is at odds with another, with the deserved rule of Caesar, and hence that justice contradicts itself. Brutus has, in short, studiously avoided facing this problem. As we will see, it will continue to haunt him, and this along with the monarchic disposition and great rhetorical abilities of Antony will bring down the conspiracy and with it, the republic.

★   ★   ★

The lack of capacity to face squarely the dilemma we have sketched, and that still haunts him, helps to explain the otherwise strange-seeming behavior of Brutus in the first meeting of the conspirators. Cassius asks the conspirators to swear an oath of allegiance to one another. Brutus objects to this with a very long harangue against oaths (2.1.114–140). The present suffering of Romans should be sufficient, he argues, to move them to act; no fear of divine sanction for failing to act as they promise is called for. Real men don't need oaths, which are used only by the weak and deceitful. "Let no oath stain the steady virtue of our enterprise nor the mettle of our spirits." Oaths, Brutus implies, are used to declare one of two things: either that "this cause is just, and I will act dutifully for it rather than for my interest," or that "this cause is unjust, but I will be reliably dedicated to it." In either case, an oath is needed owing to a perceived discrepancy between justice and self-interest. There is never such discrepancy, Brutus implies. It is only unjust causes or unjust (weak) men that need to swear oaths. Moreover, an oath implicitly calls attention to the difference between solemn vows, which are serious, and mere promises, which one might break. But mere promises are thereby made more readily broken when it is in our interest to break them. This distinction too, then, would highlight an alleged discrepancy between one's own good and justice or honesty, which Brutus will not abide. His conclusion is therefore that of what we might well be tempted to deem a fanatic moralist: even the breaking of the *smallest particle* of *any* promise "bastardizes" *every* Roman. If white lies are permissible, who can really know who his true father is? There must then be no distinction between oaths and other promises, no small white lies, but only and always frank statements of truth. There is no need ever to deceive, to flatter, to cajole.

However fanatical it may strike us, however, Brutus's argument does not differ, in kind or conclusion, from the moral consistency of Kant. And Brutus is straining mightily to be morally consistent, to make of the conspirators' enterprise something virtuous in means and ends. Still, the argument he has made[6] clearly poses a problem for any conspiracy, whose element, Shakespeare has just dramatically reminded us, is *whispering* (see 2.1.100), that is, concealment. Brutus will even feel the need subsequently to dissemble to his noble and faithful Portia (2.1.234–309) and to counsel the conspirators to (merely) *act* like noble Romans. His prolonged and morally cogent protest against oaths appears as strong as it is at odds with what he is doing. It appears to express, that is, a wish over and against what he is doing. Does it not suggest a buried doubt that what he is doing can really be justified?

The second example of Brutus's strange behavior emerges in the discussion of whether to include Cicero in the conspiracy. Cassius wants to include him, as someone who will "stand strong with us." The others readily agree, with Metellus adding that Cicero's *gravitas* will be good for public relations. But Brutus rejects the idea on the ground that Cicero would follow nothing begun by another. That is, he charges Cicero, the un-masker of the Catalinian conspiracy, with a certain injustice, with manifestly doing even just deeds *only* when they serve to enhance his own honor or when he can direct them to his own ends. If Brutus is right, there would indeed be some danger in inviting Cicero. But is he right? Or is this not merely another example of Brutus's insistence on complete moral purity, one that this time significantly impedes the conspiracy's success? Certainly in the event, Brutus's own rhetoric proves to be inadequate against that of Antony, and it is likely that not only would Cicero's have succeeded, but that he would not have permitted Antony to speak at all.

We may be less inclined to blame Brutus's tendency to permit what we have called his moral purity to trump prudence,[7] however, when we hear the third argument, concerning whether others—in particular Mark Antony—should be killed along with Caesar. Since Mark Antony's breathtakingly masterful speech will turn success to failure, everything turns on this decision. Over the objections of Cassius, who wishes to prevent Antony from exercising his shrewd contrivances, Brutus orders that *only* Caesar be killed, without malice, lest the conspirators be "butchers." With this, and his subsequent decision that Mark Antony be permitted to speak to the commoners, Brutus dooms the conspiracy. He appears hopelessly "unrealistic." Yet one must ask where such killing would end. What others of great ability will not also become suspect, after all? And where then would their liberation from tyranny stand? Do noble ends not indeed require noble means?

The thought of stopping a bloodbath of preemptive strikes leads Brutus, however, to express his warning in a peculiar way. He expresses the wish that they might kill the spirit of Caesar without killing his body, and attempts to understand the necessary deed as a kind of sacrifice, a high offering to the gods, with Caesar as victim.

> Let's be sacrificers, but not butchers, Caius.
> We all stand up against the spirit of Caesar,
> And in the spirit of men there is no blood;
> O that we then could come by Caesar's spirit,
> And not dismember Caesar! But, alas,
> Caesar must bleed for it! And, gentle friends,
> Let's kill him boldly, but not wrathfully;
> Let's carve him as a dish fit for the gods,
> Not hew him as a carcass fit for hounds. (2.1.166–174)

The conspirators are to kill Caesar as a purge—of a kind of disease or impurity—and hence as a necessity, reluctantly. It is a necessity of a medical but sacred sort, performed as a sacrifice to the gods, in order to rid the city of the spirit of Caesar.

What Brutus expresses here is not an abhorrence of killing per se; nothing he says suggests pacifism. The difficulty that prompts his abhorrence and his turn to religious imagery can rather be grasped by the fact that Brutus says nothing whatsoever to the effect that Caesar alone should be killed because Caesar alone is *guilty*. Brutus remains painfully aware, we suspect, that Caesar, this very person whom they will indeed kill, is *not* guilty but in fact worthy of rule. Brutus tries here for a second time to overcome that problem, this time by drawing an impossible distinction between Caesar and his spirit, and by making the conspirators' deed into a religious ceremony, one that would sanctify their corporeal and political act. Rather than appealing to necessity—which would in the circumstances enhance the argument of Cassius for killing still more virtuous men—he sanctifies and particularizes the necessity of killing Caesar and only Caesar. Rather than turning Caesar into an unthinking deadly beast, this attempt makes his body a gift for the gods. But like the first, this second attempt to confront the problem merely obfuscates it; it doesn't solve it.[8] Moreover, in the event, the conspirators will kill the body of Caesar, while his spirit will live on.

Our argument thus far admittedly rests on the claim that Caesar, as Brutus himself has argued, has shown himself to be worthy of rule. Is this the case? We have heard of the silencing of Murellus and Flavius, and in the next scene Brutus is able to "fashion" Caius Ligarius for the conspiracy because the latter is "sick" over having been upbraided by Caesar for speaking well of Pompey. Yet neither of these pieces of evidence shows Caesar to have operated outside of the law—the first is in fact clearly a case of upholding the law—and both appear to have been in accord with the needs of Rome after the bloody civil war ended by Caesar's defeat of Pompey. Certainly Caesar has not been ruthless with those who were aligned with Pompey, as the case of Brutus himself demonstrates. And as for Ligarius, the devotion to Pompey that has led to his present despondency may be admirable, but it does not bespeak a devotion to freedom or republicanism. His whole disposition, deftly sketched by Shakespeare in a few lines, is that of the confusedly spirited man; he considers himself ready "to get the better of things impossible" and thus to be indomitable, yet he is disposed toward Brutus—the "soul of Rome," as he calls him—as toward a monarch to whom he bows in blind obedience: "I follow you, to do I know not what; but it sufficeth that Brutus leads me on." Whether Caesar deserves to rule is thus left to be determined by what we see of him.[9]

★   ★   ★

Our second glimpse of Caesar is more revealing and more complex than the first, and helps us to understand what we saw there. The scene opens with Caesar ordering that sacrifices to the gods be offered in light of certain dreadful dreams that Calpurnia has had. Cassius's observation (2.1.195–201) that Caesar is growing more superstitious appears then to be confirmed. But Caesar's superstition is negligible compared to that of his wife, and Calpurnia appears quite weak-minded when compared in turn with Portia (whose strength of soul is displayed for us in the previous scene). Is Caesar's superstition perhaps a mere appearance designed to placate Calpurnia? It is true, against this, that Caesar orders the soothsayers to sacrifice even before Calpurnia enters. Yet the response he gives to Calpurnia's list of the bad omens of the night before is a rather stern if well-tempered rebuke of her, remarkable for its absence of hope or for its resignation:

> What can be avoided
> Whose end is purpos'd by the mighty gods?
> Yet Caesar shall go forth; for these predictions
> Are to the world in general as to Caesar. (2.2.26–29)

If the gods have indeed sent omens—and Caesar does not admit that they have—then these are *predictions* of their purposes, not warnings about what to avoid, and are, moreover, sent to all the world, making their applicability to one's own deeds or intentions dubious or boastful. While referring to himself in the third person, then, Caesar appears remarkably free of illusion about his own ultimate significance.

When Calpurnia persists, on the ground of Caesar's princely office and hence heaven's greater attention to him, Caesar's response is still more remarkable for its resignation:

> Cowards die many times before their deaths,
> The valiant never taste of death but once.
> Of all the wonders that I yet have heard,
> It seems to me most strange that men should fear,
> Seeing that death, a necessary end,
> Will come when it will come. (2.2.32–37)

Death is a necessity, coming when it will and unavoidable. This thought, bespeaking a certain fatalism, Caesar presents as the firm basis of his courage. (Cf. Xenophon, *Anabasis*, 3.2.43.) A coward's desperate and fearful attempt to avoid death is itself mortal, he suggests, to true life, valiant life. Caesar seems to imply among other things that fearful piety is a cowardly attempt to avoid death, and his understanding of the alleged portents from the gods seems close to that of Cicero. At least one of his virtues, courage, rests on an understanding of and resignation to death as a necessity. While not a philosopher, Caesar can be called philosophic. And what could be more desirable in a ruler than to be philosophic?

Yet the claim that Caesar makes concerning his disposition toward death is not quite convincing. Why after all should death, even as a necessity, not be something that one would reasonably *fear*, precisely if one's life is worth living and hence preserving? Caesar's answer is that fear *kills life*. In presenting life as valiant life (killed by every act of cowardice), Caesar moves in the direction of Cassius, who was ready with bravado to bear his body toward life's storms, all of which present themselves to Caesar as a test of courage or manliness—which they could not be were there no actual fear present to be faced and faced down. So Caesar, hearing that the soothsayers have found no heart in the sacrificed animal and so have warned against going to the capitol, responds defiantly with his own interpretation of the sacrifices and then the elevation of "Caesar" to the name of a phenomenon or abstract noun, the antithesis and fierce older, stronger twin of "danger":

> The gods do this in shame of cowardice;
> Caesar should be a beast without a heart
> If he should stay at home to-day for fear.
> No, Caesar shall not: Danger knows full well
> That Caesar is more dangerous than he.
> We [are] two lions litter'd in one day,
> And I the elder and more terrible;
> And Caesar shall go forth. (2.2.41–48)

Unlike omens, the sacrifices of Caesar's own soothsayers cannot be dismissed as unintended for himself, but they can be reinterpreted. The interpretation Caesar gives tends, however, against the resigned disposition he had shown when dismissing the omens. It moves him to elevate his own significance considerably. Having faced and apparently accepted the necessity of his own mortality—something that most certainly requires a kind of courage or valor—Caesar has, we may say, developed an enormous pride in, a self-admiration of, his capacity to do so, a pride that has led him to redefine life as valiant life and to elevate his significance as the living embodiment of valor, danger's twin. We were wrong, then, to think that Caesar might be deliberately attempting a self-deification for his or Rome's sake. We see now that his resignation to death and to other necessities has been but a step toward a boundless ambition to face and meet dangers and manifest thereby his superiority to the mass of men. Caesar would be not a god but a living idea, manifesting "fearless" courage against each new danger.

The centrality to Caesar's rule of this ambitious valor is evident both from the weightiness of the reflections that have led Caesar to it and from his earlier remarks to Antony claiming that Caesar never fears but only says what is to be feared. Were this valor Caesar's sole virtue, our assessment of his worthiness to rule would have to be negative, on the ground well summed up by Calpurnia: "Your wisdom is consumed in confidence." And it proves in the sequel to play a role in his undoing, through the very clever flattery and promises of Decius Brutus. But to see precisely what role, and to see valor's relation to other virtues that Caesar proves to manifest, and hence to address fully the question of Caesar's worthiness to rule, we must examine the sequel carefully.

Caesar initially yields to the supplication of his loving and concerned wife. When Decius Brutus enters and requests that Caesar come to the Capitol,

Caesar therefore bids him tell the Senators "that I will not come to-day. / Cannot, is false, and that I dare not, falser: / I will not come to-day. Tell them so, Decius" (2.2.62–64). "Cannot" would denote lack of ability; "dare not," of courage. The formulation reminds us that daring is possible only when ability is uncertain, when there is risk of failure. (It assumes that the abilities in question are genuine human abilities or limited in all cases by necessity; it would not mean jumping off a cliff to see if one can fly.) Daring entails perceiving the risk and not fearing it but instead testing one's ability against it, being a danger to danger. Cowardice would mean permitting a passion, mere fear of the risk, to prevent the testing. One might come, through such testing, progressively to admire one's great ability, but Caesar's pride is rather in his capacity to take such testing risks, to be, as he thinks, fearless. And this pride informs his refusal to use the excuse offered by Calpurnia: "Say that he is sick." Caesar rejects the use of this falsehood on the ground of courage: "Have I in conquest stretch'd mine arm so far, / To be afraid to tell gray-beards the truth?" (2.2.66–67). Truthfulness too, then, follows from courage; the need for deceit belongs to the weak or cowardly. Yet Caesar is not fully truthful; he cannot bring himself to tell the Senate the true reason, which is the unjust and unmanly one of deference to his superstitious wife's fearful supplications. He therefore settles on the simply defiant and unreasonable "Tell them I will not come." He is driven by a combination of tenderness for his loving, frightened wife and his pride in fearlessness to treat the republic's senators with the extreme contempt of offering no reason whatsoever for his action, and even to speak here of his battles on behalf of Rome as if they were no more than occasions to manifest his superior valor. He appears to be headed altogether away from the reasoning and mutual respect that belong to political life, and toward the image of a merely willful and arbitrary god.

Decius, careful not to dispel or defy Caesar's pride, makes a piteous appeal on his own behalf for a reason: "Most mighty Caesar, let me know some cause, / Lest I be laugh'd at when I tell them so" (2.2.69–70). The appeal, significantly, is not without effect on Caesar:

> The cause is in my will, I will not come:
> That is enough to satisfy the Senate.
> But for your private satisfaction,
> Because I love you, I will let you know.
> Calpurnia here, my wife, stays me at home. (2.2.71–75)

The love that Caesar here acknowledges for Decius as the basis of his full and private disclosure of the truth, of Calpurnia's vivid (and, in the event, remarkably prescient) dream, stands in sharp contrast with his repeated expression of contempt for the Senate. But is the contempt heartfelt? Or does it not merely express the frustration of being unable to maintain the Senate's admiration for his virtue if the truth were to be spoken?

The contempt certainly disappears altogether in the sequel, when Decius offers a remarkably cheerful reinterpretation of the bloody dream as signifying Caesar's sustenance of "great Rome," "many Romans," and "great men," a reinterpretation that Decius supports with the news that the Senate wishes to crown Caesar. He can now assure Calpurnia that she has nothing to fear. Caesar is persuaded to go not, as he had first argued to Calpurnia, because the soothsayers' findings offer a test of his valor, but because he would be crowned by great Romans for being the lifeblood of Rome. His approval of Decius's reinterpretation of the dream—which, we note, he states even before he has heard of the crowning—suggests that far from holding the Senate in contempt, Caesar desires to be held by the Senate as Rome's life-giving savior. He even makes no objection when Decius off-handedly suggests that if Caesar did not go, he would relate to them Calpurnia's dream—which Caesar had explicitly told Decius privately and on account of his *love* for him. Caesar as it were without thought now accepts Decius's hypothetical disclosure of the dream. Caesar desires in truth not just the admiration but also the *love* of the senators and indeed of all Romans—to be held as their worthy and valiant savior. His deeds are motivated not simply by pride or self-admiration. Loving Romans, he seeks the admiration and love of the great and finally of everyone in his great city indiscriminately. But this desire for his people's love, surely, belongs to the virtue of any public-spirited ruler. It is tempered in Caesar's case, the optimal case, by a self-admiration whose fundament is a remarkable if flawed capacity to admit the necessity of his mortality and hence his ultimate insignificance.

With the fulfillment of his deepest desire in prospect, Caesar greets the conspirators with a display of urbanity, affability, charm, warmth, wit, self-deprecation, and generosity such as we have seen from no one in the play and will see again from no one. Each man is hailed by name, a long story promised to Trebonius, the enmity with Ligarius made light of as concern is expressed for his health, self-reproach expressed for keeping them waiting, and wine offered to all. Caesar is no tyrant, but a self-admiring, virtuous, and dedicated ruler. The asides that we hear from the conspirators in this context make us uneasy; they seem treacherous and ill-founded. They seem the more so from what we learn in the next scene, as Shakespeare tells us of Artemidorus's prepared suit disclosing all of the conspirators by name. We don't know the source of Artemidorus's information—though the next scene suggests it may have been the slave Lucius, whom Portia cannot trust. What we do know is that Artemidorus deems the conspirators envious of Caesar's virtue. This is surely not the whole story, and Antony will in his concluding eulogy specifically exempt Brutus from this charge. But the suit does serve to show us the high regard—after we have seen its ground—in which Caesar was held by some of the nonconspiring Romans.

Act III

Any doubts we may harbor about the public-spiritedness of Shakespeare's Caesar are dispelled by the exchange between Artemidorus and Caesar and by the exchange with the conspirators before his death. While Plutarch had presented Caesar as distracted and hence unable to read Artemidorus's suit—which Caesar was still clutching when he died—Shakespeare presents him as instead declining to read it immediately for a reason that expresses the heart of public-spirited virtue: "What touches us ourself shall be last served."[10] And when the conspirators bring to Caesar the suit of Metellus Cimber, the same republican public-spiritedness, and its inherently problematical character, become manifest.

Metellus prostrates himself before Caesar with obsequious praise, and Caesar is unmoved. His reasons are of crucial importance:

> I must prevent thee, Cimber.
> These couchings and these lowly courtesies
> Might fire the blood of ordinary men,
> And turn pre-ordinance and first decree
> Into the [law] of children. Be not fond
> To think that Caesar bears such rebel blood
> That will be thaw'd from the true quality
> With that which melteth fools—I mean, sweet words,
> Low-crooked curtsies, and base spaniel-fawning.
> Thy brother by decree is banished;
> If thou dost bend, and pray, and fawn for him,
> I spurn thee like a cur out of my way.
> Know, Caesar doth not wrong, nor without cause
> Will he be satisfied. (3.1.35–48)

The harsh words are consistent with Caesar's proud manliness, and show that Caesar surely anticipated Metellus's suit for the return of his exiled brother. But they likewise bespeak Caesar's attachment to the republican principle of unchanging law, that is, to justice. To change the law, he declares, is to turn it into the "law of children," that is, a thing without reason, a mere plaything, unserious, neither high nor just. To be moved by Metellus's piteous appeal would make Caesar a rebel to impartial justice, a fool to sweet words. Caesar will not be flattered; he does not wish to be cultivated, like a despot, by slaves, arbitrarily dispensing favors. Resolutely upholding the public law stands as a fence against slippage into despotism.

Nor does he do wrong; "Caesar" will not act without just cause, for merely personal favors.[11] His own dignity requires that he remain unmoved against impartial justice, and this elevates the dignity of others, who are prevented from becoming slavish. The love of his countrymen, the deserved love of all, demands the fairness of impartiality.

Metellus's response (3.1.49f.) is no more than an admission that he would move Caesar to restore his brother with nothing but sweet words. To Caesar's shock, Brutus joins in with the sweetness, kissing Caesar's hand, while Cassius falls at Caesar's feet and begs. All of this is performed, of course, in full expectation that Caesar will remain unmoved by it; it is intended to lay the ground for the assassination of a tyrant. But it must strike us as instead considerably strengthening Caesar's case and weakening that of the conspirators, showing as it does that Caesar is one neither to demand nor yield to fawning, supplicating, slavish behavior. He is no petty tyrant or mafia don. In fact, he states next, more clearly than anyone in the play, the republican principle of proud self-sufficiency: "I could be well moved, if I were as you; / If I could pray to move, prayers would move me" (3.1.57–58). Caesar does not pray—he is resigned—and only if he did pray would he be himself moveable by prayer, by supplication, rather than by justice. Strict justice—as Brutus had himself stated in his harangue against oaths—means that there can be no exceptions. To grant exceptions means to call justice itself into question, to say that there is something higher than justice by which justice is to be judged. And what is that something? As this case demonstrates, it is the individual's good, here of Metellus Cimber and his friends. No argument from the common good is offered for his brother's pardon. Cassius simply and strikingly repeats, forward and backward, his appeal: "Pardon, Caesar! Caesar, pardon!" The plea makes no pretense to be based in justice.

The nonpartisan Caesar will not permit parties currying political favor to throw Rome back into the civil war from which it recently emerged. Only the strict republican principle of the rule of impartial law will be honored. Paradoxically, Caesar *alone* honors that principle, and hence deserves to be its sole upholder. The others look for political favoritism for one of their class. Caesar alone is to be trusted as just.

> But I am constant as the northern star,
> Of whose true-fix'd and resting quality
> There is no fellow in the firmament.
> The skies are painted with unnumber'd sparks,
> They are all fire, and every one doth shine,
> But there's but one in all doth hold his place.
> So in the world; 'tis furnish'd well with men,

And men are flesh and blood, and apprehensive;
Yet in the number I do know but one
That unassailable holds on his rank,
Unshaked of motion: and that I am he,
Let me a little show it, even in this—
That I was constant Cimber should be banish'd,
And constant do remain to keep him so. (3.1.60–73)

The analogy is to the heavens (one of the favorite objects of this reformer of the calendar). Each star shines, but only one, the north star, is constant. Only by this one can men therefore take their bearings. To be sure, insofar as they are just, all men shine brightly: Caesar denies neither that he is a man nor that others are capable of shining through justice, which he does not begrudge them. He notices only that he alone stands firmly for it, or does not "travel" or waver or change his mind about what is just.[12] For as we have seen, if justice is changeable, why be just? Why not act in accord with the principle according to which justice is changed, namely, the accommodation of one's individual good? If justice changes to accommodate this good, then is one not being just only when, and to the extent that, it suits one's interests? If, as seems to be the case, the conspirators knew Caesar would be unbending in this suit, staging it as a prelude to their assassination of him, they must somehow realize that they are murdering the one man who is living by the republican principle. Their plea is indeed, as Caesar calls it, "bootless" (3.1.75).

To put this another way: Caesar could here have practiced the virtue of clemency. He had done so, certainly, in the case of Brutus, after the defeat of Pompey. But then he was consolidating his rule over the very divided and warring city, in an extreme situation. Were he to do so now, he would be putting himself in the position of being the only one who could practice clemency, rendering others mere beings at his mercy. Caesar *abstains* from the opportunity to bend the rule of law, recognizing the consequence. He takes the opportunity to manifest his constancy. The effect must be to elevate his own virtue, his own steadfastness to the law: "Hence! wilt thou lift up Olympus?" The home of the gods, of the unshakeable justice of Zeus, will be unmoved. He is the very foundation of the home of any Zeus. Unlike the rest, he cannot be moved. But then he alone deserves to rule. So devotion to the republican principle of equality under the law must acknowledge the superior worth of him who is unsurpassingly devoted to such equality. Republicanism, by its own principle, points to the rule of one, to monarchy, as surely as it points away from despotism.

Caesar appears to have assumed that Brutus, at least, recognized this. He is mistaken. "*Et tu, Brute?*—Then fall Caesar" (3.1.77). If even Brutus seeks to kill the republican principle, then all is lost. The north star must fall from the sky. Rome has lost her virtue.

★   ★   ★

Cinna is the first to claim that the deed is public-spirited, directed against tyranny in the name of liberty. So too does Cassius, who takes the step of calling for the "enfranchisement" of the commoners, of moving Rome away from monarchy and hence toward democracy. Conspicuously, Brutus neither immediately proclaims an end to tyranny nor makes any promises. He claims only that ambition's debt is paid—that some kind of retributive justice is done. He again emphasizes that no one else will be killed, even as he proclaims that only the conspirators will bear responsibility for the deed. News that Antony has fled in fear and that others are reacting to the deed in terror of doomsday prompts Brutus to reflection on death, in which he is joined by Cassius. Brutus, as had Caesar, speaks of knowledge of the inevitability of death, but contrasts it with ignorance of its time or hour. Cassius's response is the half-jesting one that cutting off 20 years of a man's life is cutting off 20 years of his fear of death, and Brutus finishes the dark jest by saying that to grant Cassius's point would be to grant that they have done Caesar a great benefit and are his friends. Brutus, that is, does not grant Cassius's point. He recognizes that Caesar did not allow fear of death to consume him, to make his life miserable, but was instead resigned to death in a manner that Cassius, by implication, is not. Here, perhaps, is the deepest reason for the mutual affection and admiration of Caesar and Brutus. Recognizing the ground of Caesar's virtues and sharing those virtues, Brutus must be driven to try to understand or present the necessary assassination of noble Caesar as instead something altogether extraordinary, as a religious sacrifice to the gods.

While the conspirators at Brutus's command bathe themselves dramatically in Caesar's blood, Cassius and Brutus imagine future plays (like this one) about their deeds on behalf of liberty. They are moved to state the hope that in fact points to the rule of Caesar: they, and not others, will be dramatized as liberators. Brutus's description of such future reenactments contains, moreover, an implicit admission that the liberty of Rome required that Caesar's *worthiness* be destroyed through his death. And while he is now prepared to lead a procession of the blood-smeared conspirators through the streets of Rome to proclaim liberty, Brutus must instead face Antony, who has sent a slave to seek a pledge of safe passage so that Antony might learn why worthy Caesar deserved to lie in death, and Antony thereby have reason to support the conspirators. That is, *if* and only if Brutus can explain this will Antony faithfully support him, and "love Brutus living" more than Caesar dead. The moment of reckoning has arrived; the question that has been troubling Brutus must now be faced. Brutus is for his part confident that they shall have Antony as their friend; Cassius is not.

★   ★   ★

Antony, visibly moved by Caesar's corpse, from which came "the most noble blood of all this world," first asks the conspirators to kill him now next to Caesar, if they mean to kill him. Brutus reassures Antony: you see but our hands, not our hearts, which are filled with pity (3.1.169–173). Here then is Brutus's first attempt to answer Antony's question. Nothing but pity, pity for Rome, at the "general wrong" it suffered, drove from Brutus's heart pity for Caesar. There is then no need for Antony to fear; "We love and revere" Antony. Cassius adds that Antony will have as strong a say in the allocation of new dignities as any man. Will Brutus now explain, then, the "general wrong of Rome" that moved him to kill Caesar, and thereby win Antony's fidelity?

Brutus delivers only a promise to do so; they must first calm the fearful multitude. "And then we will deliver you the cause / Why I, that did love Caesar when I strook him, / Have thus proceeded" (3.1.180–82). Antony's condition for faithful friendship has not been met. Hence, while Brutus's *promise* to meet it moves Antony to profess friendship to each of the conspirators, he is once again openly moved by the corpse of Caesar, "most noble!" The just thing, he tearfully reflects aloud, is to weep for Caesar, not to be a friend to the enemies of this noble stag and heart of the world. How can one possibly be a faithful friend of a most noble man and love that friend's enemies? Cassius therefore calls Antony to state his allegiance, and Antony admits that he has indeed been swayed from friendship with the conspirators and, while wishing to be faithful to them, *must* hear the reasons why and how Caesar was "dangerous," that is, a threat to the good of Rome or Romans. The issue can hardly have been put more movingly or with greater attention to what is at stake for serious men.

But Brutus again punts: "Our reasons are so full of good regard / That were you, Antony, the son of Caesar, / You should be satisfied" (3.1.224–26). You will learn that we regarded Antony so well that we had to kill Caesar, his friend and as it were his father. Receiving this apparently preposterous promise, Antony makes his request to speak over the body of Caesar, that is, he takes his first step toward the overthrow of the conspirators, toward delivering a speech that appears from its contents—especially regarding Caesar's will—to be one to which he has already given thoughtful preparation.

It seems in other words that Antony, having seized one of the two horns of the dilemma that Brutus has not permitted himself to face—the undeniable worthiness to rule of this noble man—strongly suspected that he would receive no satisfactory answer to his question from Brutus, and has had his suspicion now confirmed. For how could killing Rome's best citizen, one worthy of Brutus's and Antony's love, be just? Brutus has alluded to the "general wrong" of Rome. But is Caesar not a part of Rome? An outstanding part? Its peak or capstone?

Brutus consents immediately to Antony's request to speak, but Cassius, sensing the danger—recognizing that neutrality in such a matter is not possible for serious men—has a private word with Brutus in an effort to bring the danger home. For a second time Brutus overrules Cassius's judgment of how best to proceed with Antony. Brutus is fully confident that by giving his oration first, showing "the reason of our Caesar's death," and publicly granting both Antony leave to deliver his oration and Caesar's corpse all proper rites of burial, their side will be advantaged. Cassius remains dubious, but Brutus immediately repeats to Antony his permission to speak, adding merely the proviso that in his oration he not *blame* them. Can Brutus not see that his offer and proviso to a man of Antony's gifts are as sensible as the offering of a weapon to a potential enemy with the proviso that he not use it against oneself? Any possibility of sanctioning a violation of Brutus's proviso rests, after all, on the assumption that whatever Antony should say in his speech, Brutus's speech will still carry the day. What is the ground of Brutus's confidence that this is so?

We will learn that ground only from Brutus's speech, but we can see already that he expects that a public display of authority, along with his public speech—he has made clear that Antony must await his public speech—will be sufficient to maintain rule. He fails to see that Antony will be able to exploit the impossibility of neutrality that Antony has now made dramatically clear—the impossibility of Brutus's wish to "love" Caesar and yet kill him. Behind that wish, as we have seen, is the inability to face another impossibility: that the man most deserving to rule Rome should by his very rule, his very activity in virtuous deeds, deprive others of their opportunity to lead virtuous lives, and hence be unjust. The right public speech seems to promise a path out of his dilemma.

Antony for his part has now no expectation of learning from Brutus's speech anything that would move him to join the conspirators. His disposition is made abundantly clear in the haunting soliloquy that concludes the scene, "Pardon me, O bleeding piece of earth." Like all of Shakespeare's soliloquies, it discloses directly to the audience the inner thoughts of the speaker, without the encumbrance of a living addressee. Unlike most other soliloquies, it has an addressee: a corpse. Its opening line expresses that what had been Caesar is now no more than a piece of earth, yet asks its pardon. It is an anguished defiance of the conspirators' attempt to destroy Caesar by reducing him to an insignificant corpse. The corpse is not just any bleeding piece of earth, after all, but "the ruins of the noblest man / That ever lived in the tide of times." Brutus had wished the conspirators to be not butchers but sacrificers; Antony proclaims them butchers. Brutus had wished to kill the spirit of Caesar without killing the body; Antony will ensure the spirit lives on. Brutus had wished to carve up a dish for the gods; Antony prophesizes— for the corpse's wounds are *like* dumb mouths begging him to speak—and proclaims a curse, a terrible unbridled destruction, led by the spirit of Caesar "ranging for revenge" and with a monarch's voice crying "havoc!" Brutus had claimed that pity for Rome vanquished his pity for Caesar; Antony implies with his prophecy that the significance of Caesar and hence of his death require that Rome suffer such horrors as to make even the mothers of infants pitiless. But he expects no gods to bring this prophecy to pass. With his speech to the commoners over the corpse of Caesar, Antony will himself, self-consciously, attempt to do it. (And as the subsequent exchange with Octavius's servant makes clear, Antony is not even sure that his speech will succeed.) His prophecy is neither a prayer nor an alleged revelation, but a prediction of what he himself intends to bring about. The spirit of Caesar is the spirit of monarchy, of the rule of the noblest man. It does not presuppose the rule of gods; it is not pious. And as far as Antony is concerned, the murder of the man who embodied that spirit warrants the destruction of public, civic life. What Brutus is counting on, public life and all that it entails, Antony in his desire to avenge Caesar is prepared to destroy.

★ ★ ★

Brutus's brief speech is a technically masterful series of tropes and figures— parallelisms, isocolon, antitheses, and anaphora—displaying the oratorical ability that moved Cicero to name one of his treatises on rhetoric after him. It openly invites its Roman listeners to judge of the wisdom of the speech; it answers their likely questions and offers in turn a series of questions. It is remarkably dialogical. Yet crucially, it also openly invites its listeners to "believe" Brutus for his honor. For his motives are at issue, and motives, always hidden, can be further concealed by speech. In this case above all, motive is everything: Brutus pits his frank love and admiration for Caesar against his perception of the need to slay Caesar for the good of Rome, and his willingness to do so.

> If then that friend demand
> why Brutus rose against Caesar, this is my answer:
> Not that I lov'd Caesar less, but that I lov'd
> Rome more. (3.2.20.22)

Brutus loved Caesar as much as anyone, but loved Rome more. But is Caesar not a Roman and even the best of Romans? How can his death be good for Rome? Putting his response to this implicit question as a question of his own, Brutus almost allows the dilemma that we have spelled out to rise to the surface: "Had you rather Caesar were living and / die all slaves, than that Caesar were dead, to live / all free men?" (3.2.22–24). Brutus aimed in his deed to secure the Romans' happiness through the securing of their freedom. But must, then, the rule of a man worthy of Brutus's and other outstanding Romans' love and admiration, entail the Romans' slavery? Brutus will not admit it. He must therefore divorce that love and admiration from anything that would suggest public-spiritedness in Caesar.

> As Caesar lov'd me, I weep for him;
> as he was fortunate, I rejoice at it; as he was
> valiant, I honor him; but, as he was ambitious, I
> slew him. There is tears for his love; joy for his
> fortune; honor for his valor; and death for his
> ambition. (3.2.24–29)

Here then is the tersely stated core of Brutus's argument. Brutus reduces love of Caesar to a private matter, isolates "valor," Caesar's great virtue, as the object of his admiration, and ascribes "ambition," a lack of public-spiritedness, to Caesar. Valor or courage easily admits of this divorce. It is of ambiguous public-spiritedness, being in the first place a capacity to face dangers and stand up for oneself and, second, something therefore possessed by criminals as well as just men. Valor can even, as we have seen in Caesar's own words, manifest in deeds that are done apparently on behalf of one's city in fact deeds that are intended to feed and sustain a self-admiration, with the city and its needs serving merely as opportunities and hence being dispensable. The case for seeing it as not in the service of Rome but in the service of Caesar rests on the claim that the valorous Caesar is turning or would turn Romans into bondsmen rather than freemen. But that merely restates the problem. Is the enslavement, to repeat, the result of an ambitious self-concern, or simply the inevitable result of the rule of the virtuous?

Brutus solves his difficulty by making a *public* appeal to the commoners' noble love of freedom, their love of being free Romans. What in the case against Caesar he divorces, he blends together in the appeal to the commoners: love of Rome, on one hand, and noble, valiant, manly love of freedom, on the other. His expectation that the *commoners* will be moved by this appeal has been called naïve or foolish, an example of a lack of "realism." Were this true, Brutus would hardly be worthy of the attention that Shakespeare devotes to him. That it is not true is shown by the great success of Brutus's speech,[13] a success that tends to be forgotten in the light of Antony's subsequent, overturning success. Brutus is *not* wrong to think that the people can be won over in this way. His turning to the people with this appeal must therefore be explained on other grounds. It is explained by the fact that the appeal is a necessity, not a choice, if he is to preserve the possibility of the virtuous life for which he stands—by the fact that the soundness or coherence of his or any human's devotion to virtue and of the honor it is accorded is here at stake. What Brutus cannot admit to, what he must at all costs refute, is that the destruction of the opportunity to practice virtue is a necessary consequence of virtue itself. It must not be the case that noble Caesar, in having sought to achieve the people's loyalty, is really moved by love of the people rather than by a self-admiration of his capacity, or that the latter (as indeed we have seen) merely tempers the former. It must instead be possible for the virtuous to rule without potentially destroying the genuine good, the virtue, of others. It must not be the case that the rule of the one most virtuous will result, willy-nilly, in the destruction of the common good; that rule must instead be destructive of that good only in the case of an *ambitious* man, whose concern for the people is that they be reduced to contented sheep for his own good, that is, of a man who lacks concern for the genuine common good, the virtue of the citizens.

The argument moves for this reason necessarily in a democratic direction; the love of Rome is the love of its citizens, but lest this be monarchic love, of a shepherd for his sheep, those citizens must themselves be capable of virtue, of being devoted to freedom or self-rule. A love of them as free, independent men, and not as the mere means to one's own glory through attention to their merely material needs, is what can distinguish the deeds of a genuinely honorable man from the ambitious deeds of an admittedly valiant Caesar. It is only by winning the commoners over with this appeal that Brutus can show that Caesar was indeed ambitious—that he wished to rule at the cost of the virtue of the rest of Rome—that his rule was directed against the common good—and thereby preserve the possibility that the honorable life of noble deeds makes sense, that the most virtuous can rule without destroying the genuine good, the virtue, of others.

Deprivation of the people's freedom is a necessary consequence of the rule of an admirable, valorous man only if the people permit it to be so—if they wish that another care for them like a shepherd, if they inevitably demand goods other than and at the expense of freedom or proud, virtuous self-rule. Brutus is counting on the existence of a certain proud virtue among the Romans in order for him to count on them to believe him for his honor—to believe that Caesar was not public-spirited and that Brutus is. They must in fact have a love of noble or honorable freedom themselves to see what he did as honorable. But he is not merely hoping for it. By putting this requirement in the form of a public question, he means to guarantee, to the extent possible and in accord with their freedom, that they will not disappoint him:

> Who is here so base that would be a
> bondman? If any, speak; for him have I offended.
> Who is here so rude that would not be a Roman? If
> any, speak, for him have I offended. Who is here so
> vile that will not love his country? If any, speak,
> for him have I offended. I pause for a reply. (3.2.29–34)

With this series of questions, we see why Brutus held off until now to answer Antony's demand for reasons for Caesar's death. Brutus waits to give the "public reasons" (3.2.7) for Caesar's death. That is to say, he waits to give the just reasons. Public speech is the home and sustenance of shame and honor, of public-spiritedness, of the common good. Public life would elevate even the vilest, whose shame must preclude publicly declaring sentiments they may harbor in private. Brutus's are the quintessential rhetorical questions; public life precludes any answer to them but a collective "none." The people's response shows to everyone their noble desire to be free, and hence shows that Caesar's enslavement of them is not inevitable but stems from *ambition*, a desire to enslave them that requires the destruction of their better, nobler selves, sustained through public life.

It is in keeping with this that Brutus, after declaring that Antony will have "a place in the commonwealth," adds "as which of you shall not?" (3.2.43–44). For to be genuine, to entail their devotion, such love of freedom and self-rule as he implicitly demands with his public questions must be steadfast. The people cannot be fickle. Brutus counts on public life, whose element is public speech, to bind the commoners, his countrymen, to their noble attachment to freedom, to give them the means to resist the blandishments of those who would win them over by base, private-spirited appeals. Public speech can even safely include Antony's praise of the virtues of a Caesar because by sustaining public-spiritedness, by permitting the expression only of what is honorable, it sustains the people's belief in an honorable man's claim to have killed the ambition of Caesar, in his attempt to seduce them with private-spirited appeals into slavery. It promises that they will not cease to believe that what they have lost in losing a Caesar and his valor is as nothing compared with their noble and nobly defended liberty.

Yet if Brutus is not mistaken to think that the people have a love of honorable freedom and that its element is public life, he is mistaken to think that it is or can be what is strongest in them, and securely sustainable by public life. His confidence rests on the expectation that he can persuade and hold the crowd of Roman commoners in the belief that he, an honorable man, acted not against the good of Rome and for his own interest but against the ambitious, self-centered concerns of a man whose rule would enslave them. Its fundamental weakness is anticipated in one of the responses of the commoners: "Let him be Caesar" (3.2.51). That is, not the people's baseness, but their very admiration of the virtue of the one who would lead them to their true good—a just sentiment—permits public acceptance of the rule of a Caesar.[14] The successful speech to the commoners thus reveals itself as open to a public attack on its claim concerning Caesar's ambition or self-concern, the discrediting of which claim would destroy its twin, Brutus's claim to honorableness. Mark Antony delivers that attack masterfully.

★ ★ ★

Antony is careful to adhere to the letter of the agreement, offering no blame of the conspirators from the pulpit but instead speaking of them as honorable men. But loving Caesar and convinced of Caesar's nobility, Antony has no compunction in bringing to bear all the persuasive appeals to passion that he can muster in order to defeat the conspirators. The honorable Brutus charges Caesar with ambition; Antony defeats the claim of honorableness by defeating the charge against Caesar. He proceeds in small steps, the first of which is an attack on Brutus's separation of Caesar's faithful love or friendship from the virtue of justice, combined with a tarring of Brutus with the reputation of the other conspirators:

> Here, under leave of Brutus and the rest
> (For Brutus is an honorable man,
> So are they all, all honorable men),
> Come I to speak in Caesar's funeral.
> He was my friend, faithful and just to me;
> But Brutus says he was ambitious,
> And Brutus is an honorable man. (3.2.81–87)

Faithful friendship includes justice; it bespeaks Caesar's justice. How could an Antony or a Brutus have been his friend otherwise? Still, Antony might be to Caesar as Brutus is to his co-conspirators, a justly treated friend engaged in a partnership of hidden crime, part of a power elite. Antony must therefore present evidence that Caesar's justice extended to all Romans, that his great valor was in the service of Rome. "He hath brought many captives home to Rome, / Whose ransoms did the general coffers fill; / Did this in Caesar seem ambitious?" (3.2.88–90). Caesar's activities benefitted all of Rome, not merely Caesar or his friends. Still, this appeal is manifestly unjust: Caesar plundered the world, extorting king's ransoms from peoples in order to fill the coffers of Rome. His valor appears like that of a kingpin of organized crime. In thus stooping to present not virtue but a full purse as the good of Romans, Antony runs the risk of having his listeners conclude that Caesar's motive may well have been as corrupt as theirs. This, we may say, is the solid reason for Brutus's reliance on the unacceptability of public declarations of private, base desires, such as the desire to be a bondman. Antony now counters this clever reliance with a judo throw, a *public* statement of Caesar's *private* motives.

> When that the poor have cried, Caesar hath wept;
> Ambition should be made of sterner stuff:
> Yet Brutus says he was ambitious,
> And Brutus is an honorable man. (3.2.91–94)

Antony makes public an account of his dear friend Caesar's private tears for the people, of his private pity for those he loves, to show that Caesar lacks ambition's coldness to the sufferings of others—that even and precisely in private the mighty and valorous Caesar harbored for the people the hope that through him every tear could be wiped away, everyone's good served. Antony thus exploits the very tension between public and private speech upon which Brutus had relied. And we have some reason, at least, to find Antony's claim credible. As we have seen, while Caesar may have wished to believe self-admiration is what moved him to virtuous deeds, he is moved in truth by a desire for the love of all Romans. Antony has noticed, and he now makes it known.

And so Antony's speech goes on, very cleverly and famously repeating in anaphora "Brutus is an honorable man" until it is reduced to sarcasm, and Antony, true to the agreement but having begun to win over his audience, is free to employ all the other rhetorical devices in his quiver—including aposiopesis ("My heart is in the coffin there with Caesar...")—to win a complete victory. He moves the people to remorse for their lack of fidelity in love of Caesar ("You all did love him once..."), using Caesar's last will and testament, in particular, to show that he deserved their love. At the same time, he absolves the people of blame, turning their remorse to a desire for revenge: the people have been wronged by Caesar's death; it is only his assassins who are unjust. With Caesar's will Brutus then turns the people's desire for revenge into a fury, the crowd into a raging mob, as he had intended.

He has carried the will at least since approaching the conspirators, and knows its contents, its "rich legacy" (3.2.128) despite the fact that it is sealed (3.2.240). With a paralepsis, he presents disclosure of the will's contents as

a breach of his agreement not to blame the conspirators, thereby making
its contents themselves a blame of the conspirators, and directing them to
take it as such:

> I must not read it.
> It is not meet you know how Caesar lov'd you:
> You are not wood, you are not stones, but men;
> And, being men, hearing the will of Caesar,
> It will inflame you, it will make you mad.
> 'Tis good you know not that you are his heirs,
> For, if you should, O, what would come of it? (3.2.140–145)

Pretending to be compelled by them to read the will, he steps down from
the podium—his agreement was to say nothing from the podium against
the conspirators—and claiming to provoke their pity but in fact bent on the
destruction of pity for any but their benefactor, he displays first Caesar's cut
mantle and then his corpse, using purple prose ("Pompey's statue…all the
while ran with blood") and an apostrophe to the gods to make the assassination appear an earth-shattering event, and Brutus, "Caesar's angel," as
having broken Caesar's mighty heart. Foul ingratitude killed mighty Caesar.
The tearful people, of course, are not ungrateful, but will demand revenge
for the "bloody treason." So does Antony turn the people's desire for gain
into an opposition to those who have killed their benefactor. He turns it
into a demand for the punishment of ingratitude—a perfectly acceptable
because perfectly just public sentiment.

So successful is Antony that he must call back the crowd, already intent
on mayhem. He now steps beyond all restraint to make them unrestrained.
He delivers a fatal blow to the foundation on which Brutus's appeal to their
honor and noble freedom had rested: public speech.

> Good friends, sweet friends, let me not stir you up
> To such a sudden flood of mutiny.
> They that have done this deed are honorable.
> What private griefs they have, alas, I know not,
> That made them do it. They are wise and honorable,
> And will, no doubt, with reasons answer you.
> I come not, friends, to steal away your hearts.
> I am no orator, as Brutus is;
> But (as you know me all) a plain blunt man,
> That love my friend, and that they know full well
> That gave me public leave to speak of him.
> For I have neither [wit], nor words, nor worth,
> Action, nor utterance, nor the power of speech

To stir men's blood; I only speak right on.
I tell you that which you yourselves do know,
Show you sweet Caesar's wounds, poor poor dumb mouths,
And bid them speak for me. (3.2.210–225)

Where Brutus had attempted to guarantee the elevation of the people through the medium of public speech, Antony pretends—with astonishing success—to be one of the people, a plain, blunt man who cannot speak cleverly of his honorableness and honorable deeds. He carefully closes their ears to the words "honorable deeds" and to any and all public reasons that the privately motivated but clever-speaking perpetrators might give the people. Antony has recognized that Brutus has been driven to found his case on the element of public speech, and hence he will overthrow any opportunity for it. His presentation of public speech as no more than the nefarious means of hoodwinking the people with appeals to what is honorable requires that he pretend to be no orator himself—to have not given reasons of his own—but to have merely listened to what the deeds themselves speak. And he has so stoked the people's passions to hearing none but his interpretation of those deeds, so prepared them for a murderous rampage, that he must again call them back to hear a reading of the will, to hear "how Caesar deserved your love." And having read the will, he makes of Caesar's name a title: "Here was a Caesar! When comes such another?" The people, not thinking for a moment that Caesar could be so generous to them only by having hoarded a vast treasure house for himself, respond with "Never!" and proceed to seek a rampaging revenge for their benefactor's death.

Antony is pleased with what his love of Caesar has moved him to accomplish (3.2.259–71). Shakespeare, however, makes clear his own opposition to the reign of popular terror Antony has unleashed by presenting as its sole example (drawn from Plutarch) the killing of a poet, Cinna, "for his verses" (3.3). Antony's desire for revenge, as fierce as his love and admiration for Caesar, has put Rome and its best and at the same time most vulnerable citizens at the mercy of its least rational part in its least rational state.

It would seem then that Brutus, while defeated by Antony's demagogic unleashing of mayhem, is proven by it to have been right: the *ambitious* rule of Caesar destroys the opportunity for a share of the noble sought by others and does so by using the people rather than elevating them, by appealing to their wallets and to the vulgar tendency to equate their benefactors with noble human beings, by exploiting the people's desire for good things obtained through the oppression and extortion of others. Antony, Caesar's faithful tongue, does indeed fully anticipate and thwart Brutus's defense of the assassination of Caesar, but he does so with a disregard or contempt for what is and can be best in human beings, twisting low things into apparently just things. But has the deed of Antony really resolved the central dilemma? Have the deeds and words of Antony clarified or not rather served further to hide it? Would *Caesar* have approved of those deeds and words? Are they not a distortion of what Caesar stood for? Does Antony not exaggerate, because he himself is so piteous, a piteous love of the people on Caesar's part? Is Antony's deception not so much of the people as of himself? Is his being fundamentally a member of the people not more than a mere act? Did Caesar himself not admire his own fidelity to a justice that is unmoved by piteous supplications that would destroy it? Does Antony not understate the desire that Caesar had for the crown, as a confirmation of Caesar's worth? Is Antony not a somewhat weepy if very talented spokesman for someone who was in truth more austere, more proud, fundamentally, of his own outstanding virtue? Would that virtue have countenanced the attack on public speech—the element of honor and disgrace—and consequent mayhem that Antony has produced? Does Caesar's last will and testament itself not demonstrate his desire to admire the prospect of his munificence rather than a desire to relieve the poor of their suffering—which he could have done immediately, after all, rather than after his death? Was not Caesar, in short, much more high-minded than Antony?

That the fundamental dilemma confronting Brutus and the virtue he stands for has not been solved but hidden by Antony's deed is made clear in the final two acts.

Act IV

We meet the new triumvirate engaged in the ghastly business of determining which senators they will put to death. Lepidus consents to his own brother's death on condition, immediately granted, that Mark Antony do so for his son-in-law Publius. The result of straying from the path of Brutus—who would consent not even to Antony's death—discloses itself as grim tyranny. Suspicion and lack of frankness mean that the rulers are "bay'd about with many enemies," but if the central reason is Brutus and Cassius and their forces, the suspicion extends even into the triumvirate itself, and turns, as did the conspirators' deed, on the question of fitness to rule. For after Antony sends Lepidus away to fetch Caesar's will (so that they may find in it some legacies to reduce) he discloses to Octavius his opinion of Lepidus as an "unmeritable man," fit to send on errands and hence unfit to share in the triumvirate's rule of the world. Lepidus was chosen by Antony, Octavius learns, solely for reasons of public relations while they engage in the dark business of choosing who must die, and Antony means to turn Lepidus out as soon as that business is done. Octavius consents, but adds in objection that Lepidus is a "tried and valiant soldier," to which Antony retorts curtly: "So is my horse." And with a long extension of the metaphor on horses he teaches the young Octavius his own understanding of fitness to rule. Loyalty and valor are insufficient for rule; required is a *spirit* given to directing matters, which Lepidus lacks and can but poorly imitate, and which Antony claims to have.

But is this the same Antony who snapped to attention to carry out Caesar's least command? (Cf. 1.2.4–10.) Was Antony, who surely admired the commanding, leonine spirit in Caesar, merely awaiting, while Caesar gave him orders, his chance to exercise that spirit in himself? And if so, for how long could he be justly expected to wait, the mere "property" as it were of Caesar? Has Brutus's deed not in fact been an enormous boon for him, turning him now from horse to human rider? And will Octavius, aware of Antony's opinion of and plan for the spiritless Lepidus, be more inclined to rebuff Antony's orders? (See 5.1.16–20.) Can he possibly take age and hence superior wisdom in human affairs, which Antony here presents as the basis of his title over Octavius, as sufficient for subordination to Antony's judgment? If so, for how long? Will the time not come, inevitably, when Octavius must have the opportunity for his own spirit to exercise itself? Was Antony's devotion to Caesar not a necessarily temporary thing, enslaving him if it were permanent? Is Brutus not right to insist on republican rule?

★   ★   ★

We learn in the next scene, however, that there is trouble also between Brutus and Cassius, the champions of the republican cause, and it too will turn on the question of who is fittest to rule, who ablest "to make conditions." But the trouble differs substantially from that of the triumvirate. Where Antony was not at all frank with Lepidus about his true judgment of him, Brutus is frank with Pindarus, Cassius's servant, about Cassius (2.6.22). He is similarly frank when Lucilius describes the treatment he has received from Cassius. To the report that there was "courtesy and respect enough," but not the old "free and friendly conference," Brutus replies, "Thou hast described / A hot friend cooling" (4.2.15–19). He then instructs Lucilius with an attack on forms that resembles his opposition to oaths. "Plain and simple faith," unaffected, is the emblem of republican virtue; form and polite courtesy belong to a monarch and his court. Brutus's lesson includes, like that of Antony to Octavius, a horse metaphor, but his metaphor suggests a wish for and admiration of genuine, frank greatness even in horses; he wants a Secretariat rather than a Sham, full and not hollow men. Characteristically, however, he omits dwelling on the difference between the horse and the one inflicting into it the "bloody spur."

On his arrival (4.2.35ff.) Cassius is as warm as he is frank: "Most noble brother, you have done me wrong." Brutus objects, calling the gods, significantly, as witnesses: he wrongs, he protests, not even his enemies, doing justice even to them—as indeed his treatment of Antony has shown. But however frank he would be, he knows enough to avoid scandal, a misunderstanding by their arrayed troops of the dispute, a perception of discord. He is keenly aware that he and Cassius are men whose example and whose unanimity matters to the unanimity of their respective armies. He implicitly admits that to disagree with someone is to dishonor him. He asks that they go inside the tent. He needs, then, forms, for the disagreements that they hide. However much he would rely upon public speech and the honor and shame that attend it to resolve his difficulties, he clearly needs private speech to address the question of who should rule. Shakespeare indicates this difficulty by according the quarrel its own scene, separate from the armies.

★   ★   ★

The cause of the quarrel is that Brutus has punished Lucius Pella for taking bribes, and ignored Cassius's missives pleading for leniency. Lucius Pella was guilty indeed, but "in such a time as this tis not meet" that justice be strictly enforced (4.3.7–8). One must turn a blind eye, or wink at, such deeds, in light of the necessity of the salvation of the army and with it, the republican cause. The necessity of war overrules strict justice. Cassius's position reminds one—is the basis—of Hobbes's contention that worth is relative: in peace one honors a judge (who aims at justice), but in war, a general (who aims at victory). Brutus altogether rejects this appeal to necessity. He immediately accuses Cassius instead of an unjust motive, of having an "itchy palm," of avarice, just as he had accused Caesar of ambition. There is no necessity; the case for justice requires necessity's absence. Noble ends always require noble means. It is here that he makes reference to Caesar's injustice:

> Remember March, the ides of March remember:
> Did not great Julius bleed for justice' sake?
> What villain touch'd his body, that did stab
> And not for justice? What? shall one of us,
> That struck the foremost man of all this world,
> But for supporting robbers, shall we now
> Contaminate our fingers with base bribes?
> And sell the mighty space of our large honors
> For so much trash as may be grasped thus?
> I had rather be a dog, and bay the moon,
> Than such a Roman. (4.3.18–28)

Will they turn themselves into rulers of thugs, supporting corrupt men, in order to attain their ends? What then of those ends? Would they not become victims of the means chosen? The money is not necessary; it is "trash"—disposable. The true necessary requirement is virtue, honor, honesty. If they become unjust, they deserve not rule but death, like Caesar. They would make being a Roman lower than being a dog. Brutus's devotion to justice remains as consistently uncompromising as ever. Cassius's position is that of one who would stoop to injustice and thereby abandon the very reason, the cause, of the fight against Caesar and his successors. Set against Brutus's position, it raises the question of who is more fit to rule in that cause.

Or as Shakespeare has them term it here, it raises the question of which of the two is more fit "to give conditions" (4.3.28–35), each claiming it for himself. So much is at stake in the insult Brutus has given to Cassius's honor that the latter expresses his readiness to kill the former. Brutus treats the threat with utter contempt: "Away, slight man." He doesn't even bother to take out his sword. "Go make your bondman tremble. You shall digest the venom of your spleen." He taunts Cassius: "I will make use of you for my mirth, yea for my laughter, when you are waspish." Cassius will be his jester. Brutus even accuses him of cowardice with respect to Caesar (4.3.61–67). With such deep contempt, such unbearable insult, we must wonder: why does Cassius not strike? What makes him endure this gross mistreatment?

Brutus's own explanation for his contempt for Cassius's threats to strike is that he is "arm'd so strong in honesty / That they pass by me as the idle wind, / Which I respect not" (4.3.67–69). Brutus's justice, his virtue, his virtue alone, holds Cassius at bay or would defeat him. On account of it Cassius cannot attack him; Brutus needs no other equipment. And astonishing as the explanation is, it is true. Cassius has been unable to answer Brutus's argument; being attached to justice, he cannot answer them. He loves Brutus for his justice, and Cassius has indeed done base things, supported unjust men like Lucius Pella. Rather than remind Cassius of that argument, Brutus presents yet another instance of Cassius's injustice:

> I did send to you
> For certain sums of gold, which you denied me;
> For I can raise no money by vile means.
> By heaven, I had rather coin my heart
> And drop my blood for drachmaes, than to wring
> From the hard hands of peasants their vile trash
> By any indirection. I did send
> To you for gold to pay my legions,
> Which you denied me. (4.3.69–77)

Cassius first denies the charge, but eventually (4.3.104) admits that he has denied Brutus the gold. He calls out for Octavius and Antony, and then the fault-finding Brutus, to kill him, as Brutus did Caesar, whom he surely loved more than he loves Cassius. Hearing this, Brutus relents, having won the encounter. Virtue has triumphed.

More surprising than Cassius's deference to Brutus's virtue is his deference to it in light of the implicit victory that Cassius's argument has in fact won over Brutus's argument. Brutus needed the money from Cassius for his troops, after all, because Brutus had none, and he had none because he would not soil his own hands for what this Stoic for a second time calls "trash." Cassius taxed the peasants under his troops' command; Brutus would not. Brutus needs something in addition to virtue—virtue is *not* sufficient—but his own virtue will not allow him to obtain what he needs. His concern for his own virtue makes him willing to turn Cassius into his henchman to keep his virtue pure. (He was even prepared to say nothing of Cassius's flaws "till you practice them on me.") This has been called the "ugly ...hypocrisy" of Brutus,[15] and it is indeed ugly insofar as it discloses a lack of self-knowledge. More importantly, it shows the impossibility of the virtue to which Brutus aspires or claims to live by. That virtue must render Cassius a mere vicious instrument to Brutus's own self-admiration. It entails an unjust subordination of Cassius to Brutus, a subordination that cannot be said to be for the common good.

Cassius, who surely sees this, does *not* exploit it. He is, unlike Brutus, prepared to sacrifice his virtue, not indeed for the common good but for the sake of the existence of that virtue in another, for the very possibility of admiring and loving that virtue, unalloyed with vice, in a Brutus. Lest this sacrifice seem improbable, we would do well to remember that a version of it is practiced all the time, as it were, in parents, who sacrifice their own leisure and wealth and the virtues that these would permit them to practice, giving them up for the sake of their practice by their children. And lest our interpretation seem askew, we note that Shakespeare provides still further evidence of this devotion on Cassius's part.

For when the two are reconciled, claiming that they spoke in anger, Cassius expresses his surprise that Brutus could ever be so out of sorts. When Brutus replies that he is "sick" on account of "many griefs," Cassius upbraids him. "Of your philosophy you make no use, if you give place to accidental evils." No Stoic himself (but as we will soon hear, a would-be Epicurean) Cassius wishes that Brutus live up to his Stoicism, according to which virtue is sufficient for happiness and so all other things accidental to it. Brutus then delivers the lightning bolt: "No man bears it better: Portia is dead," at her own hand, in despair at the growing strength of Octavius and Antony. The news moves Cassius to apostrophize the "immortal gods." The news is made the more moving by its late disclosure in the scene, which seems to speak indeed for Brutus's stoic virtue. But the disclosure of the news also makes explicitly manifest that it has affected Brutus—that it is behind his anger toward Cassius, and is even Brutus's open excuse for it. The happiness of the virtuous man turns out to rely on others, loved ones, to whose happiness he is devoted. Virtue is then but a means, one among many, to happiness. It is not the end in itself that it must claim to be. Moreover, Brutus's angry (and confused) intransigence on behalf of a purity of virtue and, finally, on behalf of the possibility of the purity of his own virtue—his angry redoubling in his argument with Cassius of a demand for it—is said to be *caused* by his grief at the death of Portia. Could his virtue, then, like that of the spirited Caius Ligarius, be traceable to a desire to "get the better of things impossible," to make himself worthy of immortality in the eyes of the "immortal gods"?

However this may be, when Titinius and Messala deliver the news that not 70 but 100 senators have been killed, including Cicero, Cassius is stunned by the news of Cicero's inclusion. (According to Plutarch, the triumvirate debated a full day over Cicero, with Octavius holding out the longest.) Brutus for his part questions Messala concerning news of Portia. Messala claims to have none, but finally delivers the awful report that Portia is dead. Brutus, feigning indifference, claims that the "meditation" that she must die at some point gives him patience to endure it now. This edifying moralism has the desired effect on Messala, who proclaims that "[e]ven so great men great losses should endure." This half fraud is perpetrated in the presence of—with the implicit consent of—Cassius, who is moved at no point to intervene. The silly poet who now arrives and who can hardly rhyme and who demands their reconciliation after it is already accomplished and who claims title to do so merely on the basis of his superior age (4.3.124–138) sees, then, neither that his subject matter as a poet is the conflict of thoughtful men, nor the depth of their reconciliation. Cassius not only admires Brutus's flawed capacity to endure the news of Portia's death, but wishes that capacity to be known as pure or unflawed. His subsequent bowing to Brutus's (wholly mistaken) judgment that it is better to march to Phillipi than to wait for the enemy further bespeaks his abiding deference to Brutus and his virtue—despite all the failure it has meant for their political efforts. His desire to avoid a fatal tactical division in their ranks is merely the political expression of a desire to avoid a division in his own soul; he wishes that there be a fully virtuous Brutus to whom he can bow, and for whom he would give up his own virtue and rule. But this has the result of making him consider himself less worthy than he, by his own understanding of worth, is.

It has been argued that had Cassius's judgment reigned rather than that of Brutus, the republican cause would have succeeded. This claim may be true, but the central problem that Shakespeare has brought to light would thereby have been hidden from us. The conspirators believed that they needed the noble Brutus if they were to have any hope of success, and it is tempting to think that this concern for public relations is sufficient to explain their turning to Brutus. Shakespeare shows us in Act IV that this concern is insufficient to explain the thinking of a Cassius, who needed to bow to Brutus for deeper reasons than the mere use of him for the conspiracy. But the bowing depends on a mutual if tacit acknowledgment of the need for fraud, a joint turning away from the truth concerning the insufficiency of virtue or a joint obfuscation of the necessities that would show its impossibility. Little wonder, then, that Act IV closes with Brutus haunted in his sleep by the ghost of Caesar, the killing of whom Brutus cannot shake from his Roman conscience.

Act V

Brutus's decision to take the fight to Phillipi is so imprudent as to be unexpected by Antony, who concludes that it must be a "show of bravery." In the dispute with Octavius that follows—over the placement of their soldiers against the oncoming enemy—we see the troubling result of their earlier discussion of Lepidus and a foreshadowing of what will follow (in *Antony and Cleopatra*): Antony orders Octavius to take the left side of the field, but Octavius orders him to take it. "Why do you cross me in this exigent?" Antony thunders. "I do not cross you; but I will do so," Octavius responds, with a double entendre. Octavius's display of the very spirit that Antony views as indispensible for a ruler, as a title to rule, brings to a head the fact that one or the other must become the horse and the other his rider. Monarchy can be just only over a slavish people, from whom either an Antony or an Octavius would never have arisen, to say nothing of a Brutus or Julius Caesar.

Antony calls for a parley with Brutus and Cassius, the double theme of which is public speech versus public deeds, and the justice of those who engage in them. Octavius and Antony together charge the "good words" of Brutus with being a mere veil for foul deeds; Antony cites the conspirators' false words to Caesar as they stabbed him, but Cassius reminds Antony of his own theft of all speech by his sweet speech, his robbing the Hybla bees and leaving them honey-less. Antony points out that his speech left them "stingless"—unable to harm him—which Brutus answers with a taunt about him "buzzing" now before he stings. This hits home, and Antony berates his opponents angrily for this mocking of his present frank warnings, they who treacherously, cowardly, killed Caesar not only without warning but with flattery, the mere pretense of admiration. Cassius, scoffing at the charge, blames Brutus for having overruled him and thereby permitted this "tongue" to now offend them. Octavius would have the battle prove who is right in the argument. He, another Caesar, will avenge Caesar's wounds, or else make the "traitors" also slaughterers. Brutus denies that they are traitors, and proudly, magnanimously states that even were Octavius (as he is not) the "noblest of thy strain," he could die no more honorably than at Brutus's hand; he implies that even Julius Caesar would have been honored to die in battle at Brutus's hand. Cassius adds that Octavius is unworthy to do so, and belittles Octavius's and Antony's worth with contemptuous epitaphs, prompting Antony to call him "Old Cassius still," that is, one who must enviously tear down the great and mistake their worth. Octavius utters a final defiance of them as traitors and possible cowards, thus bringing to an end a parley that has brought out both the abiding desire of Antony for revenge and the extraordinary high-mindedness or self-admiration of Brutus, whose honorableness Cassius seconds even as he faults him for having overruled him in the matter of Antony.

After the parley Brutus speaks privately with Lucilius. From what we learn later (5.4.5–25 and 5.5.54–59), we know that Brutus is here instructing him to act if needed as a decoy for Brutus, who will then be free to commit suicide. Brutus already anticipates here, that is, a possible defeat and makes provision to be able to die at his own hand. Cassius, meanwhile, in an exchange with Messala, is also coming to terms with the prospect of defeat. "Against my will," he declares, he is compelled like Pompey to wage this single battle for their liberties. He goes into battle deferring, that is, to Brutus's will—as Pompey had deferred to the senators' will at Pharsalia—despite the fact that Cassius continues, as we have just seen, to blame Brutus for overruling him in the matter of Mark Antony. His compelling need to do so, to bow to the nobility of Brutus, has led him to a battle that he now suspects or half believes is actually *doomed* to be lost. For as he tells Messala, he now disowns his Epicurean opinion (about omens), having come to believe "partly" that the activities of birds he has recently seen are omens presaging their defeat. Only partly believing these, he finds himself still resolved "to meet all perils very constantly." Full belief in the birds' activities as omens, that is, would sap his resolve with the full expectation of defeat and hence make him defeatist; there would be no possibility of victory or indeed of any free human action or liberty. Given Cassius's previous dispute with Brutus over traveling to Philippi, it would seem that his noticing of the flights of birds of significant symbolism, whose activity corresponds with what he expects—with his forcefully expressed, rational misgivings over the battle, rejected by Brutus—have *led* him to conclude that the birds' activities may well be what others have said: omens. But his abiding resolve seems to be countervailing evidence that makes his belief in omens only partial. He has been led, we may say, through his compelling need to bow to Brutus to the realization that it will lead now to a final defeat, and rather than abandon his reverence for Brutus and his virtue he would instead explain that defeat as something divinely ordained, but nonetheless requiring of him his full resolve on behalf of the republican cause.

If Cassius does partly think the omens presage defeat, he hides this altogether from Brutus, telling him instead that "[t]he gods to-day stand friendly, that we may, / Lovers in peace, lead on our days to age!" (5.1.93–95). He introduces the question of what Brutus will do if they are defeated as a topic induced merely by the uncertainties of the affairs of men. Brutus first answers that he will adhere to the "philosophy" that led him to denounce Cato's suicide, that is, Stoicism, which Cassius has hitherto admired in him but which requires patient endurance of what divine providence sends. To the Stoic suicide is not a gift from the gods, as Cassius had told the pious Casca it is—a gift ensuring liberty from tyranny—but is instead a rebellion against their providential rule. Brutus will not, therefore, commit suicide. But while he speaks of his denunciation of Cato's suicide, he says nothing of the suicide of Cato's daughter, the manly Portia, whose manliness he had admired and understood to be the ground for her demand for an equal share in his deliberations (2.1.919–32). And since Brutus has already made anticipatory arrangements with Lucilius, we can see that his statement here is false.

The two friends appear then each to have offered an edifying tale to the other, the one concerning the gods' friendly stance and the other concerning stoic patient endurance of whatever evils the gods in their providence send, or the sufficiency of virtue to bear what Cassius had earlier called "accidental evils" (4.3.146). But this stoic response is no longer or in this dire situation sufficient for Cassius. Can the man whose virtue he has admired and bowed to and attempted to keep pure be prepared to end their labors with no more than a humiliating acceptance of defeat? Can these be the wages of virtue? He now forces Brutus to face concretely what the result of foreswearing suicide would mean for Brutus: "You are contented to be led in triumph / Through the streets of Rome?" And Brutus, with breathtaking alacrity, unceremoniously drops his pious stoicism or rather his pretense to it: "No, Cassius, no: think not, thou noble Roman, / That ever Brutus will go bound to Rome; / He bears too great a mind" (5.1.110–112). Brutus will, we now learn, *not* be governed by the outcome of either divine or human rulers if that outcome entails the public humiliation of shameful bondage. He will instead commit suicide. He and Cassius will therefore meet again only, as he states, if their side wins the battle, and so they now say their contingent "eternal" farewells. On the basis of their common ground of being not base but noble Romans, Brutus tells

Cassius the grim yet welcome truth. Brutus's high mindedness or greatness of soul, his high self-admiration, something he assumes that his fellow noble Roman will of course grasp immediately, will not abide the public humiliation of enslavement. Indeed, had Brutus's very appeal to the commoners not hinged on their public repudiation as noble Romans of any base or vile readiness to be bondsmen? Yet was that appeal not made precisely to have them realize and sustain their *liberation* from the rule of a noble Roman, the great-souled Caesar? Of a man whom Brutus, as we have just seen, thinks would have been honored to die in battle at Brutus's hand? Does Brutus's great-souledness, his being the peak of Roman virtue, not point to the necessity of his rule, over Cassius and certainly over all lesser Romans?

Cassius's abiding resolve to fight on in what seems the losing republican side, resting as it does on his admiration of the great-souled nature of Brutus, rests on something that leads to monarchy and hence enslavement rather than to republicanism.

We are thus not altogether unprepared and hence not altogether surprised to discover in the penultimate scene that Titanius (of whom we have barely heard), and not Brutus, who has "ruled" Cassius throughout the play, is Cassius's "best friend," the one whose death leads Cassius to suicide.

★   ★   ★

The respective and quite different suicides of Cassius and Brutus, and their aftermaths, dominate the final scene and give us the final elements of the great human dilemma that the play has brought to our attention. The myopic Cassius sends Titanius to investigate a distant part of the battle and so must rely upon his slave, Pindarus, to describe for him the result. Pindarus misdescribes it as the taking of Titanius, and Cassius, ashamed to have lived while his best friend is taken, orders Pindarus to kill him—to obey Cassius in accord with the oath he swore when Cassius spared his life in battle at Partia—and to thereby be liberated from his slavery. He commands a slave to, as it were, do to him what he had done to Caesar, to kill his master and be liberated. Against his own wishes Pindarus immediately dares to obey that order and, recognizing himself in astonishment as now free by dint of his daring act, runs far from the sight of Romans to keep his freedom secure. If Caesar is thus avenged, as Cassius's final words declare him, the principle upon which Cassius had sought Caesar's death is shown by Pindarus's deed to have been sound. We may even say that in ordering his slave to liberate himself by taking Cassius's life, Cassius has exceeded Caesar in nobility, at least with respect to those of low and even the lowliest rank.

Titanius and Messala arrive too late with the true, good news of Brutus's victory over Octavius's troops. They find, as Titanius puts it, that "the sun of Rome is set." Titanius rightly attributes the suicide to "mistrust of my success," while Messala thinks it is "mistrust of good success," that is, of the good success of their side. Messala delivers an oration against "hateful error," and departs to find Brutus, leaving Titanius to deliver an anguished soliloquy, not to error in the abstract but to the dead Cassius, about his specific error concerning Titanius and his mission. After crowing Cassius with a crown sent from "thy Brutus," with Cassius's sword Titanius slays himself, in grief over his lost friend, dying as a Roman, that is, in the manner that Cassius would have admired and expected of him. Cassius dies alone, yet his death is mortally devastating to his faithful friend.

Brutus and his entourage arrive to find the bodies of Cassius and Titanius, and Brutus blames the horrible scene on "the spirit of Caesar" that is now taking its revenge. "The last of all the Romans," as he calls Cassius and Titanius, "fare thee well." Like Titanius, Brutus sees in Cassius's death the end of Rome, of the republic that was Rome. Yet he fights on, and will have no funeral lest it discomfort the troops. He must believe that so long as he lives Rome still lives, and goes forth to a second battle.

Lucilius is taken alive while acting the part of Brutus, while the latter in another part of the battlefield asks first Clitus, then Dardanius, then Volumnius, to help him take his life. All as friends refuse—it is not the part of a friend to slay a friend. But the ghost of Caesar—of Brutus's friend whom he slew—has appeared to him again, he discloses to Volumnius, and their enemies press them to the pit. "It is more worthy to leap in ourselves, / Than tarry till they push us." They have all refused. Yet Brutus is determined, and after saying his farewells to them, declares his joy:

> Countrymen,
> My heart doth joy that yet in all my life
> I found no man but he was true to me.
> I shall have glory by this losing day
> More than Octavius and Mark Antony
> By this vile conquest shall attain unto.
> So fare you well at once; for Brutus' tongue
> Hath almost ended his live's history.
> Night hangs upon mine eyes; my bones would rest,
> That have but labor'd to attain this hour. (5.5.33–42)

Finally a sleepy Strato, whose life has, Brutus states, "some snatch of honor in it," consents to hold the sword while Brutus runs on it. "Caesar, now be still: / I kill'd not thee with half so good a will" (5.5.50–51). Here then is how Brutus has solved his problem and the problem of Rome, the "tragic" problem of political life at its peak. Brutus's friends have been loyal to *him*, and *he* will have glory through *losing* the hard-fought battle. This is no mere sour grapes, or a making lemonade of lemons. One cannot say that Brutus sought to lose, but he is indeed happy with the outcome, the loss of the hard-fought battle. He has attempted to keep Rome a republic, and while unsuccessful, his defeat, unlike the victory of Octavius and Mark Antony, brings *him* glory. Had he won, he would, like them, have had to rule Rome, and thereby enslave Romans, or lose their loyalty. Brutus's *own glory* is in the end, quite explicitly, his primary concern—the republican cause was his instrument. All his life he has labored to attain such a glorious end; he has not labored all his life for Rome or for the republic. Defeat in the noble republican cause provides what he has sought. Unlike the melancholy suicide of Cassius, Brutus's is a happy death; he is indeed twice happier to take his own life, in this circumstance, than he was, with his never-resolved dilemma, to have taken Caesar's. And as Strato tells Octavius and the captive Messala, "Brutus only overcame himself, / And no man else hath honour by his death" (5.5.56–57). The great-souled Brutus has stolen from the conquerors the opportunity for obtaining the honor that might have been theirs in killing him. His glory is thus completely his.

★   ★   ★

Octavius is drawn to make Strato, the man anxious to declare Brutus's achievement, through suicide, of a monopoly of honor, one of his own men. Only with Messala's permission will Strato agree to this. Messala agrees once he has heard that Strato held the sword upon which Brutus ran himself, that he performed the last service for his "master." The difference between Pindarus, the aid to Cassius's suicide, and Strato, the aid to Brutus's suicide, is striking. Cassius offered Pindarus, a mere slave, his liberation, which he obtained by daringly following his master's orders against his own wish. Brutus would have none aid him in the deed but who had at least a "snatch of honor," finally settling for Strato. His criterion reflected a concern for his honor, a concern to have someone who was worthy enough to have a share of the deed of killing him. Strato met the condition, but obtained by the grim deed not liberation but only—after seeking his superior's permission—faithful service to the new ruler of Rome. Nor does any friend commit suicide over Brutus's death. His friends had, it is true, departed before he killed himself, but his final words to them about the attainment of his own glory are hardly such as to have moved them to do for Brutus what Titanius did for Cassius. This is not to say that Cassius's virtue is superior to that of Brutus, but to say that as the great-souled Brutus approaches his end, as that end comes into his possession, we see clearly its relation to others and its detrimental, ultimately enslaving effect.

Mark Antony, whose eulogy of Brutus almost concludes the work, had seen the use being made by the conspirators of Brutus's honor and hence the need to discredit Brutus's honor in the eyes of the people. But Antony's deep love of and admiration for Caesar, along with his wait for his opportunity to exercise his ruling spirit, also allowed him to perceive at least dimly (and to exploit) the dilemma behind Brutus's actions, and hence the impossibility of Brutus's position. We may say on this account that Antony truly and understandingly says of Brutus in the end that "this was the noblest Roman of them all"—meaning, as he quickly makes clear, of all the *conspirators*. He alone "in a general honest thought / And common good to all, made one of them." Antony's condemnation of the others for envy of Caesar should not hide the fact that he has declared them nonetheless noble Romans, just not the noblest. His praise of Brutus ascends, however, to a declaration that on account of Brutus's gentleness and the mixture in him of "all the elements," all of nature would proclaim of him, *"Here was a man."* To Antony Brutus, great and gentle and troubled Brutus, is the natural peak of humanity. As long as there is public life, a victorious Antony must be ultimately but a foil and noble eulogizer of a Brutus. The greatest honor does indeed come from dying in the impossible task of trying to save republican Rome from the rule of the human being who most deserves it.

But it is perhaps the case that the weepy Antony says more than he knows. He is impressed by Brutus's action because he believes that it was for the general good. Yet in truth, as we have seen, it was ultimately for Brutus's own glory. Little more than Brutus does Antony permit himself to see clearly the fundamental problem or its resolution. That problem will now fade altogether from Roman political life, however, as Octavius rises. He is given the last word, and it indicates his disposition toward Brutus:

> According to his virtue let us use him,
> With all respect and rites of burial.
> Within my tent his bones to-night shall lie,
> Most like a soldier, ordered honorably. (5.5.76–79)

In sharp contrast to Antony, Octavius will honor Brutus only as one who possessed the virtue of a soldier. This may be prudent—for how could Brutus, the assassin of Caesar, have acted for the common good, and be among the conspirators the "noblest Roman of them all," much less nature's very manifestation of a man? But Octavius's limitation of Brutus's honors also reflects the disposition of which we have had a glimpse, in his exchange with Antony over Lepidus. All who will be left in Rome, all who can now find a home there, are good soldiers, valiant men who take orders. The gentleness of a more human (and humane) virtue, wrought paradoxically in the competitive world of high republican politics, will be lost. The soldier's virtue will, paradoxically, eventually bring peace to the known world[16] under Octavius. But the cost will be the loss of men like Brutus, who struggled mightily in the losing cause of trying to resolve the great dilemma of political life at its peak.

CHAPTER 2

MACBETH: AMBITION DRIVEN INTO DARKNESS

With *Macbeth* we move from Roman to Christian times, from a deep sense of honor and pride in noble acts to sin and remorse; from a debate between an Epicurean and a Stoic to a fight between dark forces of hell and angelic forces of heaven. The politics of eleventh-century Scotland seem very strange in comparison with what we have seen of high political life in Rome, and they are. But the human problems perdure. The changes that Christianity brings to political life are, as we will see, real and far-reaching, but they do not destroy the permanent political questions. We are shown in the rule of Macbeth and Lady Macbeth the peculiar tyranny of bad or half Christians, and the eventual curing of Scotland by Malcolm, who is in contrast to his father, the pious Duncan, decidedly non-Christian.

Act I

Under stormy skies, three hags open the play speaking in a baffling, eerily confounding manner. In the questions put by the first hag, "When shall we three meet again? / In thunder, lightning, or in rain?" (1.1.1–2), three forces found together in nature are treated as if they could somehow be split up. The second hag's reply is equally perplexing in its equivocation: "When the hurly-burly's done, / When the battle's lost and won." And despite the looming storm and what will soon be referred to as the "fog and filthy air," the third hag speaks of "the set of sun." The hags have some knowledge of the future: they know that Macbeth will win the coming battle ("Upon the heath / There to meet with Macbeth"). They also have each a pet spirit with an ugly name, whose summonses they alone hear and creepily obey. What strange and spooky world have we entered? The hags mention air, fire (lightning), and water (rain); they don't mention earth; they are, as Banquo will say of them, unearthly creatures (cf. 1.3.41–42).

Their conclusion, uttered in unison, makes the deep confusion explicit and universal: "Fair is foul, and foul is fair" (1.1.11). Shakespeare has taken characters from a late episode in Holinshed's chronicle[1] and used them to set the preternatural stage upon which the politics of a Christian Scotland will play themselves out.

But who is this Macbeth to whom the hags have referred? He is introduced, but only by report, in scene two, where we also learn more generally of the political and military situation of Scotland. The Sergeant who reports Macbeth's deeds has come recently from battle, "bloody" (1.2.1), the military action he describes began as "doubtful" (1.2.7). He delivers his report to the king of Scotland—Duncan—and his son Malcolm, recently held captive by Macdonwald. The latter is in rebellion against the king. Scotland is a very unsettled monarchy, and Macbeth leads the fight against the rebels. The Sergeant tells of how, "disdaining Fortune," Macbeth cut "the slave" Macdonwald in half, navel to chin, and then beheaded him. And we learn from the report of Rosse (who, intriguingly, has suffered no wounds) that when the king of Norway came to Macdonwald's relief, Macbeth defeated him as well. Macbeth thus appears immediately as a fierce fighter, a lion or an eagle, "Bellona's bridegroom." Or as the Sergeant had described both him and Banquo, with a Christian metaphor, "Except they meant to bathe in reeking wounds / Or memorize another Golgatha, I cannot tell." Macbeth's martial valor is said to arm justice (1.2.29), that is, Duncan's monarchic rule. But does Macbeth, like these faithful Christian followers of Duncan, consider that rule good and hence worth defending, or does he fight for other reasons?

We aren't told what motivates the rebels but are left to gather it from the speeches of Duncan and his partisans. Duncan is as delighted with Rosse's report of Macbeth's success ("Great happiness!" [1.2.58]) as he had been with the Sergeant's, and declares Macbeth the new Thane of Cawdor, to replace the one who joined the rebels and whom Duncan now condemns to death. Duncan is fully confident that Macbeth deserves this title—remarkably so, given the betrayal he has just suffered from its former holder. He sees only that Macbeth has fought valiantly on his behalf; it does not occur to him that Macbeth might be engaged in martial deeds for his own glory. The sequel will show Duncan's judgment to be mistaken: Macbeth, the new Thane of Cawdor, will turn out more treacherous than the old. Duncan is, then, a less than wise, even a naïve, king. And he is soft: he does not lead his men into battle but relies for his victories on tough men like Macbeth. Holinshed had traced the rebellion against Duncan to the fact that he was too soft in punishing criminals; the taunting Macdonwald, Holinshed reports, called Duncan "a milksop, more meet to govern a sort of idle monks in some cloister, than to have rule over such valiant and hardy men of war as the Scots were."

Shakespeare is far less direct, but what he leaves us to gather of Duncan is in agreement with this taunt.

The hags reappear in the third scene, with lines not just baffling but ugly. They are consumed by petty events and vulgar jealousies; they are gluttonous, selfish, vengeful, and delight in human misery. With all the vices of teenagers and none of their virtues, they appear as powerful and hence monstrous children. Their powers, given them by their spirits, are limited, however: they cannot down the ship on which sails one of their enemies. And so they need to try to work a charm to defeat him. Before Macbeth meets up with them, he utters his first words, which echo the hags' opening and deeply ambiguous speech: "So fair and foul a day I have not seen," he tells Banquo (1.3.38). Macbeth is disposed to be in their thrall.

Banquo, while questioning the hags, describes their repulsive appearance: withered, wild in attire, possessed of choppy fingers and skinny lips, and bearded. Macbeth gives them an order and then a question: "Speak, if you can. What are you?" (1.3.47). They respond with a threefold, prophetic greeting to Macbeth as Glamis, Cawdor, and King hereafter. And from Banquo's words we learn of Macbeth's fearful reaction to this greeting: "Good sir, why do you start, and seem to fear / Things that do sound so fair?" (1.3.51–52). Macbeth doesn't reply, so we are again left to discover the reason. That he has heard fair things from foul lips isn't sufficient to make so stout a man fearful. And the sequel makes impossible the thought that he loves the king and so fears the words that bespeak his demise. Has he, perhaps, already been plotting against Duncan, and fears that his plot is now public knowledge?

The hags have, Banquo declares, granted "noble" Macbeth the prediction "of noble having and of royal hope," and he now fearlessly demands (as in Holinshed) to learn his own future from them. They comply, but with more maddening ambiguity:

> Lesser than Macbeth, and greater.
> Not so happy, yet much happier.
> Thou shalt get kings, though thou be none.
> So all hail, Macbeth and Banquo! (1.3.65–68)

Macbeth has now recovered enough to command the hags to stay and explain the how and the why for of their "prophetic greeting," but they vanish: "what seemed corporal melted." Banquo questions whether they were real, but Macbeth states simply that "your children shall be kings," and the two repeat the predictions. Rosse and Angus arrive and confirm the veracity of the first prediction: Cawdor's confessed treachery has overthrown him, and Macbeth is now Cawdor. Yet the announcement is strange.

Rosse claims of Duncan that, upon hearing of Macbeth's role in the fight against the rebels, Duncan's "wonders and his praises do contend / Which should be thine or his. Silenc'd with that,..." Whatever does Rosse mean by telling Macbeth that Duncan could not decide "which" of his "wonders and praises" should be Macbeth's or Duncan's? Is it really unclear to Duncan to whom the praises rightfully belong? Is his reaction as reported by Rosse not as baffling as the hags' statements?

The responses of Macbeth and Banquo to the confirmation of the hags' first prophecy come in a series of asides by Macbeth, both to himself and with Banquo. Shakespeare here departs notably from Holinshed, who presents Banquo as a coconspirator with Macbeth; Banquo is instead made a steadfast foil for Macbeth's wavering. Upon hearing Macbeth's new title Banquo had exclaimed, "What? Can the devil speak true?" indicating immediately his Christian disposition. Macbeth then tells himself in an aside, "Glamis, and Thane of Cawdor! / The greatest is behind" (1.3.117–118)—our first indication of his royal ambition. But when Macbeth inquires of Banquo about his hopes for a similar confirmation of the hags' predictions of the kingship of his progeny, he is met with a private rebuke:

> That, trusted home,
> Might yet enkindle you unto the crown,
> And oftentimes, to win us to our harm,
> The instruments of darkness tell us truths,
> Win us with honest trifles, to betray's
> In deepest consequence.(1.3.120–126)

Banquo warns against taking the hags' predictions as license to pursue, by means fair or foul, the ends they promise. Yet it is only if there are "instruments of darkness," and only if the promised rule is a "trifle" compared to our deepest concern—our immortal souls—that Banquo's advice makes sense. His is the warning of a devout Christian.

But Macbeth is unmoved by it. In a second aside to himself, he calls the hags' two truths (Glamis, Cawdor) "happy prologues to the swelling act / Of the imperial theme" (1.3.128–129). He is, however, troubled by the moral ambiguity of "[t]his supernatural soliciting," which "[c]annot be ill; cannot be good,"

> If ill,
> Why hath it given me earnest of success,
> Commencing in a truth? I am Thane of Cawdor.
> If good, why do I yield to that suggestion
> Whose horrid image doth unfix my hair
> And make my seated heart knock at my ribs,

> Against the use of nature? Present fears
> Are less than horrible imaginings:
> My thought, whose murther yet is but fantastical,
> Shakes so my single state of man that function
> Is smother'd in surmise, and nothing is
> But what is not. (1.3.131–142)

Macbeth is terrified by the image of murdering that has arisen from this "supernatural soliciting." He implicitly rejects Banquo's claim that dark forces can win us "with honest trifles," however: the truth, Macbeth thinks, cannot belong to what is "ill," nor is the hags' prediction a "trifle." The image of Duncan's murder is "horrible," yet it grips him, owing to the "earnest of success" that has been given through the confirmation of the hags' first prediction. Macbeth is between two worlds, pagan and Christian, driven by a guilty ambition for what he perceives to be good, but which would be achievable only through doing "ill." His terror abates when he recasts what he had called the "supernatural" as chance: "If chance will have me king, why, chance may crown me / Without my stir" (1.3.143–44); he is not doomed or fated to murder Duncan. The others call him back from these reflections, and he says, quite truthfully, that his "dull brain was wrought / With things *forgotten*" (emphasis added). For as we will soon learn, he has indeed before now planned, with Lady Macbeth, to murder Duncan. He promises Banquo to speak freely of "what hath chanc'd," but this promise will remain unkept. The words and deeds of Duncan and of Lady Macbeth will silence Macbeth's fears, and so make Banquo and his heirs an obstacle to his desires.

★ ★ ★

From Malcolm's account of the death of the former Thane of Cawdor we learn that Macbeth's predecessor was torn between dutiful Christian devotion to Duncan and a desire to unseat him. His end, significantly, puzzles Malcolm:

> I have spoke
> With one that saw him die; who did report
> That very frankly he confess'd his treasons,
> Implor'd your Highness' pardon, and set forth
> A deep repentance. Nothing in his life
> Became him like the leaving it. He died
> As one that had been studied in his death,
> To throw away the dearest thing he ow'd,
> As 'twere a careless trifle. (1.4.3–11)

A non-Christian too, of course, may die as one "studied in his death"—a Brutus or a Prospero—but in Cawdor's case that study is linked to "a deep repentance," and to the treatment of life as a "careless trifle." We have seen Banquo refer to becoming Thane of Cawdor an "honest trifle," deprecating political titles; we see here that the former Cawdor himself, taking this Christian position to its logical conclusion, considered life itself a "trifle," which indeed it must appear to one who dies in hope of eternal bliss. Malcolm implicitly disagrees with this Christian teaching, calling Cawdor's life "the dearest thing he ow'd." This initial disagreement will, by the fourth act, have become a quiet but firm rejection of Christian doctrine by Malcolm, upon whose shoulders the salvation of Scotland will rest.

Malcolm's father Duncan has, however, no such trouble with Christianity. Rather, its troublingly paradoxical nature comes through in him. Reflecting on Cawdor's death, Duncan merely regrets that there is

> no art
> To find the mind's construction in the face:
> He was a gentleman on whom I built
> An absolute trust. (1.4.11–14)

But as we have seen, a Caesar was able to discern much in the face of a Cassius. Duncan's lament reflects in truth his own deficiency in this art, his overtrustfulness or naiveté, as Shakespeare makes abundantly clear by concluding the lament with Duncan's greeting of the man we have just heard speak of murdering him: "O Worthiest cousin!" Duncan's defect is tied to his Christianity: "The sin of my ingratitude even now / was heavy on me," he declares, a "sin" that he has, as he sees it, incurred by not rewarding Macbeth sooner for his recent deeds.

This guilt leads Duncan to deliver quite bluntly a graceless but significant paradox to Macbeth:

> Thou art so far before,
> That swiftest wing of recompense is slow
> To overtake thee. Would thou hadst less deserv'd,
> That the proportion both of thanks and payment
> Might have been mine! (1.4.16–20)

Macbeth's having been virtuous—as Duncan can only have wished—makes Duncan sinful in not having bestowed on him sooner what he deserves. Duncan must therefore wish, as he says, that Macbeth had deserved *less*, since Macbeth's deserving is the source of Duncan's *sin*, and Duncan does not wish to be sinful. Duncan here states this self-concern quite frankly. We are thus confronted with a new kind of paradox, one that is introduced by Christianity. The classical problem of virtue, as we saw in *Julius Caesar*, is that the more virtuous one is, the more one inevitably deprives others of their share of virtuous deeds. This new paradox, by contrast, rests on a new understanding of virtue, one with a peculiar, frank self-concern at its heart. That it should do so may seem quite surprising, inasmuch as Christianity calls for a self-renunciation, over and against prideful pagan self-admiration. But Shakespeare's portrayal is not without solid ground. For the concern for one's immortal soul—deep-seated and acknowledged, to be sure, by pre-Christians—was not an explicit, acknowledged concern of classical *political* life. It became so only in Christian political life. As St. Augustine puts it (in his argument against Varro's Roman civil theology), it is "for the sake of eternal life alone that we are Christians" (*City of God*, 6.9). Duncan's rule embodies that concern. His most devoutly Christian follower, Macduff, will eventually tell Malcolm,

> Thy royal father
> Was a most sainted king; the queen that bore thee,
> Oft'ner upon her knees than on her feet
> Died every day she liv'd. (4.3.108–111)

As this already suggests, however, the explicit and even official path to the great good of eternal life is one of renunciation of the goods of *this* life. Hence, when Duncan concludes his greeting of Macbeth with the words "More is thy due than more than all can pay" (1.3.21), Macbeth responds with an expected public total self-renunciation:

> The service and the loyalty I owe,
> In doing it, pays itself. Your Highness' part
> Is to receive our duties; and our duties
> Are to your throne and state children and servants;
> Which do but what they should, by doing every thing
> Safe toward your love and honor. (1.4.22–27)

Renunciation of worldly goods in a selfless, dutiful service to the king—to him whose body Macduff will call "the Lord's anointed temple" (2.3.68)—is demanded of the Christian subject. Macbeth publicly accedes to that demand. But if nature is at odds with it—if it is a demand that goes too far, infantilizing and enslaving all but the king, as his "children and servants"—we can expect politics to suffer from the actions of men who must despise themselves for trying to meet it. Their natural desire for a share of worldly honor will—especially in the case of those who entertain some doubts of eternal life—be driven into dark, private channels, there to do its "sinful" work.

And so it is with Macbeth. Duncan accepts his profession of selfless service without the slightest doubt of its sincerity, and then makes an announcement that betrays an astonishing ignorance of his faithful defender's actual ambition. So moved to joy is Duncan by the faithful, selfless deeds of Macbeth and Banquo that…he names *Malcolm* his lawful heir, making him Prince of Cumberland and announcing that they will all travel this day to Macbeth's castle at Enverness. Were Macbeth's and Banquo's professions of selfless devotion simply sincere, of course, this announcement would make perfect sense. But the ascension of Malcolm is in truth more than Macbeth can bear. He gives, to be sure, another public profession of his total devotion to Duncan: "The rest is labor, which is not us'd for you." And Duncan for his part accepts it at face value: "Worthy Cawdor!" But Macbeth has in truth now begun to resolve again upon the murder of Duncan, as we learn through his aside:

> The Prince of Cumberland! that is a step
> On which I must fall down, or else o'erleap,
> For in my way it lies. Stars, hide your fires,
> Let not light see my black and deep desires;
> The eye wink at the hand; yet let that be
> Which the eye fears, when it is done, to see. (1.4.48–53)

No public justification is available to contest what the Christian king has decided. The "light" has room only for the kind of totally selfless duty Macbeth has professed. In fact, his desires are even "black" in his *own* judgment. He needs the darkness to hide the deeds that will win him what he somehow senses that he, rather than Duncan or Malcolm, ought to have.

★   ★   ★

At Enverness Lady Macbeth reads a letter from her husband in which he describes to her, "my dearest partner of greatness," the hags' predictions and the fulfillment of the first of them. The letter omits any mention of Banquo and his heirs, and so this part of the hags' prediction remains, significantly, outside of all of Lady Macbeth's subsequent deliberations and deeds. Of more immediate importance, the letter was clearly sent *before* the previous scene took place, since it says nothing of the need to prepare for the king's impending visit (cf. 1.5.30–33). It was sent, then, before the announcement of Malcolm as heir to the throne and Macbeth's consequent resolve to commit the murder. In Lady Macbeth's reaction to the letter we (therefore) learn that she and Macbeth had been plotting

Duncan's murder before that announcement, indeed even before Macbeth encountered the hags:

> Glamis thou art, and Cawdor, and shalt be
> What thou art promis'd. Yet do I fear thy nature,
> It is too full o' th' milk of human kindness
> To catch the nearest way. Thou wouldst be great,
> Art not without ambition, but without
> The illness should attend it. What thou wouldst highly,
> That wouldst thou holily; wouldst not play false,
> And yet wouldst wrongly win. Thou'ldst have, great Glamis,
> That which cries, "Thus thou must do," if thou have it. (1.5.15–23)

Lady Macbeth has clearly discussed with her husband Duncan's murder, and found him wanting, not in ambition but in "the illness should attend it," that is, cruelty. Too full of the milk of human kindness, he would attain the high only "holily."

We have seen Brutus wrestle with a similar problem, in his "It must be by his death" soliloquy. But we see now a distortion by Christianity of that problem that was so clearly present in classical political life. Brutus was gentle in his nature, a characteristic praised even by Antony. To Lady Macbeth, however, kindness is akin to holiness, and is the result of a natural feminine weakness that obstructs the means to "greatness." She can see kindness or lack of cruelty only as an officially sanctioned weakness. Yet like Macbeth, she nonetheless *accepts* the Christian understanding of right and wrong: to win the crown by murder is to win it "wrongly," but so would she have Macbeth win it. Human greatness has in Christian times become, it seems, so discredited by the elevation of Christian "supernatural" virtues that those who long for greatness, as she does, are disposed to accept that seeking it is "sinful" and hence are disposed to view cruelty—also sinful—as its natural accompaniment. Her moral universe has no place for human greatness that includes gentleness or a sense of remorse. She is open to finding in the ugly hags' predictions, therefore, as had Macbeth, an alternative, evil, "metaphysical" or supernatural aid to the greatness they both seek.

To achieve her end, Lady Macbeth can and must, as she sees it, overcome her feminine—gentle, compassionate, moral—nature, with the help of dark spirits. After a messenger has announced the king's coming, she delivers her famous soliloquy:

> The raven himself is hoarse
> That croaks the fatal entrance of Duncan
> Under my battlements. Come, you spirits

That tend on mortal thoughts, unsex me here,
And fill me from the crown to the toe topful
Of direst cruelty! Make thick my blood,
Stop up th' access and passage to remorse,
That no compunctious visitings of nature
Shake my fell purpose, nor keep peace between
Th' effect and [it]! Come to my woman's breasts,
And take my milk for gall, you murth'ring ministers,
Wherever in your sightless substances
You wait on nature's mischief! Come, thick night,
And pall thee in the dunnest smoke of hell,
That my keen knife see not the wound it makes,
Nor heaven peep through the blanket of the dark
To cry, "Hold, hold!" (3.5.38–54)

Such a prayer does Christianity produce in this woman who seeks its antithesis. We may better appreciate its Christian character by comparison with the pleading of Portia in *Julius Caesar*. She had laid claim to hear of her husband's troubles on the ground that she was a noble woman, daughter of Cato, and wife of the noble Brutus. She had indeed stabbed herself to show her courageous capacity to endure pain above what is usually expected of a woman. But she had said nothing of being unsexed by spirits, nor of anything supernatural having power over the natural, nor, monstrously, of sightless substances taking her milk for gall. There was no talk of hell and its "dunnest smoke," or of heaven crying "hold." In Lady Macbeth, on the other hand, we see a craving for the antithesis of Christianity's promise of overcoming, by the purity of self-denial and remorse for sin, nature's limit to "mortal" life. If Christianity has effeminized men through self-denying virtues, the hellish spirits included in its teachings can unsex a woman. "Dark" spiritual forces are sought out to justify and to achieve political greatness.

Greatness remains the theme as Macbeth enters: "Great Glamis! worthy Cawdor! / Greater than both, by the all-hail hereafter!" Lady Macbeth is transported, she declares, by Macbeth's letters, from the present to the future, where he is king. The future is now; the supernatural, in the form of the hags' prophecies, has promised that it will be so, and this is taken as permission to make it so. Is Duncan to take his leave tomorrow? "[N]ever / Shall sun that morrow see!" The whole of what is to be is to be changed, so that what might have been—what Duncan intended—will not be so. Once the dark deed is done, what appears in the light will be different. But for this to be accomplished, Lady Macbeth cautions, darkness, hiddenness of intention, deceit, is required: to beguile the time, look like the time, like an innocent flower, but be the serpent under it. A glance at the speech of Brutus again discloses the significant change of the political landscape. Brutus had to convince himself that Caesar was a serpent ready to be hatched; Lady Macbeth is advising her husband to be a serpent himself. Brutus endeavored to preserve his honorable virtue intact, in service to Rome; with that proud virtue now publicly deemed to be a splendid vice, Lady Macbeth turns to what dark forces say is possible, if one but call upon them and follow their ways. Brutus tried mightily to avoid deception, to remain trustworthy, needing no oaths; Lady Macbeth advises deception, like the serpent in the garden. She will take care of the rest.

★ ★ ★

Duncan's arrival at Enverness, as A. C. Bradley notes, is one of only two scenes of sweetness and light in *Macbeth*. Its serenity is ironic; Duncan is taken in by the sweetness, as is Banquo: a bird building its nest on the castle confirms, he declares, that "heaven's breath smells wooingly here." The naïve Christian omen sets the stage for the second of Duncan's Christian paradoxes, his catechizing greeting of Lady Macbeth:

> See, see, our honor'd hostess!
> The love that follows us sometime is our trouble,
> Which still we thank as love. Herein I teach you
> How you shall bid God 'ield us for your pains,
> And thank us for your trouble. (1.6.10–14)

Since we trouble you, offer your trouble up as a sacrifice to God for our sake, and be thankful that we grant you the opportunity to do so. Duncan's astoundingly ungracious words may be facetious, but they sit squarely with his Christian beliefs. Common sense would say that the king should be grateful for the hospitality he has imposed; Duncan believes, to the contrary, that trouble, self-sacrificial service, is to be performed with an eye to moving God, an opportunity to ease the guests' way to heaven, an intercession performed out of love. An opportunity to manifest earthly virtue is thus reinterpreted in the light of divine rewards, becoming thereby a compounded opportunity for selfless love. Lady Macbeth goes along with this teaching, at least for the most part: "twice done, and then done double," she declares, all our service is poor measured against the honors, old and new, you have bestowed. For these, "we rest your 'ermits." As hermits do for God, so are she and Macbeth prepared to do for him—to live a spartan existence for his sake, who have honored them so.

But Macbeth is strangely absent, and when Duncan asks after him, he receives no answer. The king then recounts how Macbeth, out of great love, arrived before them; love spurs zealous acts of devotion. But then, where is Macbeth? With no response from Lady Macbeth, Duncan gently reminds her of the situation and hence of her duties: "Fair and noble hostess, / We are your guests to-night." She replies with more standard hypocrisy: What's ours is yours. But where is Macbeth?

He is in fact being kept offstage by an inability to "beguile the time" as Lady Macbeth had advised. For he is now troubled by doubts, which he considers decisive, against the murder of Duncan. And while the scene and hence Act I will end with Macbeth fully resolved to murder Duncan, Macbeth comes to that resolution only when driven by certain accusations of Lady Macbeth and her assurances of an easy success. This is strange: we would expect here, in Macbeth's "If it were done" soliloquy (1.7.1–28), to hear his justification of the seizure of the throne. What we get instead is a claim that there is no justification, nor anything to be gained in the attempt.

> If it were done, when 'tis done, then 'twere well
> It were done quickly. If th' assassination
> Could trammel up the consequence, and catch
> With his surcease, success; that but this blow
> Might be the be-all and the end-all—here. (1.7.1–5)

If killing Duncan were the end of the matter, Macbeth reasons, then it were best done quickly. The problem is that it isn't the end, for two reasons. The first has to do with the afterlife: "But here, upon this bank and [shoal] of time, / We'ld jump the life to come" (1.7.6–7). Eternal life is risked as a consequence of murder. This does not, however, trouble Macbeth much at all. He is quite willing to take the risk, for the sake of success "here"—to keep his one-in-the-hand instead of wagering it for two-in-the-bush. But (as Pascal would later argue) these are bad odds, since the loss would in fact be infinite. Yet Macbeth accepts them with little trouble, and without proffering any argument against the possibility of "the life to come." He is not sufficiently serious about the life to come to be serious about adhering to the divine justice that attaining that life would require. Thoughts about his immortal soul will indeed continue to trouble him, as we'll see, but not sufficiently to stop his murderous activities and in fact only enough to encourage them, through an embittered despair.

The second stated reason that killing Duncan may not be the "end" of the matter brings out more clearly Macbeth's lack of seriousness about justice: "But in these cases / We still have judgment here." Macbeth now considers strictly human justice. There is an obvious link between what would condemn him to eternal damnation and what is condemned here on earth by human beings. Yet Macbeth does not link the human longing for eternity and the devotion that humans have to justice "here." Instead, he *separates* them. Having no deep longing for divine justice himself, he reflects now only on what others will be moved to feel against his deed, and so is led to that petty moral advice according to which what goes around, comes around:

> We still have judgment here, that we but teach
> Bloody instructions, which, being taught, return
> To plague th' inventor. This even-handed justice
> Commends th' ingredience of our poison'd chalice
> To our own lips. (1.7.8–12)

That he would by his unjust action teach others bloody instruction against himself is all that "even-handed justice" means to him. His reflection is about policy, not justice; he has left the consideration of justice behind.

Macbeth even turns divine justice into a mere metaphor for the justice others practice: what human beings will say will be *like* the pleadings of angels, because Duncan's Christian virtues are so manifest to them:

> He's here in double trust:
> First, as I am his kinsman and his subject,
> Strong both against the deed; then, as his host,
> Who should against his murtherer shut the door,
> Not bear the knife myself. Besides, this Duncan
> Hath borne his faculties so meek, hath been
> So clear in his great office, that his virtues
> Will plead like angels, trumpet-tongu'd, against
> The deep damnation of his taking-off;
> And pity, like a naked new-born babe,
> Striding the blast, or heaven's cherubin, hors'd,
> Upon the sightless couriers of the air,
> Shall blow the horrid deed in every eye,
> That tears shall drown the wind. (1.7.12–25)

Kinsman and host, trusted to protect the king, Macbeth would doubly violate trust in killing Duncan. But what troubles him is that in the eyes of others, the killing, and the horrible death of one with the manifest Christian virtue of meekness, would be seen as damnable. Pity for Duncan's fate would create a public relations disaster.

Finally, Macbeth does not himself feel offended, hard done by, or rankled by Duncan's rule. He oddly decouples his ambition from any sense of his own worth or desert:

> I have no spur
> To prick the sides of my intent, but only
> Vaulting ambition, which o'erleaps itself,
> And falls on th'other. (1.7.25–28)

Macbeth feels nothing that would move him, against the inevitable public outcry, to dare the deed; not only has he no publicly acceptable cause to do it, but he himself accepts Duncan's Christian virtue of meekness as a genuine virtue; he does not rail against it as foolish, nor doubt the justice of honoring the weak king, even if, as seems likely—especially in light of his later claims—his ambition is in truth driven by a sense of his own desert. And so, expecting that no good but only trouble will result from Duncan's murder, he is against the deed, and tells the entering Lady Macbeth, "We will proceed no further in this business."

Yet she wins him over. Lady Macbeth appeals first to his royal hope, formerly so fresh; then to his love of her, which, she now claims, looks as pale as his hope; and above all to his sense of valor or manliness. He wants and esteems something highly as the ornament of life; he thinks it a good thing. But he is like a silly beast, a cat that wants the fish in the pond but abhors wetting its feet. He lacks the daring that becomes a real man, who will do what must be done. Since he desires what is desirable, only cowardice can explain his reluctance to take it. Macbeth replies that he dares what becomes a man, but she has a rejoinder: were you a beast, then, when you swore to me that you would do it? (The oath to which she refers—of which we learn here for the first time—gives us a clear confirmation that they had discussed the murder before.) Beasts swear no oaths. She now impresses upon him the significance of abiding by his oath:

> I have given suck, and know
> How tender 'tis to love the babe that milks me;
> I would, while it was smiling in my face,
> Have pluck'd my nipple from his boneless gums,
> And dash'd the brains out, had I so sworn as you
> Have done to this. (1.7.54–59)

These horrific lines are made the more so by the absence of her child, who must be dead. She speaks not of mourning it but of being prepared to kill it. We see now the full meaning of "unsex me": she claims the ability to uphold a sworn oath even if it would mean killing her own suckling infant.

"And if we should fail?" Macbeth asks. "Screw your courage to the sticking place, / And we'll not fail." She will inebriate the guards, and they will bear the guilt. Macbeth comments that she should bring forth only men children; her mettle should compose nothing but males. It is an ambiguous comment, since she isn't a man and such mettle doesn't become a woman; there is something monstrous, that is, in her lack of female virtue. Yet his only remaining question is: Will others believe it? "Who dares receive it other?" she replies, again with a manly confidence, "As we shall make our griefs and clamour roar / Upon his death?" This settles Macbeth on the deed; he will now "mock the time with fairest show." Macbeth's devotion to the Christian king has been upended not by the prophecy of the hags, which came late in the couple's deliberations and which neither of them mentions in this decisive dialogue—but by his devotion to his wife, whose manly valor stands in striking contrast to Duncan's meekness. He admits that he has not only a false face but also (to Duncan) a false heart. Brutus was, by contrast, driven to have only a false face turned to Caesar, whom he loved.

Act II

With Macbeth resolved to commit the murder, Banquo and his son Fleance become a problem for him, and so are called to center stage, though they have doubtless been on Macbeth's mind, as on ours, since the hags' prophesying. Macbeth's ambition cannot be sated by his ascension to the throne if Macbeth—as we have just seen that he does—wishes progeny. Banquo for his part expresses the wish that "[m]erciful powers" should restrain in him "cursed thoughts" that nature would permit in sleep. What he has dreamt of, as he soon tells Macbeth, is the hags, "the weird sisters." His fight against their tempting prophecies explains Banquo's testing disposition toward Macbeth: Banquo speaks of the bounteous gratitude of the king, but he thereby suggests the less than bounteous hospitality of the Macbeths, and Macbeth himself has remained noticeably, gauchely, absent all night. Macbeth excuses these faults: "Being unprepar'd, / Our will became the servant to defect, / Which else should free have wrought." With this Banquo declares, "All's well." Or do the hags' predictions perhaps provide a better explanation for Macbeth's faulty hospitality? When Banquo speaks of them, Macbeth lies again: I haven't given them another thought. He then promises Banquo to speak further on the matter, but adds that he will bring honor to Banquo if, when the time comes, Macbeth can count on him. Banquo proffers another polite rebuff to this offer of increased honor:

> So I lose none
> In seeking to augment it, but still keep

My bosom franchis'd and allegiance clear,
I shall be counsell'd. (2.1.26–29)

They depart on good terms.

The vivid, dramatic scene of Macbeth's vision of a dagger follows. It appears to have behind it the question of whether forms of things can press themselves upon the mind without any material beings there, and yet be real, that is, a version of the question of whether there are separate forms, incorporeal and hence eternal, or whether the forms or kinds of things are there only when we perceive them in actual beings. Macbeth enters into a philosophic dialogue with himself on this subject. He notes that he sees but cannot touch the dagger, and offers on this basis a materialist doubt of the dagger's existence (2.1.35–39): either he can also touch what he can see, or what he sees is a mere creation of "the heat-oppressed brain"; touch is for him the deciding sense, and the "brain," not the mind, is the source of the image. But he wavers for a moment: perhaps his eyes see something that his other senses have no access to? What convinces him that "[t]here's no such thing" is that the form visibly changes: it starts to bleed. He therefore concludes that it is "the bloody business which informs" his eyes. He defeats the fear that the image would provoke by defeating the image, through a materialist reasoning.

But that the brain can so distort our awake senses with images of things that are not shows that the real world, the world that is, is manifestly dependent on perception by beings with the requisite senses. Macbeth does not go so far as to say that nature, the world of natural necessities, exists not when it is not perceived. But he comes close to saying so: "Now o'er the one half world / Nature seems dead, and wicked dreams abuse / The curtain'd sleep" (2.1.49–51). This "seems" turns into something more like "is," moreover, when he goes on to describe what occurs at night: witchcraft lives; the wolf becomes not merely an animal but a sentinel for Hecat. So he would not have the "firm set earth" (still sensibly there) hear his steps, "for fear / The very stones prate of my whereabout." Macbeth's world is divided into the daytime, awake world of the senses and the nighttime world, in which, with humans asleep, other beings have a chance to be that are dispelled by the light but that can affect what is in the light. This nighttime world is the dark spiritual one to which both he and Lady Macbeth have already made appeals, a world in which their deeds will take place and have an effect, but remain as if never done because it is unperceived, like a magic trick. The murder of Duncan is a "horror" that "suits with" the night time. Macbeth's belief that he acts in a time in which the full working of nature is suspended is something he holds alongside of his abiding Christian beliefs: when the bell tolls, he declares: "Hear it not, Duncan, for it is a knell, / That summons thee to heaven or to hell" (2.1.63–64).

* * *

Lady Macbeth too, having gotten the guards drunk, speaks of the life of night as differing substantially from the life of day. A hooting owl at first alarms her, but she assures herself that it is "the fatal bellman, / Which gives the stern'st good-night." She understands "nature" as life, against which "death" contends; "I have drugg'd their possets, / That death and nature do contend about them, / Whether they live or die" (2.2.6–8). Death is not for her a part of nature, but a separate force fighting it. It is hard to tell whether the Christian doctrine of the resurrection, of death being overcome by life, has permeated her perceptions, or whether she would have this understanding without it. We see in any case our first clear evidence that her plea to be "unsexed" has been limited, for she says of Duncan: "Had he not resembled / My father as he slept, I had done't." The cruelty she sought is checked by a pity provoked by paternal resemblance.

Macbeth, too, proves to be troubled by a version of Christian remorse, with the slaying of Duncan. After describing his bloodied hands as a "sorry sight," he describes the guards:

> There's one did laugh in 's sleep, and one cried, "Murther!"
> That they did wake each other. I stood and heard them;
> But they did say their prayers, and address'd them
> Again to sleep ...
> One cried, "God bless us!" and "Amen!" the other,
> As they had seen me with these hangman's hands.
> List'ning their fear, I could not say "Amen,"
> When they did say "God bless us!" (2.2.19–27)

Macbeth is genuinely puzzled by this inability to conclude a prayer. Lady Macbeth, intent on repressing these budding, pious, troubling thoughts in her husband, implores him to "consider it not so deeply," but they continue to haunt him:

> But wherefore could not I pronounce "Amen"?
> I had most need of blessing, and "Amen"
> Stuck in my throat (2.2.28–30)

Strikingly, Macbeth still believes that he needs and can obtain a blessing after murdering the king—so completely had he separated the nighttime world of his deed from the world of daylight and perception. At the same time, he realizes that for some reason (!) he cannot give the consent required, the Amen, for the blessing. And now Macbeth is hearing voices, which are taken to heart by a man who clearly knows the value of a good night's sleep, the sleep of the innocent:

> Methought I heard a voice cry, "Sleep no more!
> Macbeth does murther sleep"—the innocent sleep,
> Sleep that knits up the ravell'd sleeve of care,
> The death of each day's life, sore labor's bath,
> Balm of hurt minds, great nature's second course,
> Chief nourisher in life's feast. (2.2.32–37)

To Macbeth "great nature" offers sleep as the reknitter of tattered, awake life, or as a balm, or even as the *main course* in life's feast, to which the cares of working life whet the appetite. Whatever else we may think of him, Macbeth is no slacker or spoiled man of wasted leisure. He is a weary worker, so much so that waking life is but a burden for him, a string of troubles. Yet something tells him that he can no longer look forward to sleep, the one deep pleasure that he has known.

It is understandable that his wife should to these reflections reply, "What do you mean?" Is this all that life has been? How, indeed, can this be, for a man who has not lived hand-to-mouth? How can sleep, "death's counterfeit," as Macduff will call it, have become so desirable for him? It would seem that service to the Christian king has been so utterly exhausting, and the pretense of its unselfish nature so inhuman, as to make him crave sleep, a kind of death, as a welcome relief, a reward. Christianity, to be sure, offers an "eternal repose" for the just: "Come to me, ye who labor and are burdened, and I will give you rest." The suggestion here, however, is that it is Christian service itself that robs life of its joy, in a man who would otherwise have had every reason to enjoy life. Innocent sleep alone has hitherto offered a recompense. But no longer:

> Still it cried, 'Sleep no more!' to all the house;
> 'Glamis hath murther'd sleep, and therefore Cawdor
> Shall sleep no more' (2.2.38–40)

The ambitious one, Glamis, has done the murder, and so the one who has obtained a step to the rank he desired, Cawdor, will lose the pleasure of sleep in his new rank. What had lain in the back of Macbeth's mind, unexamined and almost moribund, haunts him now, to his surprise: he has through the murder ruined his prospects of deserved rest and of eternal rest.

Lady Macbeth tries to buck up her husband:"Worthy thane" and "noble strength," as she calls him, you think "brain-sickly of things." These voices do not exist; they are what Macbeth himself had guessed the dagger to be: a "false creation" of a "heat oppressed brain." She advises him in his distraction to get some water and "wash this filthy witness from your hand." We recall that at Brutus's request the murderers of Caesar had washed their hands in his blood, as "sacrificers." Here, the blood is but a "filthy witness"; once washed away, it is gone, done, cleaned. It and the deed are purely material things, or so Lady Macbeth would believe. "A little water clears us of this deed," she scoffs, in the play's most ironic line. But she believes it, and would have Macbeth believe that his misgivings about covering the guards with blood are childish. "The sleeping and the dead are but as pictures; 'tis the eye of childhood that fears a painted devil." Macbeth, for his part, remains filled with remorse: his hands cannot, he thinks, be cleansed by all the seas. And he expresses the wish that the knocking on the castle door could wake Duncan.

★　★　★

Hearing that knocking, the drunken Porter of "Hell's Gate," with his series of knock-knock jokes, affords us some welcome comic relief, but relief given by a man whose playful allusions to hell and to the devil touch on the play's serious themes. The first arrival to hell is a suicide farmer made miserable by a good, bounteous harvest for all, his own good ruined by the common good. The third arrival is an "English tailor" who has "stolen out of a French hose." The first and third arrivals are thus men damned for selfish sins in what we may call the economic or private realm. Theirs are violations of commandments from the second half of the decalogue—of the fifth and the seventh commandments (in the Catholic list), sins that any political order would have to proscribe. In the language of Christian theology, they are violations of "natural law" or injustices that are intelligible to unassisted reason. They surround the second or middle arrival, who has, by contrast, violated a commandment from the first half of the decalogue, that is, the commandment against swearing an oath to God in vain. He is an "equivocator" who "could swear in both the scales against either scale," and could "commit treason enough for God's sake." The Porter may be referring to the Jesuit Garnet, who was implicated in the gunpowder plot. The equivocator's sin is in any case clearly tied to the nonprivate, political realm, and brings out the great problem posed to that realm by Christian revelation. The Christian is enjoined loyally to obey his rulers (cf. 4.2.44–53), but he is also enjoined to seek first the kingdom of God and its righteousness, to "teach all nations" the truth as revealed by God. Rulers are to be judged not only

by their service to the common goods obtainable in this life, but by their
devotion to the Christian God and His transpolitical demands, which are
not simply natural or intelligible to unassisted reason. These demands make
"treason for God's sake" possible, as it never was in pagan regimes with civic
gods. Attempting to meet them can make the foul fair. The "meek" Duncan
is for his part clearly devoted to these transpolitical Christian ends, but his
being so cannot but make men like Macbeth, who seek this-worldly honor,
into his political enemies. The equivocator, the central arrival at Hell's Gate,
presents in a nutshell the underlying problem of the play, the problem of
Christian politics.

Macduff has come early, as he tells Macbeth, to meet the king, and as
he goes to do so, Lennox describes the strangeness of the night, both what
he saw (his chimneys blown down) and what has been reported by hearsay
(lamentations, "strange screams of death, / And prophesying, with accents
terrible, / of dire combustion and confus'd events"). Should Shakespeare
with this report lead his audience to believe that heaven and earth are
affected by the murder of Duncan, he is also careful to maintain the distinction between what undoubtedly actually happened—which is rationally
explicable—and what is merely reported by hearsay. The subsequent outcry
of the pious Macduff, who has seen Duncan's corpse, is compatible with
the latter:

> O horror, horror, horror! Tongue nor heart
> Cannot conceive nor name thee! ...
> Confusion now hath made his masterpiece!
> Most sacrilegious murther hath broke ope
> The Lord's anointed temple, and stole thence
> The life o' th' building! (2.3.63–69)

After this direct declaration of the murder as a sacrilege, Macduff awakens
the whole house, and Lady Macbeth begins her act.

Quite ridiculously, Macduff forbears from telling this "gentle lady" of
the murder yet blurts it out in her presence as soon as Banquo enters. Her
response, "Woe, alas! / What, in our house?" immediately invites suspicion,
since it shows her too eager to appear distraught not over the murder but
over its having occurred in her house. Banquo calls her out on this: "Too
cruel any where." Macbeth and Lennox reenter with (curiously) Rosse,
who was neither called by Macduff nor had been seen hitherto. Macbeth's
reaction to the discovery of the body appears more sincere than his wife's:

> Had I but died an hour before this chance,
> I had liv'd a blessed time; for from this instant
> There's nothing serious in mortality:
> All is but toys; renown and grace is dead,

The wine of life is drawn, and the mere lees
Is left this vault to brag of. (2.3.91–96)

It is difficult to know how much truth is in this professed remorse. Macbeth's deprecation of life is, in contrast to that of his predecessor, not made with a view to the next life, but with a view to the king he had served in this one. His words are those that a faithful servant—Lear's Kent—could honestly use. But Macbeth cannot be a Kent.

The entrance of Malcolm and Donalbain cuts short any genuine remorse that Macbeth might still feel, especially since the first response of the astute Malcolm to the news that his father is murdered is a curt "O, by whom?" All now learn, through the reports of Macbeth and Lennox, that Macbeth has killed the blood-smeared guards. Macbeth excuses this deed by reference to his furious loyalty to the king whom he loved, which, he claims, silenced wisdom, temperance, neutrality, and reason. He excuses his deed, that is, by reference to a tension among the virtues, especially to the forgivable devotional love that trumped his reason. His words are followed by Lady Macbeth's swoon, which might well be an act, performed to guard her husband from growing suspicion. It seems more likely, though, especially in light of her subsequent remorse, that the final two lines of Macbeth's speech have gotten the better of her: "Who could refrain," he has asked, "That had a heart to love, and in that heart / Courage to make's love known?" These words apply equally, after all, to Macbeth's love for Lady Macbeth herself, who is the prime mover of the murder. Macbeth has now proven his love for her, which she had claimed to doubt, by having the courage (which she likewise doubted) to murder Duncan. The full responsibility for what she has done will certainly begin soon to weigh heavily upon her. The limits to Christian transformation of men have a parallel, as we will see, in the limits to women being "unsexed."

Banquo calls for a full investigation and—unlike Macbeth, who had spoken of "great nature"—he "stands" (as he says) "in the great hand of God," and therefore "[a]gainst the undivulg'd pretense I fight / Of treasonous malice" (2.3.130). He seems prepared to disclose at this point the hags' tempting predictions. But Malcolm and Donalbain, fearing that they are next, have already decided to flee, and their flight hands Macbeth a perfect means to pin all suspicion on them. They have not, or at least not yet, felt sorrow for their father's death, as Malcolm somewhat shockingly admits (2.3.136–137 with 123). They flee to England and Ireland, respectively.

★ ★ ★

Rosse's curious conversation with a superstitious old man closes the second act. When the old man, who is aware of the murder, remarks on how unprecedentedly strange and dreadful was the previous night, Rosse responds, ingratiatingly, that the heavens were and remain troubled with men's acts. The old man then offers an allegory or omen: a mere owl killed a falcon. Rosse's response is remarkable. After Rosse describes the wildness that came over Duncan's beauteous horses, "as they would make / War with mankind," the old man replies, "'Tis said, they eat each other." And Rosse presents himself as an eyewitness of that impossible deed: "They did so—to th' amazement of mine eyes / That look'd upon't." Either Rosse is being allegorical, referring indirectly to Donalbain and Malcolm, or he is telling a whopper of a tale, claiming to have witnessed something impossible. The former is out of the question, since he has not yet heard of the flight of Duncan's sons. We must conclude that Rosse is a bald-faced liar, perfectly willing to augment the old man's wildly superstitious tales that make heaven and earth appear to have been moved with signs of horror at the murder of the king.

Rosse's subsequent exchange with Macduff, who comes with news, betrays more of his dubious character. He asks first, "How goes the world, sir, now?" To which Macduff replies with astonishment, "Why, see you not?" Rosse then asks whether the doer of the bloody deed is known. He—who saw Macbeth kill the servants—doubts that they did it. "What good could they pretend?" he asks Macduff. Cui bono? is his leading question; he doesn't consider possible grudges, jealousies, hatred, anger, resentment, and so on, but only cold self-interest as a possible motive. His question is made the more powerful by what he says when he learns that Donalbain and Malcolm are fled, so that suspicion falls on them. "'Gainst nature still!" he declares. Rosse understands "nature" to entail the pursuit of one's own good; if killers, Malcolm and Donalbain, would represent "[t]hriftless ambition, that will ravin up / Thine own live's means!" So Rosse doubts their guilt, too, but their departure helps to provide his answer to the cui bono question: "Then 'tis most like / The sovereignty will fall upon Macbeth." And Macduff discloses that Macbeth is indeed already gone to Scone to be invested. Macduff himself, perhaps suspicious, will go to his own castle at Fife rather than to Scone. But Rosse will go to Scone—pursuing his own good. How far this shady character will go in that pursuit and what the outcome of his efforts will be remain to be seen.

Act III

With Duncan dead and Macbeth king, Banquo becomes the center of Macbeth's attention. Banquo's reflections on the hags' predictions open the central act, in which Macbeth's rule becomes tyrannical in pursuit of Banquo and other potential enemies. Banquo suspects most foul play by Macbeth, but also now has hopes for the crown for his own posterity. Yet he again silences these hopes and where they might lead and will perform his duties under the new king. Curiously, he appears to have no suspicion that Macbeth will act against him or his son, Fleance—not even when Macbeth asks him where he is going, how long he will be gone, and whether Fleance is going with him. Banquo simply promises to return for the state dinner in Macbeth's honor, and departs.

Macbeth then excuses his royal self from the company of others for the rest of the day, in order, as he says, "To make society / The sweeter welcome" (3.1.41–42). He will starve himself for company in order to enjoy it more, as one might fast before a meal, avoiding a surfeit of pleasure. It is not a very gracious excuse, and signals his movement to tyranny, which is usually characterized by the lack of enjoyment of the company of others. And toward tyranny he proceeds to move. His true reason for leaving his guests, as we learn in the "To be thus is nothing / But to be safely thus" soliloquy, is to plan the murder of Banquo and Fleance. He offers to himself three reasons for doing so. The first is, significantly but not surprisingly, expressed by way of a parallel with the great Roman Mark Antony: Banquo's virtues—his dauntless, daring valor guided by wisdom to act in safety—make Macbeth fearful of Banquo, "and under him / My Genius is rebuk'd, as it is said Mark Antony's was by Caesar" (3.1.54–56; cf. *Antony and Cleopatra* 2.3.19–38). Macbeth's political education, as we might have suspected, is Roman. Yet while Antony simply fled to Egypt to stay clear of Augustus Caesar, Macbeth seeks Banquo's life. His second argument explains why: he wants his own children, not Banquo's, to rule; he is driven by a desire for a certain kind of immortality, the earthly kind that is through one's children. Third, and finally, Macbeth does not wish to have given up his immortal soul, as he thinks he now has, for the sake of Banquo's progeny. That is, he is certain at this point that he is damned to hell, and this belief contributes to his bloody action against Banquo. If he believed that he had paid a lesser price than his immortal soul for the crown, he would be less troubled by the small payoff of a lifetime kingship without heirs, and so would not continue murdering. A strange and deadly combination of Roman and Christian education and principles guides Macbeth down the road to bloody tyranny.

This combination's precise character includes contempt for the virtues of the very Christianity that has caused Macbeth to consider his immortal soul damned. This contempt is visible in his securing of the two men who are to murder Banquo and Fleance. Macbeth had on the previous day slurred Banquo to them, painting Banquo rather than himself as the source of their former troubles. He now poses to them a question:

> Do you find
> Your patience so predominant in your nature
> That you can let this go? Are you so gospell'd,

To pray for this good man, and for his issue,
Whose heavy hand hath bow'd you to the grave,
And beggar'd yours for ever? (3.1.85–90)

The Christian gospel and its demand for love of enemies and patient endurance of wrongdoing stands, as Macbeth reminds these men, against a natural desire for vengeance. When one potential murderer responds, "We are
men, my liege," Macbeth taunts them further: Are they really men? Can they
distinguish themselves by natural worth, natural gifts, natural rank? Or has
Christianity left them men only in name? Having suffered all their lives, they
vow that they are ready to kill him whom they now perceive as the cause
of their troubles, and thereby win the love of Macbeth. Their desire for justice, suppressed, finds now a most frightening outlet. What Shakespeare is
careful to disclose only through this deadly conference of murderers is what
Holinshed states explicitly as a problem with Christian virtue: it is responsible
for encouraging the rule of men who fail to avenge wrongs, leading to political disorder.[2] Macbeth gives the murderers instructions on how to do away
with their common enemy Banquo and his son Fleance. Yet in the concluding words of the scene we are shown for a third time Macbeth's abiding belief
in the immortality of the soul: "It is concluded: Banquo, thy soul's flight, /
If it find heaven, must find it out to-night" (3.1.140–141). Macbeth's contempt for Christian virtue and flight into dark deeds is done with an abiding
Christian faith in, or perhaps attachment to the notion of, the afterlife.

★   ★   ★

Lady Macbeth has for her part found their chosen path to be one of
doubtful joy, "without content." The cause is her husband, whom she now
upbraids for reflecting alone, as she thinks, remorsefully. "What's done is
done," she tells him. But it isn't done, even as Macbeth's soliloquy, which her
words echo, had predicted. Macbeth suggests that there is more to be done
(3.2.12–15), but he still does not disclose to Lady Macbeth the action he has
set in motion against Banquo, nor its reason. In fact, he leads her to believe
that his thoughts are only with the dead Duncan. And in part they are. For
Macbeth has, we now learn, been suffering terrible dreams; he expresses
envy of Duncan's peaceful state:

Better to be with the dead,
Whom we, to gain our peace, have sent to peace,
Than on the torture of the mind to lie
In restless ecstasy. Duncan is in his grave;
After life's fitful fever he sleeps well. (3.2.19–23)

Tortured by ambition, Macbeth had sought peace by killing Duncan but finds life still a "fitful fever." He attempts, through the murder of Banquo and Fleance, to cure it.

Lady Macbeth encourages him to be bright and jovial at dinner, but his response is disappointing: yes, he says, let us "make our faces vizards to our hearts, / Disguising what they are." She'd have been content to do so before, but wishes now for genuine delight, with their true hearts no longer in need of being hidden. "You must leave this," she declares. And only now does Macbeth let out a hint of his worry: "Banquo and his Fleance lives." She replies that "in them nature's copy's not eterne," not realizing that everything depends, for the royalty of her own progeny, on when they die. Macbeth hints that he has a dreadful deed in store for them, but states that she is to remain innocent of its knowledge, and calls night and its "black agents" to his aid. She is clearly horrified: "Thou marvel'st at my words, but hold thee still: / Things bad begun make strong themselves by ill" (3.2.54–55).

The murderers act in scene three, killing Banquo but missing Fleance. One puzzling fact is that there are not two but three murderers. Who is the third, and what is he doing here? He knows all the instructions, and he knows the ways of the court and the ways of Banquo: he knows that Banquo and the other "men" (i.e., the nobles) dismount before the final mile to the castle and "make it their walk," that is, their constitutional, their exercise. And he (alone) recognizes Banquo, when a light is shone in his face. The third murderer is someone from the castle.

The subsequent dinner scene opens with Macbeth half absent still. He gives directions to his guests and to himself as if reading from cue cards, or directing a play. And when the first murderer gives him news of Banquo's death and of Fleance's escape, "then," he exclaims, "comes my fit again. I had else been perfect" (3.4.20). He sees and decries Banquo's ghost in his seat, and Lady Macbeth attempts to assure the guests that his imaginings are an old ailment of Macbeth's. She tells him, sternly, that such imaginings belong in old wives' tales by the fireplace. But her husband is genuinely terrified by the apparition, by "that which might appall the devil" (3.4.59). He bids it take any shape but the one it has, and manages in the end to drive it away, along with his guests. He then turns his suspicions against Macduff, whose servants he has suborned as spies, and prepares to visit the hags for counsel.

We note three peculiarities of this dinner scene. First, before he sees Banquo's ghost, Macbeth publicly accuses Banquo of unkindness for not showing up, and Rosse seconds it: "His absence, sir, / Lays blame upon his promise" (3.4.42–43). Was the sycophantic Rosse perhaps the third murderer? Second, in the course of arguing that murder has always been common and that it is not murder but the appearance of ghosts of the murdered that is strange, Macbeth expresses a longing for a peculiar kind of ancient time:

> Blood hath been shed ere now, I' th' olden time,
> Ere humane statute purg'd the gentle weal;
> Ay, and since too, murthers have been perform'd
> Too terrible for the ear. The [time] has been,
> That when the brains were out, the man would die,
> And there an end; but now they rise again
> With twenty mortal murthers on their crowns,
> And push us from our stools. This is more strange
> Than such a murther is. (3.4.74–82)

Macbeth's understanding of the "olden time" is of a situation that obtained before human law "purged the gentle weal," that is, of a lawless situation in need of purging in order to become gentle. We tend to associate this understanding of our original state with modern political thought, which (beginning with Hobbes) teaches the existence of a warlike "state of nature." It is, though, also present in classical thought, most obviously in the opening of Thucydides's work and in Lucretius's poem, but in more muted form in Plato's *Laws* and the first book of Aristotle's *Politics*. It is a teaching that stands in contrast to the biblical teaching of a perfect beginning. In referring to it, Macbeth again makes mention of "brains," the material basis of the mind, and expresses an astonishment that the state of such matter is no longer decisive, as it once was, in determining life or death. Or rather, he is astonished that men now "rise again." The term is Christian, used in the gospels to refer to Christ's resurrection, the forerunner of the resurrection of all on the last day. We might have expected Macbeth's astonished, regretful observation to lead him to attribute the apparition, as he had the knife that led on to Duncan's room, to his own "heat oppressed brain," as indeed Lady Macbeth suggested to him (3.4.60–61), but he fails to do so. Macbeth, who would be a materialist, is remarkably unable to see how his Christian beliefs have shaped his mind and thoughts, unable—at least to this point—to cast off what haunts him, as we have seen before but are shown here dramatically in his own reflections.

By the end of the scene, Macbeth has, to be sure, driven away the image of Banquo's ghost, by command, and is resolved, finally, to do all things for his own good:

> for now I am bent to know,
> By the worst means, the worst. For mine own good
> All causes shall give way. I am in blood
> Stepp'd in so far that, should I wade no more,
> Returning were as tedious as go o'er. (3.4.133–37)

And to this end he seeks the hags' advice. He here makes clear, however, that until now he had indeed hoped to return, to end the bloodshed and find legitimacy, if not redemption. No more. Now—only now—he has made the determination to act strictly for his own good. And having resolved thus, he also blames his youthfulness in crime for his present troubled soul: he must, and he will, grow more accustomed to murder. He thus takes the final step toward the silencing of his conscience and hence toward limitless crime, the first and crucial one having occurred with his reflection on the sale of his immortal soul for what would be too low a gain should Banquo's progeny become kings.

★ ★ ★

Before Macbeth meets the hags, we see them (for a third time) without human company, this time with Hecat, and with speeches that invite reflection on the question of the best disposition toward death. Hecat is upset that she has had no part to play in the hags' activities: "[H]ow dare you / To trade and traffic with Macbeth / In riddles and affairs of death" (3.5.3–5). But her biggest complaint is puzzling: all they have done, she laments, has been done for Macbeth, a "wayward son, / Spiteful and wrathful, who (as others do) / Loves for his own ends, not for you" (3.5.11–13). How strange to believe that anyone would love for these hags' sake! And why should Hecat be angry that the hags have acted for a selfish man? Perhaps they could have acted for a more saintly or innocent one, but such a one would surely not have loved for their sake. Is Hecat, too, imbued with Christian principles? The hags are in any event to make amends for these two faults, in such a way as to help us to understand these puzzles.

First, Hecat will now be included in the deliberations and deeds. This settles her first complaint. Second, she devises a scheme such that Macbeth is not merely their instrument for vile ends but the very object of their labors; he, the selfish one, will now *suffer* from his hopes. Hecat will work the illusion with "artificial sprites," who

[s]hall draw him on to his confusion.
He shall spurn fate, scorn death, and bear
His hopes 'bove wisdom, grace, and fear;
And you all know, security
Is mortals' chiefest enemy. (3.5.29–33)

What might seem to most of us to be "mortals' chiefest enemy," death, is not so, according to Hecat. Is death somehow not even our enemy? Certainly wisdom, grace, and fear are presented as alternatives to what is our chiefest enemy, *security* from death. Now, that Hecat calls fear one of the three alternatives to "security" is not surprising, but fear is, after all, only a passion—if a helpful one. As for the "grace" of which Hecat speaks, it is not something received but rather something possessed by an individual and manifest in his deeds; it is "grace under pressure," as we still say. It is part of all moral virtue, the keeping of one's wits about one, and not only with the sternness or steadfastness that one associates with courage. It goes beyond this. As Malcolm will indicate in the next act (4.3.91–95), "grace" entails a steadiness of soul, a being undaunted despite what may await one. But this necessarily requires some awareness of what awaits one, a freedom from illusion about it and a grasp of its limits. And so it leads to the third alternative to the "chiefest enemy," that is, to wisdom. Wisdom would entail a full awareness of one's inevitable mortality, and a resignation to it, as a necessity, something that cannot be escaped or admits of no "security." Wisdom is the opposite of hope in security. It entails not despair (the obverse of hope) but rather, fully awake acceptance of death as inevitable—a somewhat flawed version of which we have seen in Julius Caesar.

Hecat speaks of the illusion of security that draws one on to confusion, to a spurning of fate, a scorning of death, and a bearing of high hopes. The false security, which Macbeth will soon receive, is tied to a hope for the impossible; it is a certain security against mortality—which Macbeth comes to believe in owing to the personal revelation that he is about to receive. The world is such, he will come to believe, that he will not die at any man's hand. But there is, of course, another type of security from death, equally based on a revelation, that is much more prevalent in Scotland and England. The hope with which Hecat will ensnare Macbeth is a variant of the more universal hope for security through divinely guarded justice. As the threatened Lady Macduff will soon put it, "Whither should I fly? / I have done no harm" (4.2.73). So we can see that Macbeth, having given up hope for what he still holds to be his immortal soul, remains vulnerable to the hope for security afforded by supernatural beings who reveal the future to him. This is the heart of his abiding Christian hope, which, in his lack of seriousness about justice, he has never confronted. In Shakespeare's presentation—guarded by its placement in the mouth of Hecat—this hope is the opposite of wisdom.

The middle act ends with Lennox discussing with another lord, gingerly and with a dissembling demanded by the political situation, both the tyrant Macbeth and Macduff's recent flight to England, where he is paying a visit to the "holy king." Lennox's hope is that an invasion of Scotland led by English lords, "with Him above to ratify the work," will free the Scots from tyranny. In flight to England to deliver a message to those lords, Macduff acts like "some holy angel." His deed is the first inkling of the forces of light. As we will see, however, those forces—led by Malcolm—are of a decidedly non-Christian stamp.

Act IV

The hags boil their hell broth with ugly things, and Shakespeare thereby indicates that the hags belong to the Christian world: among the things they consider ugly is "the blaspheming Jew" (4.1.26). Hecat commends their "pains," and promises that every one shall share "i' th' gains" (4.1.39–40); she conceives of their painful efforts as productive of a common good. When Macbeth enters, he speaks to them in a bold but informal manner. He is no longer frightened by them, but conjures them by their professions to answer him, suggesting at the same time that they are agents of nature's destruction. They promise to answer him, and do so through a series of apparitions. The first apparition warns Macbeth to beware of Macduff. The second is of a bloody child, which enjoins him to be bold, bloody, resolute, laughing to scorn the power of men, for none of woman born, the apparition states, shall harm Macbeth. The second apparition thus implicitly contradicts the first, as Macbeth briefly notes (4.1.82). Yet he dismisses the contradiction, deciding instead to make "assurance double sure." This is Macbeth's crucial failure; he fails to question the revelations in light of their contradiction. Had he done so, he would have doubted them altogether and eschewed the hope that they induce. The third apparition is a child crowned and, with tree in hand, prophesying that Macbeth will not be vanquished until Burnan wood comes against him to Dunsinane hill. "That will never be," Macbeth concludes, reverting now to judging by the possible and impossible. He does not stop to wonder how this very apparition can "be." He remains caught between a strictly material nature and a belief in spiritual forces with a concern for him. The final image, given at his demand, shows Banquo's issue reigning in the kingdom. This moves Macbeth to damn all who trust the hags; they have not given him what he wished to see. In spite or because of this, he will trust only what they have revealed that corresponds to his wishes or hopes.

★   ★   ★

Hearing from Lennox of Macduff's flight to England, Macbeth resolves to kill Macduff's wife and children immediately. And so the action shifts to Macduff's castle, for the darkest scene in this dark play. There we find Macduff's wife mystified by her husband's flight; it seems to her prompted by a fear-induced madness. Rosse, counseling her to patience, suggests that wisdom, not fear, drove her husband away. But she is not persuaded: it seems *unwise* of Macduff to have left her and their children behind. But then she has another thought: he loves us not, and fears only for himself. He "wants the natural touch"; even the wren protecting its brood shows more love. But if fear did induce Macduff's flight, it remains an unwise fear, since it has moved him to leave all that he has behind.

Rosse's response to this lament is guarded and puzzling: Macduff, he says, is

> noble, wise, and judicious, and best knows
> The fits o' th' season. I dare not speak much further,
> But cruel are the times when we are traitors,
> And do not know ourselves. (4.2.16–19)

Does he refer in this odd conclusion to Macduff, or to Macbeth, or to himself? He would now take his leave, but he states that he will return soon, and then exclaims to the Macduffs' son, "Blessing upon you!" Lady Macduff pleads for her boy: "Father'd he is, and yet he's fatherless." But Rosse will not stay. "I am so much a fool, should I stay longer, / It would be my disgrace and your discomfort. I take my leave at once" (4.2.28–30). He seems to mean that with Macduff now disgraced, so would he be were he to linger. Or does he, like the messenger who soon arrives and departs with the words "Heaven preserve you! / I dare abide no longer" (4.2.72–73), know just what is in store for Lady Macduff and her children, and so wishes to leave them?

After the pathetic scene of Lady Macduff with her charming and shrewd son—who recognizes the preponderance in the world of traitors and liars to honest men—that messenger arrives to warn her to flee, prompting Lady Macduff's surprised reflection:

> Whither should I fly?
> I have done no harm. But I remember now
> I am in this earthly world—where to do harm
> Is often laudable, to do good sometime
> Accounted dangerous folly. Why then, alas,
> Do I put up that womanly defense,
> To say I have done no harm? (4.2.73–79)

Lady Macduff has guided her life on the presumption of the operation of justice, according to which to those who do no harm, no harm shall come. Reflecting now on the absence of such justice "in this earthly world," she accounts this presumption a "womanly defense." It is a defense that goes together with the presumption of a non-"earthly world." True manliness would, by her account, consist in *not* presuming that "heaven," that is, the God of that other world, will "preserve" one, as the messenger had wished or prayed for Lady Macduff and as she herself continues to presume, hoping her husband is in a "sanctified" place free of murderers (4.2.81–82). Manliness would consist in a renunciation of hope in divine care and a resolve to preserve oneself and those for whom one cares.

The "womanly defense," as we will soon see, has guided Macduff as much as it has his wife. Their son, who has no such hopes, is the most gallant of anyone we have seen thus far, defying the murderers who now arrive and telling his mother to flee (4.2.79–85). His murder is the low point in the play; his defiance signals the return of light, the ascent of Malcolm, and, as we are about to learn, the restoration of Macduff to manliness.

★　★　★

That restoration begins in England. Macduff attempts there to persuade Malcolm to return to Scotland and, with an invading force, to overthrow Macbeth. But Malcolm is suspicious; he expresses doubts about this man who once loved Macbeth and who has not yet suffered at Macbeth's hands. Perhaps Macduff has in truth come to ensnare Malcolm in a trap?

> He hath not touch'd you yet. I am young, but something
> You may discern of him through me, and wisdom
> To offer up a weak, poor, innocent lamb
> T'appease an angry god. (4.3.14–17)

Malcolm here utters the first pagan words in the play, though they are, to be sure, used only as a metaphor. But they accord with Malcolm's distrust, which stands in striking contrast to his trustful father. It persists even as Macduff protests that he is not treacherous. "A good and virtuous nature," Malcolm replies, "may recoil / In an imperial charge" (4.3.19–20), and even a fallen angel appears an angel still. When Macduff declares that he has lost all hope, Malcolm presses him: why did you leave your beloved children and wife behind? The question of the previous scene thus recurs. If Macduff did not entrust their safekeeping to Macbeth, then to whom did he trust their care? Macduff does not answer the question; despondent, he prepares to leave.

But Malcolm now begins an elaborate act (whose original is found in Holinshed). With it, the deceitfulness that has been in evidence throughout the play is stood on its head, as at last someone who is virtuous pretends to be vicious, in order to put off imprecations that he return home and seize rule from the tyrant Macbeth. Malcolm's act provides us with a classic statement of the premodern title to rule—that is, to rule on the basis of the manifest inequality of human virtues and vices. He begins by claiming that he would bring more vices to the throne than those that are possessed by

Macbeth. Macduff protests that hell could produce no worse, and Malcolm then lists his vices. The first is voluptuousness or lust; Macduff does not find it a particularly serious or troublesome vice in a king, and offers to provide a bevy of harlots for him. Malcolm's second vice is avarice, which Macduff finds worse, but offers that there is wealth enough in Scotland for him, if one weighs his other graces (virtues) with them. But Malcolm protests that he has none of the king-becoming graces, none of the virtues that grant title to rule: justice, verity, temperance, stableness, bounty, perseverance, mercy, lowliness, devotion, patience, courage, fortitude. He lacks them all, and would pour the sweet milk of concord into hell. Am I, he concludes, fit to govern? The despairing Macduff replies: "Fit to govern? / No, not to live" (4.3.102–103). If worth is determined by virtues and vices, Malcolm deserves not rule but capital punishment. It is here, in his grief and his despondency, that Macduff offers the earlier quoted portrait of Malcolm's father and mother as "sainted," dying to this world and its allurements.

With Macduff's intention now clear, Malcolm relents, and discloses that he has been putting on an act:

> I put myself to thy direction, and
> Unspeak mine own detraction; here abjure
> The taints and blames I laid upon myself,
> For strangers to my nature. I am yet
> Unknown to woman, never was forsworn,
> Scarcely have coveted what was mine own,
> At no time broke my faith, would not betray
> The devil to his fellow, and delight
> No less in truth than life. My first false speaking
> Was this upon myself. What I am truly
> Is thine and my poor country's to command. (4.3.122–132)

Significantly absent from Malcolm's new list of virtues, however, is any claim to be merciful, lowly, full of devotion, or patient, which his first list had mentioned. Malcolm, who delights, as he says, in "life"—he does *not*, we recall, consider it a trifle—makes no promise to possess any such distinctively Christian virtues. And he has already gathered, as he now discloses, a force of 10,000 men, under his English uncle Siward, who are ready to invade Scotland, and therefore his hopes of success are as good as his cause is just; he does not for a moment presume the victory of unarmed justice.

This conference is interrupted, oddly, by a doctor, who now establishes the medical motif of the rest of the scene and indeed of every subsequent scene. The doctor reports on the faith healings of England's king (Edward the Confessor). The healings are confirmed by Malcolm. He voices no doubts about the English king's type of healing, which he in fact calls "a most miraculous work." Yet his description of the healings makes clear that he does not understand them nor will attempt to emulate them. The king's "strange virtue," he says, obtained mysteriously by how the king "solicits heaven," allows the king to heal the "strangely-visited," ulcerous people of something called "the evil," by his touches alone (4.3.141–159). These healings stand in striking contrast to the healing of Scotland that Malcolm is about to bring about, beginning with the curing of Macduff.

That curing is set up by Rosse, who now arrives and, after Macduff's warm greeting of him, is recognized by Malcolm. Rosse relates how bad things are in Scotland, but when asked about the newest grief, he does not mention the murder of Macduff's family. Even when Macduff asks him point blank, "How does my wife?" Rosse lies: "Why, well," and he lies again when asked about the children, and then again when pressed: "they were well at peace when I did leave them" (4.3.176–77). Or is this last statement not a lie, but a horrible truth? (For the term "at peace," see 3.2.20.) Strikingly, it is only after Rosse has received directly from Malcolm a confirmation of the rumor of an impending invasion that he discloses the truth concerning Macduff's wife and children: they are all murdered. We surmise that Rosse has held this truth back until he could learn where his political interests lie. He is not about to infuriate his listeners with terrible news if he will be returning to Scotland soon, but he delivers the news once he knows that Macbeth's fate is sealed. And he is then able to clear himself of the suspicion that he took part in the murderous deed by being the one to report it. We, however, are given some reason for that suspicion by the fact that Rosse knows the full manner of the murders, which he here forbears from relating on the ground that it would be too hard for Macduff to bear (4.3.205–207). If he is not one of the murderers, Rosse has at the very least talked with the murderers. That this shady character and likely murderer will now join forces with England, to silence those who know of his deeds on behalf of the tyrant, and will be at the end of the play as unbloodied as at its opening, is perhaps the most disturbing (and therefore least trumpeted) aspect of the entire play.

Macduff is beside himself with grief, unable even to speak. But now Malcolm takes charge. "Give sorrow words," he commands Macduff. "The grief that does not speak / Whispers the o'er-fraught heart, and bids it break" (4.3.209–210). The grief is real, and must be acknowledged, *not* hidden. Once it is acknowledged, its cure will come through a second medicine: "Let's make us med'cines of our great revenge," Malcolm tells Macduff, "To cure this deadly grief." And a bit later: "Dispute it like a man" (4.3.213–215, 219). These tough words from the future king are needed because Macduff is (to use Macbeth's word) "gospelled." "Did heaven look on," asks Macduff, "And would not take their part?" (4.3.223–224). His question provides us, finally, with the reason that Macduff left his wife and children behind: he trusted their care to heaven, to providence. By expressing this trust now as a question, of course, Macduff finally confronts the absence of providence, doubts it—perhaps for the first time in his life. He attempts to bury this brief doubt, however, by blaming himself—his sins—for his family's horrific suffering:

> Sinful Macduff,
> They were all strook for the! naught that I am,
> Not for their own demerits, but for mine,
> Fell slaughter on their souls. Heaven rest them now! (4.3.224–227)

But Malcolm will have none of this. "Be this the whetstone of your sword, let grief / Convert to anger; blunt not the heart, enrage it" (4.3.228–29). According to Christian doctrine, of course, anger is one of the seven deadly sins. Malcolm correctly perceives that that doctrine blunts the heart of Macduff, and Malcolm encourages anger over and against that doctrine. This finally begins to have an effect on Macduff:

> O, I could play the woman with mine eyes,
> And braggart with my tongue! But, gentle heavens,
> Cut short all intermission. Front to front
> Bring thou this fiend of Scotland and myself;
> Within my sword's length set him; if he scape,
> Heaven forgive him too! (4.3.230–235)

While still speaking of "gentle heavens" and of forgiveness, Macduff is now clearly prepared to fight and kill Macbeth in face-to-face combat. "This tune," says Malcolm, "goes manly." Macduff has now moved from what his wife had called the "womanly defense"—reliance on providential care of the world—to manliness. And while Malcolm himself soon adds that "the pow'rs above / Put on their fighting instruments," this is a cheering declaration, not the reading of any Christian prophecy. It is preceded, significantly, by Malcolm's declaring that "*our* power is ready" (4.3.236; emphasis added). The coming of daylight after a long night, the curing of Scotland, has in this way begun.

Act V

The medical motif, or rather the question of what is Scotland's sickness and what is its cure, continues, as another doctor takes center stage. He has been called in to observe Lady Macbeth's sleepwalking. She has visibly failed to lose the milk of human kindness or to have "the passage of remorse" stopped up. She has now with her at all times, we learn, a candle, because, as she puts it, "hell is murky" (5.1.21–23, 36), and she is ever attempting to cleanse her hands of a "damn'd spot," an indelible stain made worse for her by her knowledge of Lady Macduff's murder. The question that she had put to Macbeth she here repeats in her trance: "What need we fear who knows it, when none can call our pow'r to accompt?" (5.1.37–38). Her servant woman supplies the answer. For like Lady Macbeth, the servant believes (quite literally) that "heaven knows what she has known" (5.1.49). To both women the foul deeds matter, have a cosmic consequence, because, as they believe, a powerful, just, providential God rules the universe, and condemns the Macbeths' deeds. And so the doctor concludes: "This disease is beyond my practice" (5.1.59). When Lady Macbeth repeats advice she had given to Macbeth—"Banquo's buried; he cannot come out on's grave ...What's done cannot be undone" (5.1.63–68)—the doctor states unambiguously, "More needs she the divine than the physician." He is no confessor, to whom "infected minds...discharge their secrets" (5.1.72–74). Lady Macbeth no more than her husband would seek salvation through such a confessor. But what is the doctor to do? Will he tell Macbeth? "I think," he says, "but dare not speak" (5.1.79).

On the field of battle, meanwhile, Scottish troops marshal to join Malcolm, Siward, and Macduff, in whom "revenges burn" and motivate the political and military action that is to cure Scotland (5.2.3). Angus surmises that what we might call a certain natural justice is now overtaking Macbeth:

> Now does he feel
> His secret murthers sticking on his hands;
> Now minutely revolts upbraid his faith-breach;
> Those he commands move only in command,
> Nothing in love. Now does he feel his title
> Hang loose about him, like a giant's robe
> Upon a dwarfish thief. (5.2.16–22)

The fear of human justice, which was stronger in Macbeth than fear of divine justice, has, thanks to Macbeth's continuously murderous rule, proved to be warranted. The revolts are real. But Angus is mistaken concerning the "secret murthers sticking on his hands," or what we might call the stings of conscience—the instrument of divine justice. Not Macbeth, but, as we have just seen, Lady Macbeth feels those stings. And when Menteth too remarks on Macbeth's "pester'd senses," Cathness responds:

> Well, march we on
> To give obedience where 'tis truly ow'd.
> Meet we the med'cine of the sickly weal,
> And with him pour we, in our country's purge,
> Each drop of us. (5.2.25–29)

Not any remorse, but instead Malcolm's troops, burning with revenge, are the medicine that is to cure Scotland.

Lady Macbeth's doctor, meanwhile, reports his findings to Macbeth, in a remarkable scene. Macbeth is embattled, but he remains desperately confident in the words of the hags' revelations. He accordingly does not fear Malcolm, who is "of woman born." His heart, he declares, "Shall never sag with doubt, nor shake with fear," and he moralizes against the "false thanes" and "English epicures" who oppose him, suggesting that they seek pleasure rather than remaining true and virtuous. Macbeth considers himself and his cause, his rule, just, and so abuses his servant for appearing to be afraid: "The devil damn thee black" (5.3.1–12). Macbeth's anger is not bestial, but arises from his perplexity:

> Seyton!—I am sick at heart
> When I behold—Seyton, I say!—This push
> Will cheer me ever, or [disseat] me now.
> I have liv'd long enough: my way of life
> Is fall'n into the sear, the yellow leaf,
> And that which should accompany old age,
> As honor, love, obedience, troops of friends,
> I must not look to have; but in their stead,
> Curses, not loud but deep, mouth-honor, breath,
> Which the poor heart would fain deny, and dare not.
> Seyton! (5.3.18–29)

What is left to Macbeth is hardly worth having. He would have been content with honor, love, obedience, troops of friends, but they are lost to him now. There is but one servant who is not cowed by Macbeth, the one for whom he here thrice calls: Seyton. This servant arrives, fearless, and without addressing Macbeth by any title, simply asks Macbeth his pleasure. Seyton knows (without having been present) what has just been reported to Macbeth. And he contradicts Macbeth when he calls for his armor: "'Tis not needed yet." The doctor, who has witnessed all of this, manages discretely to state, when asked, what the problem is with Lady Macbeth: "she is troubled with thick-coming fancies, / That keep her from her rest" (5.3.38–39). The doctor's prudent statement affords us all the indication we need that Shakespeare is fully alive to the problem of persecution, and so of the need to write with discretion. That he has Macbeth now served by a character named "Seyton" (Satan) serves that end.

Macbeth asks the doctor for a drug for Lady Macbeth that would cure "a mind diseas'd," that is, put an end to her remorse:

> Canst thou not minister to a mind diseas'd,
> Pluck from the memory a rooted sorrow,

Raze out the written troubles of the brain,
And with some sweet oblivious antidote
Cleanse the stuff'd bosom of that perilous stuff
Which weighs upon the heart? (5.3.40–45)

What was to take place in the dark and hence remain there has, Macbeth
now knows, continued to trouble the mind of his wife. But the patient, the
doctor says in reply, must "minister to himself." He may be referring, daringly, to Macbeth rather than (or as well as) to Lady Macbeth, but Macbeth
himself speaks only of Lady Macbeth, and he searches for a material remedy
for her "brain." Damning "physic," he now asks the doctor for a means to
find the disease of the land, to purge it of the English with a purgative drug,
and restore it to "a sound and pristine health." Macbeth clearly considers
not himself but the English, and the thanes who fly from him, to be the
disease of the land. The doctor makes a fearful exit.

In the field, meanwhile, Malcolm directs his troops to cut each a
bough from Birnan wood, in order to hide their numbers on the march
to Dunsinane. Malcolm's subsequent words echo those of Macbeth: "none
serve with him but constrained things, / Whose hearts are absent too"
(5.4.13–14). Fear of death is recognized by both as alone responsible for
any remaining obedience to Macbeth. Malcolm's patient, Macduff, appears
now altogether a soldier: "Let our just censures / Attend the true event, and
put we on / Industrious soldiership" (5.4.14–16).

At Dunsinane, Macbeth hears a noise, and Seyton discloses its source:
cries of women. Macbeth, almost forgetting fears, had failed to recognize it.
For he is, as he had hoped to be, inured to horrors. But Seyton delivers the
news that the Queen is dead, prompting Macbeth's final, famous soliloquy:

She should have died hereafter;
There would have been a time for such a word.
To-morrow, and to-morrow, and to-morrow,
Creeps in this petty pace from day to day,
To the last syllable of recorded time;
And all our yesterdays have lighted fools
The way to dusty death. Out, out, brief candle!
Life's but a walking shadow, a poor player,
That struts and frets his hour upon the stage,
And then is heard no more. It is a tale
Told by an idiot, full of sound and fury,
Signifying nothing. (5.5.17–28)

The "fools" to whom Macbeth refers would be those who invest their lives
with a moral significance that, in truth, it lacks. The brevity of life speaks
against any such significance, which would require not merely an extension

of years—against eternity, even hundreds of thousands of years are as noth-ing—but a being "heard" outside of the life itself, by an eternal being who remembers our deeds. This would indeed lend life a significance, a meaning, bestowed by a being who assessed it, thereby saving life from being utterly contingent, idiosyncratic, particular—told by an idiot. Life's sounds would then be signs of something beyond itself, so that it signified something. Our sense of dignity, of worth, would then be more than a brief strutting and fretting on a stage. But, Macbeth claims, it is not.

If Macbeth genuinely accepted what he here states, it would not induce in him any anger, desperation, fear, shame, hurt, humility, or any other moral passion. He would be without hope, resigned to having his long-ings for eternity unmet. He might even achieve a certain serenity. But Shakespeare makes it clear that Macbeth does not accept his own words. For as soon as Macbeth hears from a messenger that Birnan wood is mov-ing toward Dunsinane, he becomes startlingly angry: "Liar and slave!" (5.5.34). He maintains still the hope instilled by the hags' revelation, which he now denounces as "th' equivocation of the fiend / That lies like truth" (5.5.42–43). Macbeth is angry that the hags have lied to him, and wishes "th' estate of the world were now undone" (5.5.39). He sees (and hates) an order to things. Yet he is, or appears to be, resolved to die defiant, armed, "with harness on our back" (5.5.51).

And die he will. Malcolm, Siward, and Macduff arrive at Dunsinane, where Malcolm—prudently—instructs Siward and his son to take the lead in the battle. Macduff, now utterly transformed, calls for the trumpeters as "clamorous harbingers of blood and death" (5.6.10). Young Siward is the first to find Macbeth, and while anxious to kill the "abhorred tyrant," he is slain by him. Macbeth then discloses an abiding faith in the revelation concerning any "man that's of woman born" (5.7.14). But Macduff is seek-ing him out, imploring "Fortune"—not God—to let him find Macbeth and avenge the death of his wife and children (5.7.14–22). Macduff obtains his wish. For Macbeth's remaining people switch sides (5.7.24–25), and Macbeth—failing to return fully to the Roman virtue that would have him now die on his own sword, an act that he calls the part of a "Roman fool" (5.8.1)—remains alive for Macduff's revenge, preferring to kill others but also holding an abiding hope in his security.

Macduff destroys that remaining hope. Calling Macbeth "hellhound," he calls upon him to face him. Macbeth, amazingly, bids Macbeth leave: "Of all men else I have avoided thee, / But get thee back, my soul is too much charg'd / With blood of thine already" (5.8.4–6). Macbeth continues to believe in a soul that can be "charged" with sin, and warns Macduff—with striking generosity—of his own "charmed life," his invulnerability to any that are of woman born. Macduff now discloses, however—referring to himself now, like a Roman, in the third person—that "Macduff was from his mother's womb untimely ripped" (5.8.15–16). This final evidence of the equivocation of the hags' revelation moves Macbeth to again curse those "That keep the word of promise to our ear, / And break it to our hope" (5.8.30–31). His hopes dashed, Macbeth refuses to fight Macduff. But told to surrender and be mocked, Macbeth decides to fight on, in manly fashion, to his death. Only now, freed of hope, does he appear at last fully a Roman, and meets his end.

★ ★ ★

In the play's conclusion we are assured that Malcolm will heal Scotland of the disease that has troubled it. Rosse, unsurprisingly lacking any wounds, tells Siward of his noble son's noble death. Siward wishes to know only that his son's wounds were in the front, not in the back. When Rosse reports that they were, Siward is (or pretends to be) fully satisfied:

> Why then, God's soldier be he!
> Had I as many sons as I have hairs,
> I would not wish them to a fairer death.
> And so his knell is knoll'd. (5.9.13–16)

But Malcolm will not let this be; to him it is yet another unhealthy pretense of contentment with service and sacrifice to God. "He's worth more sorrow," he responds, "And that I'll spend for him" (5.17–18). Siward persists: "He's worth no more; / They say he parted well, and paid his score, / And so God be with him!" It was of course just such pious denial of any worldly rewards or honors that underlay Duncan's rule, and that had driven the Macbeths to seek in Christianity's apparent antithesis dark forces to aid their worldly ambition. Malcolm is having none of it. He is hailed as king by Macduff—his cured patient—who bears Macbeth's head, and who invites all present to hail Malcolm not only in their minds but aloud, with their voices.

When all present do so, Malcolm announces that he will soon

> reckon with your several loves,
> And make us even with you. My thanes and kinsmen,
> Henceforth be earls, the first that ever Scotland
> In such an honor nam'd. (5.9.26–30)

Shakespeare thus takes from Holinshed a fact—the first Scottish naming of earls by Malcolm—and makes Malcolm himself state it as a significant event. Malcolm adds that he will not fail to punish the "cruel ministers / Of this dead butcher and his fiend-like queen" (5.9.34–35), nor fail to perform all else that is needed "by the grace of Grace." He thus does not omit, for his listeners' sake, a brief reference to the Christian God. Yet in these concluding statements of his intention to honor those who act justly and to punish supporters of tyranny, Malcolm makes abundantly clear his intention to restore honor and hence healthy political life to Scotland, and thereby cure it of its sickness.

CHAPTER 3

THE MERCHANT OF VENICE: ROMAN VIRTUE IN A CHRISTIAN COMMERCIAL REPUBLIC

Shakespeare chose the Christian commercial republic of Venice as the setting for his play about a merchant and his Jewish opponent. While the play's most riveting drama concerns Shylock's attempt to destroy Antonio, that drama is secondary to the broader one between Antonio and Portia. Antonio is sometimes understood to embody Christian virtue in his willingness to lay down his life for his friend Bassanio,[1] but it is noteworthy that Bassanio praises Antonio for being more than anyone in Italy an "ancient Roman"—an Antony—and Antonio's own understanding of the virtue he practices toward his friends resembles pagan munificence rather than Christian charity.[2] Portia, too, though careful to keep up the appearance and traditions of her pious Christian father and his wishes, displays virtues more appropriate to her Roman namesake. In her attempt to curb what she considers to be the troubling profligacy of her Christian husband's affection, she also has more in common with the pre-Christian Shylock, who recognizes that profligacy, than with Bassanio. More importantly, her cunning, deft exploitation of Antonio's plight permits her to subordinate him, and his affection for her husband, to her own marital bliss, and it is her "pagan" understanding of virtue and of law, here as in her dealings with her suitors, that directs her actions and permits her to succeed. In the drama between her and Antonio we see Shakespeare's transposing of Roman virtue to the context of a Christian, cosmopolitan world, where it is able to secure the private happiness of a couple against the threats that that world poses to it. In Rome, Antony triumphs over Brutus and Portia; in the commercial republic, Portia defeats Antony.

1.1: Antonio and Bassanio

The play opens with sadness and dialogic attempts to explain that sadness; it will close with a beloved woman's restoration of some joy to all concerned. Antonio is at the heart of the dialogue; he is sad but claims to know not why. The true reason, as we are subsequently led to see, is that his beloved friend Bassanio is hoping to marry (119–121), which would mean a curtailing of their deep friendship. Friendship and love and the worthiness for these, in their exclusivity and hence harshness, are the chief theme of the play.

Salerio and Solanio offer their explanations for Antonio's sadness: he has noble and splendid ships on the sea, to which other ships bow; he is anxious; the fleeting, temporary nature of all good things is brought home to him by images of shipwreck. These guesses fail to hit the mark, Antonio responds; he has prudently diversified his assets, risking his all on none of them. Is it love, then, they ask? He denies that it is. But the false diagnoses begin to elaborate upon the play's chief themes. Unlike the shipping of goods, devotional love or friendship does not admit of diversification; the lover is moved to devote his all to the beloved. Love entails a willingness to give up on all other good things, promising at the same time to compensate for their loss or their fleeting nature.

In the end Solanio gives up on his guesses: you must, he concludes, be one of those creatures who is simply by nature sad, as strange a fellow as one who laughs at bagpipes. But this too misses the mark: Antonio is not by nature sad. Yet however mistaken his companions' guesses, they have shown us incidentally both that Antonio is a great merchant and that his friends are all classically trained. They depart quickly when Bassanio, Lorenzo, and Gratiano appear, perhaps anxious to leave this sad man to others. Perhaps what they would do to make Antonio merry cannot be done in the presence of these others, particularly of Bassanio?

Lorenzo, knowing the friendship of the others, offers to leave. But Gratiano addresses Antonio before he does so. He remarks on how changed Antonio looks, and attributes the change, as had the others, to too great a concern for worldly affairs. That concern will be the death of Antonio, he predicts. But Antonio again rebuffs this explanation, and now offers a different one of his own: the world is a stage, on which every man must play his part, and his is a sad one. He is resigned to play a script. There is some great difficulty, he suggests, for some people that simply cannot be overcome or escaped, and to which he clearly attempts to be resigned. The garrulous Gratiano, whom Lorenzo thinks hardly worth listening to, proposes (perhaps because of the metaphor) that Antonio's sadness is all an act, intended to convey to the world, as he says with open disdain, "wisdom, gravity, profound conceit" (92). He takes Antonio's expressions of sadness as bombast intended to give the appearance of depth of soul. To appear cheerful risks appearing light-headed or shallow, untroubled because ignorant, naïve, sheltered; so to appear wise, Gratiano concludes, Antonio is appearing sad, grave. He fishes for the opinion of wisdom with the pretense of gravity. "Fish not," Gratiano admonishes (101–102). While there are undoubtedly such people as Gratiano claims, Antonio is not one of them: there is a good reason for his sadness. Gratiano thus appears immediately to us as too cheerful: he fails to see that there are reasons for sadness in life, if not also for joy. He is light or thin-souled.

When Gratiano and Lorenzo depart we learn what is troubling Antonio: Bassanio has planned a "pilgrimage" to a lady, Portia, to overcome the effects of his prodigality. He has a plan to clear himself of all the debts this vice has brought him, and Portia is the key to it. Antonio asks to know the plan (135–140). He could of course simply *give* money to Bassanio but, we must infer, this would destroy their friendship, the friendship of equals; Bassanio's honor would be lost were he to become indebted in this way to Antonio. Aware of this, Antonio is driven to become part of the scheme to restore a self-sufficiency to Bassanio, who gingerly suggests his plan (with a metaphor from archery [146–152]). Antonio is, however, insulted by the gingerly nature of Bassanio's request for money; his wallet is ever open to his friend (153–160). The plan is to win over the very wealthy Portia, and for this, Bassanio needs to be a prince and hence needs a loan.

But who is Portia? Antonio is eager to know. She is fair, of wondrous virtue, "nothing undervalu'd / To Cato's daughter, Brutus' Portia," declares Bassanio (165–166). Shakespeare thus points us back emphatically to Rome and to the virtue of Rome's women, to the wife of Rome's most celebrated champion of republicanism. He points us back to the virtuous republic but to its private virtue, the virtue of Portia, who rested her claim to know the conspiratorial thoughts of her troubled husband on the basis of her lineage from noble Roman men, of her legal marriage to Rome's worthiest citizen, and of her "constancy."[3] What is left of public virtue in the commercial republic is, or is most visible as, wealth.

The description of Portia immediately shifts to ancestral Greece: She has many suitors, many "Jasons" coming for her golden fleece. As we know, according to myth, Jason, son of a Greek king who had been expelled by his brother, had returned and reclaimed his kingdom. The usurper agreed to step down if Jason could bring back the golden fleece from the Hellespont (Colchis), where Phryxos left it as a gift to his father-in-law. It is the fleece of a golden ram, sent by the gods. Jason sails with the Argonauts (Theseus, Herakles, etc.) to win the fleece, and succeeds because the king's daughter, Medea, a sorceress, falls in love with him and therefore helps him obtain the fleece. But Jason then betrays her and marries the queen of Corinth. The upshot of the allusion to this myth is that Bassanio is simply out for Portia's money. If it is meant to comfort Antonio, it fails: he would be in the position of Medea.

Antonio is willing, however, to put up the money. Since his assets are not liquid at the moment—they are tied up in his investments at sea—he offers his credit, and all that remains is to find a creditor. The two therefore end up at the house of Shylock, who lends money at interest. Antonio, perhaps still sad, is now doing something for his beloved friend.

1.2: Portia

When we meet Portia, she too appears to have troubles; she is a parallel of sorts to Antonio, and as we have already been led to see, his rival for Bassanio's affections. She is not sad, but claims to be weary of this great world. Her servant Nerissa offers an explanation: surfeit, which is as bad as starving. The mean or middle, it seems, is best. But Portia will soon have the chance to use some of her unmiddling, indeed great, wealth to obtain the object of her desire. In the meantime, she calls Nerissa's advice good but not something she will follow. It is, she notes, not so easy to part with money, which offers security and many consolations, of a sort, for a life of miseries.[4] The reasoning of Nerissa, Portia adds, "is not in the fashion to choose me a husband." She will not settle for a middling man. But she cannot choose a husband in any case. Her father's last will and testament prescribes a test of suitors of three caskets—of gold, silver, and lead—stipulating that he who chooses the correct casket wins Portia. She finds this lawful arrangement "cruel," while Nerissa defends the arrangement on the ground that Portia's father was virtuous and "holy," and so the casket lottery scheme he designed as he approached death will "no doubt" work out; the one Portia should rightly love will choose correctly (27–33). Portia gives no evidence, however, of finding her father's holiness, nor the trust in providence that it seems to bespeak, to be a sufficient ground for accepting his "cruel" scheme.

The father's scheme is, to say the least, risky. An unsuitable suitor could by accident choose correctly, and Portia's lifelong companion be thereby made the source of her lifelong misery. Her "holy" father must have been driven to it through mistrust of Portia's own judgment. Perhaps his daughter is too taken with outward appearances and therefore apt to choose a suitor who is similarly misled. In any event, Portia may be cleverer than the old man reckoned when devising his scheme. She may find a way around it. As the remainder of the scene suggests, she certainly has decided opinions of what she does not want in a suitor—what she finds defective or repulsive. And so by contrast we learn what she would find attractive in a prospective husband.

The first of seven suitors she and Nerissa discuss is "the Neopolitan prince," who is like a racecar driver but one who fixes the engines and changes the tires himself. He likes horses, and Portia explains this predilection by saying that his mother had a dalliance with a mechanic, a horseshoe smith. She does not want someone in the menial arts but wants a leisured gentleman, who shares her tastes for the high use of leisure. And she traces vice to the parents' blood or genes.

The second suitor, the "County Palantine," is a weeper or sad man—precisely what Antonio had appeared in the opening to be. Portia declares that she does not want such a one even if he is a philosopher in old age. A weeping philosopher, one who is preoccupied with the sufferings and sorrow that nature holds in store for man, or who is inclined to be resigned to nature's austerity, is not her type. She seeks someone who is festive, merry, happy. This doesn't mean, however, an empty-headed Gratiano. It could mean, as she subsequently discloses, a "scholar."

The third suitor is "Monsieur Le Bon," whom Portia describes as "every man in no man." He is never steadily himself but is an actor, a drama king, a chameleon, a Robin Williams. In dismissing him, Portia reveals, however, a certain act of her own: "I know," she tells Nerissa, "it is a sin to be a mocker: but…" Portia honors the Christianity she professes, it seems, in the breach. She winks at her sins, and unlike her father, lives as a human being, not as a saint. Here as in the rest of the scene, Portia shows no inclination to follow the teachings of Christianity.

Falconbridge, the fourth suitor, a British baron, is a "dumb show." He can't speak Latin, French, or Italian (and Portia can). He is an empty suit, but an Italian, French, or German suit. He is as we might say the perfect multiculturalist, that is, a fraud, a would-be cosmopolitan who mistakes the superficial manifestations of particular ways of life—clothing, and so on—for the full and serious devotion to any one of them, and so finds them easily adapted or assimilated to his speechless ways. He possesses no genuine way of his own. His behavior or mores are bought everywhere. He is a nonconversant clotheshorse, with Armani ties, Yves St. Laurent pants, and John Lobb shoes. He is, in short, another boaster.

The fifth suitor is a Scottish Lord, and Portia proves to be repulsed by his pugnacity. She doesn't want a scrapper, a man so unsure of his own worth, so thin-skinned or short-wicked, as to challenge every apparent affront to his dignity. She is looking for a more self-assured and therefore genuinely gentle man.

Finally, she expresses her contempt for the German Duke—a drunk. She wants a man not indebted to intoxication for his sociability, or one who is fundamentally sober. And she discloses now that she is not above thoughts of trickery in the business of the caskets: put some Rhenish wine near a wrong casket, she tells Nerissa, and the German Duke will go for it. He and the other unsuitable suitors are leaving, and as Portia says, "I pray God grant them a fair departure." Her piety contains, at the very least, a dose of irony.

Nerissa now mentions Bassanio, "a Venetian, a scholar, and a soldier." He is a citizen of Portia's own city, a learned man, and brave or valorous. She finds him deserving, too, of a fair lady in his *looks*. This last condition is not, as it turns out, least in Portia's judgment, as we learn from her rejection of the Prince of Morocco (1.2.130ff.). Portia is moved by looks, and she is unattracted to Moors or Arabs for this reason. Perhaps this is why her Christian father mistrusted her judgment. She is in any event frankly determined in her judgments by national characteristics—and national vices—and by a predilection for the cosmopolitan virtues of one who is at the same time a handsome Venetian.

1.3: Shylock

Modern sensibilities have decried Shakespeare's presentation of Shylock as a reprehensible slur upon Jews, second perhaps only to that of Marx in *On The Jewish Question*. While we know that the presentation is historically inaccurate—Shakespeare had no direct experience of Jews, since they were excluded from England—it is, as we will see, at least as much a condemnation of Christians as it is of this Jew. It is also such as to suggest a certain superiority of Judaism to Christianity.

Antonio is, as Bassanio has informed Shylock, to provide the bond on a loan, at interest, of 3,000 ducats. Shylock declares Antonio "a good man," that is, good for his money—though he indicates that he knows Antonio's money is tied up in five perilous voyages. Shylock expresses the wish to speak with Antonio, and Bassanio offers to have dinner with both of them. This prompts Shylock to deliver these famous lines:

> Yes, to smell pork, to eat of the habitation which
> your prophet the Nazarite conjur'd the devil into. I
> will buy with you, sell with you, talk with you,
> walk with you, and so following; but I will not eat
> with you, drink with you, nor pray with you. (1.3.33–37)

Shylock knows the Christian scriptures, and hence that the Christian way of life is at odds with the Mosaic law by which he directs his life. The *limited* means to overcoming the fundamental differences between him and Bassanio is commerce, but it is means enough for what Bassanio purposes.

Just how limited the means are is suggested when Antonio appears, and we hear, in an aside, of Shylock's hatred of him, spawned by Antonio's contempt—a hatred that will inform all of Shylock's deeds. Shylock hates Antonio for being a Christian, but hates him more for his "simplicity," his stupidity in drawing down interest rates in Venice. Antonio's simplicity in this appears "low" to Shylock: the cleverness of maintaining the conditions for profit-making is by contrast "high" because the profit is needed for high ends, for a high or dignified life. The obliteration of the distinction between high and low that would follow from the leveling, indiscriminate lending practiced by Antonio would destroy the material basis for the high. And the high life as Shylock conceives it is a life bound up with service to his "sacred nation" and hence to its God; his ancient grudge has its roots in Antonio's hatred of (and Shylock's love of) "our sacred nation." For the universalism of Christianity, its deprecation of the particular, *must* deny above all the perduring sacred character of Shylock's particular nation; its universalism rests on this denial. Antonio has, moreover, railed at Shylock, at his lending practices—at his "well-won profits." For this, Shylock vows, on the sacredness of his tribe, that he will never forgive Antonio—never practice *the* Christian virtue of forgiveness: his deepest devotion is not to his profits but to his nation and its dignity. And as he lets out, he has been waiting for his chance to strike and avenge his grudge. His provoked hatred directs him, consumes him, and even distracts him from the business at hand: though he has twice repeated the term of the loan, he asks to be reminded of it. While he too lacks the 3,000 ducats at the moment, he declares that Tubal, "a Hebrew of my tribe," will provide them— apparently without interest (1.3.54–57).

The first words of the arriving Antonio confirm the essential difference to which Shylock has alluded: Antonio declares that he is breaking his custom, law, *nomos* never to lend or borrow at interest. He does so to supply his friend's "ripe wants." He has in the past mercilessly abused Shylock for lending at interest (106–129), and Shylock now brings that dispute to a head, justifying his practice by reference to the practice of Jacob, "from our holy Abram...the third possessor." He mentions the device through which Jacob managed to get all the strongest ewes to conceive spotted sheep for him—that is, how he outwitted Laban, who had been cheating him.[5] Jacob saw "a way to thrive," Shylock concludes, "and was blest: / And thriving is blessing, if men steal it not" (89–90). As he presents it, Jacob did not break the letter of his agreement yet used his skill as a shepherd to get the better of Laban. Antonio, who might have cited other Hebrew scriptures against usury (see, e.g., Psalm 15.5) instead counters that Jacob had served for his reward (91–95), and that it was not in his power to bring the reward to pass: blessing is from "the hand of heaven." The devil, he warns the Christian Bassanio, can quote scripture, and he likens Shylock to a smiling villain.

With this insult, the long-standing acrimony between the two rises to the surface, as Shylock reminds Antonio of his past reviling and cruel contempt of him for his usury and his "misbelief," of his spitting on his "Jewish gabardine" and on his beard (106–113). Shylock has borne it all patiently, "For suffrance is the badge of all our tribe." Patient endurance is not an exclusively Christian virtue. Shylock's patience—like Jacob's before him[6]—is prudent: He asks if, hitherto reviled, he should now bow low like a slave and grant their request for a loan: simple reciprocal justice is on the side of his dignity in denying it, a justice that stands against Christian humility.[7]

Shylock's stance has the remarkable effect of bringing out how un-Christian Antonio has been and remains in his deeds. Antonio denies none of the contemning deeds and, asserting that he is likely to do them again, requests that the money be lent by Shylock not in friendship but rather "to thine enemy." He is determined to remain Shylock's enemy not on the basis of Christian faith—which, after all, commands love of one's enemies—but rather on the classical ground that usury is against nature. "[F]or when," he asks, all but quoting the pagan Aristotle rather than any Christian source, "did friendship take / A breed for barren metal of his friend?"[8] It is true that when Shylock offers, in feigned friendship, to have but a pound of Antonio's flesh as bond, "in merry sport," Antonio finds that "[t]he Hebrew will turn Christian: he grows kind" (178). But Antonio himself has not even a pretense to Christian charity; he simply accepts the terms of the bond, confident that his ships will come in.

2.1: Portia with Morocco

While Antonio is thus getting himself into trouble, Portia is avoiding it. At the announced arrival of the Prince of Morocco she had remarked, saucily, that if his soul be saintly but his complexion devilish (black), "I had rather he should shrive me than wive me" (12.129–131). However attractive it may be to God, saintliness is not attractive to Portia, at least when measured against looks. Her Christian father's casket scheme rests on the separation of appearance and worth, but Portia finds them inseparable. Not that looks are everything to her; as we have seen, she has a list of disqualifying vices and hence of qualifying virtues. But looks trump virtues in being a sine qua non for her husband. So when Morocco—who claims to have in spite of his looks (about which he worries) outstanding courage or valor—chooses wrongly and departs, Portia muses, "may all of his complexion choose me so" (2.7.79).[9] She does nothing, moreover, to dispel Morocco's high opinion of his own worth and consequent regret that fortune will determine the outcome, though her doing so would have mitigated fortune's role in that outcome.

2.2: Launcelot

Shylock had described Launcelot his servant as an "unthrifty knave" (13.176). Launcelot's opening soliloquy is no less harsh to Shylock. It is a dialogue on "conscience," which Christianity calls a faculty of the soul and which Shakespeare is ever careful to have only Christians speak about. Launcelot would run away from Shylock's house, but his conscience opposes it, counseling honesty. The devil, on the other hand, admonishes him to be brave, that is, to act fearlessly for his own good and depart. To Launcelot as to Hamlet, conscience goes together with cowardice.[10] If he does what is right and stays, he will be ruled by a devil (Shylock); if he leaves, he will do so at the behest of the devil. With no good choice, he observes that the devil offers friendly advice against the hard, Christian advice (of patiently enduring wrong). But once Launcelot has decided in this way to run from Shylock, his blind father appears, and he deceives him, in a send-up of the biblical story of Isaac and Jacob in which the details of the biblical account are comically turned on their head.[11] Finally Launcelot convinces his father to give the gift of doves he has brought for the Jew Shylock to the Christian Bassanio, who is fitting out "rare new liveries," and when Bassanio happens by, father and son stumble over one another to plead for a new job for Launcelot. As it happens, Shylock has already offered Launcelot to Bassanio, and so the latter accepts him into his service—in the livery of a jester.

It is significant that Shylock could not himself so use Launcelot. There is a lack of jesting, of cheer, in his life; his only "merry sport" is the deadly deceit through which he is attempting to secure a pound of Antonio's flesh. Or, stated positively, there is a sobriety to Shylock's life, and a parsimony that contrasts with the cheerful, spendthrift ways of Bassanio. Shylock makes his way in a tough world by his wits and by adhering to the law of his tribe. While Bassanio appears to be growing closer in friendship with him—"my best esteem'd acquaintance," Bassanio calls him (172)—and even to have won his agreement to dine (!) at his home, it is as we soon learn all part of an effort on Shylock's part to exploit Bassanio's great profligacy in order to ruin him.

That Christian profligacy is not confined to money matters begins to be suggested in the sequel, in which Gratiano enters and demands to go with Bassanio to Belmont. The provisos that Bassanio makes to the invitation that he now offers Gratiano explain why Gratiano had not hitherto been invited: he must be less wild, rude, bold, and liberal with his words; he will have to be politic and appear modest, lest he be misunderstood. That is, while Bassanio himself enjoys Gratiano as he is, he fears that his taking of liberties will give offense to strangers. Gratiano agrees to be sober in dress, respectful in speech, pious, demure, civil, "like one well studied in a sad ostent," so that even his grandmother would approve. He will in other words lose his youthful liberality, pretending to be—like Shylock. His normal behavior—welcome to the Christian Bassanio—is a foil for what is missing in Shylock's life: festive merriment, as will now be confirmed by Shylock's daughter.

2.3–2.5: Jessica among the Christians

Jessica tells the departing Launcelot that her father's house is a "hell," which the merry devil Launcelot alone had made bearable. As he is leaving, tearfully, so she too will leave, her secret intention being to convert to Christianity and marry Lorenzo. This, she expects, will end the strife in her heart: Christianity does not demand the honoring of one's father if it stands in the way of heaven.[12] As Launcelot—who here equates being a Jew with being a pagan (11)—followed what seemed the easier way, so does Jessica. She sends a letter with Launcelot to Lorenzo, who, with Gratiano, Salerio, and Solanio, is pushing a hastily cooked-up conspiracy to take her away during the evening's masquerade. To Lorenzo's joy, the letter discloses Jessica's intent to steal away from her father's house with gold and jewels.

Whether leaving Shylock's house is wise is the question raised in the next scene. Shylock warns Launcelot that life with Bassanio will be worse for him: he will be unable to eat, sleep, snore, and wear out clothes as he has been doing in Shylock's house. Shylock has a good opinion of his treatment of Launcelot, and we see clearly what guides the latter's life: his body and especially his stomach. Launcelot for his part rejoices in his newfound freedom to say and do things without the bidding of Shylock, but he will of course have another master. Shylock prepares now to depart for Bassanio's dinner "in hate, to feed upon / the prodigal Christian" (14–15). And when he hears of the planned masque, he similarly warns Jessica not to go out to gaze on "Christian fools with varnish'd faces / ...Let not the sound of shallow foppery enter / My sober house" (33–36). The sobriety that marks this follower of Jacob—by whose staff he swears (36)—stands again in marked contrast with Christian prodigality and merriment. It would seem that, in Venice at least, Christianity's emphasis upon the next world has made Christians improvident in this one. To Shylock this improvidence is hateful, and he now lets out that he has agreed to let Launcelot go into Bassanio's service to have him "help to waste his borrowed purse" (50). Jessica would appear, then, to be justified in leaving one so eaten up with malice. But is she? If Shylock goes too far here in his hatred—and he does—we must nonetheless wonder about the Christians who, improvident, cruelly drive him to his hatred of their ways by and while condemning his sobriety and parsimony.

The brief discussion of love between Salerio and Gratiano that opens the next scene, occasioned by the late arrival of Lorenzo, certainly does nothing to dispel this wonder. Salerio contrasts, on one hand, the speed or zeal with which "Venus' pigeons fly," to, on the other, their uneasy fidelity once they are sworn to each other. Gratiano agrees, and extends the thought from love to all appetites—even those of animals and inanimate things—attributing the changed disposition of successful pursuers to their disappointed satiety. "All things that are / Are with more spirit chased than enjoyed." Life is prodigal, a leaky sieve; we hunt pleasures, but end up disappointed. The man who proclaims this is about to promise his undying affection to Nerissa. Here then is the downside of those who chase merriment, pleasure, diversions: their desire for a thrilling change from their present discontent can never be settled, but must ever be renewed. They are neither steady nor reliable nor trustworthy, and they too easily assimilate erotic longing, which leads serious human beings to devotion, to a bestial pleasure that must ever be on a hunt. Shylock's sobriety bespeaks by contrast both a deeper and a steadier soul.

Jessica, tossing the casket of gold ducats down to Lorenzo, declares ambiguously that she is "much ashamed" of her "exchange." She means not her change from a faithful Jew to a lover of a Christian, but to the appearance of a boy. Cupid himself would blush, she declares, if lovers could see their pretty follies, like this one. Yet she, the lover, does see it as a folly, and is aghast to hear that she will be the torch-bearer: "I should be obscured." Her remark would make sense only if the world sees what she sees—that she is Jessica dressed as a boy—rather than seeing, as they will, a boy. She appears unable to fathom that the disguise will disguise her, as Lorenzo indeed reminds her. Or is it not rather the case that Jessica is indeed ashamed of something else, which she fears cannot be so easily hidden: the betrayal of her father and her people?

At Belmont, meanwhile, Portia observes the wrong choice of casket by Morocco, to whom appearances are indeed decisive: Portia deserves to be in gold, so gold it must be. Portia, we also see, is not above making use of her father's scheme for her own ends, encouraging Morocco in what she knows is the wrong choice (2.7.61–62). She does not, however, violate the convention established by her father. She appears ready to submit to its judgment, just as the suitors must; she uses the convention effectively. And so the Prince of Morocco takes his leave.

From Salerio and Solanio, however, we learn that Shylock has learned of his daughter's elopement and is now beside himself with anger, and mocked in it by all the boys: "my stones, my daughter, my ducats!" (2.8.15–26). He vows that Antonio will pay for the suffering he has undergone. We know that this makes no sense: Antonio had nothing to do with Jessica's stealing away. But this is now the awful situation: the only way Shylock has left to redeem his honor and satisfy the vengeance that his dignity demands is through "the law." Salerio and Solanio speak indeed of the kind gentleman Antonio and his generous love for his friend Bassanio, but they have never experienced the obverse of that love: Antonio's deep, abiding, and harsh hatred of his enemy, Shylock.

As Antonio's fate grows darker with the deepening of his enemy's hatred, Portia's brightens with the failure of another detested suitor at her hands. For we now learn that the suitors are required to swear three oaths before submitting to the testing by caskets: they must not tell which casket they have chosen, must never woo a maid, and must leave immediately if they fail. The central of these three oaths raises the stakes of failure, and surely deters most suitors from even attempting the test of the caskets. We do not yet know whether the prescribed oaths are Portia's or her father's doing, but we would not now put it past her to have invented them. Aragon, the next suitor, rejects the lead casket on the basis of its poor looks. He rejects also the gold casket, since its inscription speaks of what "many men desire"; he is keen to distinguish himself from the multitude, whom he condemns for judging on the basis of looks (as he has just done with respect to the lead casket). Aragon is a snob, pretending to be above the many while remaining fundamentally of them. The inscription on the silver casket promises to give him what he deserves, and since this is in his opinion much, he chooses it. But before he assumes his desert, he gives a disquisition on desert (40–49), revealing himself to be, as Portia will put it, a "fool." He delivers sentences in the overbearing, hortatory subjunctive ("Let none presume ..."), and his expressions of disappointment with the world ("O that estates ...") are the ridiculous product of foolish hopefulness. He is ever wishing that the world were perfectly just and so ever disappointed to discover that it isn't. "If only" is his pathetic watchword: if only men were not corrupt! If only the truly deserving (like himself) received their due!

So deep runs his hope that he can scarce believe that he has not won the prize. Portia must remind him of his third vow ("Too long a pause ..."), and since even then he argues the result, she must rebuke him, reminding him that he is not the judge. The note inside the casket declares him a fool, and he leaves. "Deliberate fools," as Portia calls those who pride themselves on such deliberations, "when they do choose / They have wisdom by their wit to lose" (80–81). The outcome, that is, is good for them, since if they should win, she would make their lives miserable. For unlike them, she has no high hopes in the world's justice. She will take things, rather, into her own hands. In fact, we can see that she has already done so: the note in the silver casket tells Aragon "Take what wife you will to bed" (70), revealing to us that Portia, not her father, is responsible for the second daunting oath. And in conformity with her reasonable hopes, Bassanio is now arriving, bestowing gifts on the announcing messengers, who are completely won over by them. Portia for her part prudently suspects that self-interest rather than disinterested admiration lies behind the messengers' praise of Bassanio; she realizes how easily one's benefactors are equated with noble-hearted humans, that is, how easy it is for most of us, thinking well of ourselves, to assume that good things that come our way are what we deserve, as the noble-hearted recognize. Not that she doesn't think highly of herself, but she does not see her good fortune as resulting from her worth. She and Aragon would have been oil and water.

3.1: Shylock's Hope for Divine Vengeance

If to this point Shakespeare has given us cause to see in Shylock a reasonable if flawed alternative to Christian profligacy, we now see Shylock turned, by the apparent losses of his enemy Antonio, into a man wholeheartedly bent on the fulfillment of an ugly hope in bloodthirsty vengeance. Antonio, we learn from Salerio and Solanio, has lost a second ship at sea. And Jessica, Shylock declares, is damned for rebelling against him. He thereby justifies the fears of Salerio and Solanio that he will exact vengeance for his loss of her upon Antonio who, he declares, was once smug, called him usurer, and lent money for a mere Christian curtsy. Shylock has been humiliated, disgraced, mocked, lost friends, and gained enemies at Antonio's doing, "because I am a Jew."

Shylock's famous reply to these wrongs—"Hath not a Jew eyes? etc." (I2.1.58–73)—brings out the desperate plight of his dignity. For the attributes that Shylock mentions are all, save revenge, bodily; they belong to any mammal. Shylock abstracts from the distinctively human, the virtues upon which worth or dignity rests. The cultivation of those virtues was the highest end of premodern political life but Venice, the commercial republic, must move away from their cultivation precisely if it wishes to maintain peace among its various subjects. Revenge, to be sure, is distinctively human, but having a desire for it is hardly a reason to treat someone with respect, as Shylock himself admits: he has learned revenge from the Christians, he claims, and will now outdo them in its villainy. He will demand for his revenge the stipulated pound of Antonio's bodily flesh. How the laws of the commercial republic address—as they must—this distinctively human desire will be disclosed in the trial of Antonio.

And trial there will be. For Tubal, sent to Genoa in search of Jessica, feeds Shylock's desire for revenge, alternating news of Jessica's shopping spree with news of Antonio's growing losses on the seas. Jessica, Shylock states, is no longer his daughter; having betrayed him and taken his ducats—which were for him to give her—she is dead, and as he tells Tubal, he will have revenge. He now makes clear that he has not in fact learned this desire from Christians, but that Antonio's misfortunes have merely provided the opportunity for sating it. He thanks not fortune but God for providing this opportunity: he will execute divine justice, plaguing and torturing Antonio. Yet his response to the last of Tubal's disclosures—of Jessica's exchange of a ring for a monkey—shows us again the depth of soul that is now moving him to seek revenge, a depth conspicuously absent, as we have seen, from the Christian Gratiano. Shylock had this ring from Leah, his wife, when he was a bachelor, and would not have exchanged it "for a wilderness of monkeys." If as the Christian Launcelot has suggested, to be a Jew is to be a pagan, then pagans display a devotional love unmatched by Christians, who appear profligate in theirs. The loss of his beloved daughter—and with her, his dignity and his hopes—now manifestly moves him. If the world is to make sense, if it is to be a place in which a just God does rule, then there will have to be some compensation for his suffering. And so he is driven to seek the arrest of Antonio.

3.2: Portia and Bassanio

As Bassanio is about to choose among the caskets, Portia makes it clear that she loves and wants him, asking him to stay a few more days or even months before choosing. He requests to be given the test, however, and she complies, stating that if he wins, "Then music is / Even as the flourish when true subjects bow / To a new-crowned monarch" (48–50). It will have all the joy and majesty of a high political event. She calls for a song, this time, to accompany the choosing, and before the song, she offers a comparison of Bassanio's deed to a scene from pagan mythology, one that contains the helpful counsel to choose hardship: "I stand for sacrifice" (54–62). The song she has chosen, too, provides Bassanio with hints: each of its first three lines ends in a word rhyming with "lead," and by speaking of love born in the eyes that will die in the cradle where it lies, the song prompts Bassanio's reflections on the caskets. They are, like Aragon's, about worth, but with none of Aragon's pious moralizing, scolding, or laments about the world's injustice. They are instead about the artifices and ornaments that hide vice and beautify what is ugly. These reflections lead him to choose rightly.

Portia can scarce contain herself for her joy, and Bassanio waxes eloquent about the portrait of her that the lead casket holds; he is indeed a lover. He can scarce believe that he has won, but Portia confirms she is his, and for a brief moment, all is happiness. She wishes that she had more to give, but whatever she has is now his—so long as he wears her ring. He for his part eloquently describes his speechlessness: like a buzzing multitude after a fair oration by a beloved prince, he says, is the confusion of his powers. As with Portia, so with Bassanio, the comparisons that are made to bring out the joy of his choice are to political life, but that life is thereby made the more conspicuously absent in Belmont. He vows to wear Portia's ring faithfully to his death. Gratiano and Nerissa announce that they too will be married. And as soon as that is agreed to, Gratiano reverts to his old self with the demand for a bet on who will have the first child, followed by a dirty joke and—as Salerio and Lorenzo arrive—a crass reference: "We are the Jasons. We have won the fleece" (241).

But suddenly all is not well; a letter from Antonio causes Bassanio to turn pale, and Portia remarks that it must mean that a dear friend is dead, "else nothing in the world / Could turn so much the constitution / Of any constant man" (245–247). Her words announce immediately the problem that Antonio will pose to her in vying for first place in Bassanio's heart. Shakespeare now has her echo what the Roman Portia said to her Brutus upon noting the trouble that the conspiracy to kill Caesar had brought to his soul: "With leave, Bassanio: I am half yourself, / And I must freely have the half of anything / That this same paper brings you" (248–250).[13] In response, Bassanio discloses that his claim to have no wealth was a boast: he has engaged himself to a dear friend, and that friend to his mere enemy, "to feed my means." Unlike Brutus, he is—owing to his Christian profligacy—in debt. Like Brutus, however, he presents the situation in the classic political terms of friend and enemy rather than with any reference to the religious question. And Salerio confirms that the contents of the disturbing letter are true: all of Antonio's five ships are wrecked, and Shylock is stubbornly demanding "justice," his bond. Jessica, too, confirms that Shylock has sworn to Tubal and Chus, "his countrymen"—not his tribesmen, not his fellow Jews, but his countrymen—that he would prefer Antonio's flesh to 20 times the loaned ducats. While the dispute between Shylock and Antonio is unintelligible in abstraction from that of Christian and Jew, here, at the heart of the play, the issue is understood in strictly political terms, as it would have been in the pre-Christian city.

So too when Portia asks if it is Bassanio's friend who is thus in trouble, Bassanio responds with this striking praise of Antonio:

> The dearest friend to me, the kindest man,
> The best-condition'd and unwearied spirit
> In doing courtesies, and one in whom
> The ancient Roman honor more appears
> Than any that draws breath in Italy. (292–296)

These words appear to stand in sharp contrast to Shylock's (confirmed) accusations, but not to what we have seen of Antonio. For they say nothing of any Christian virtues—of which we have seen none in Antonio; they stress instead his devotion to ancient Roman honor. "Before a friend of *this* description / Shall lose a hair through Bassanio's fault" (301–302; emphasis added), asserts Portia, 12 times the owed sum should be paid out. As Bassanio had led us to expect, Portia, too, is moved no less than her Roman namesake by concern for honor.

But she begins already here to reveal a superiority to Brutus's Portia, disclosing the wit to use the superior position in which she finds herself. For though she tells Bassanio that he will have gold to pay the debt "twenty times over," she has heard already that Shylock will not accept even this amount, and that he can be thwarted in his intention only by "law, authority, and power" (289). She knows, that is, that her offer, while generous, is likely to be rejected, and as the rest of the play discloses, she has another plan up her sleeve. She is careful to go with Bassanio "to church" to make their vows public and solemn, in accord with Christian law, but as we will see, she will not—as she suggests to Bassanio—sit idly if faithfully by with Nerissa and await the outcome. The reason she gives for her generous action tells us why: "For never shall you lie by Portia's side / With an unquiet soul" (305–306). The statement certainly expresses affection, and Portia undoubtedly loves Bassanio. But it also puts Portia first, and even has her referring to herself, in the proud, Roman manner, in the third person. Even in love, Portia acts clear-sightedly and proudly for her good. Bassanio's reading of the contents of the letter confirms what she must now suspect: Antonio wishes that Bassanio come, moved by love, to witness his end. Hearing the contents of the letter Portia exclaims, "O love," and bids Bassanio be gone to Venice. He then vows to Portia his fidelity.

3.3: Virtue in a Commercial Republic

Shylock has had Antonio arrested, the jailor has allowed him out to speak once more to Shylock, and we see Antonio asking to be heard. But Shylock is closed to speech. He takes the jailor to be supporting a plea for mercy. "I'll have my bond," he thrice states, rejecting Antonio's request to be heard. Shylock claims by his own words to have become now subhuman: you called me a dog, watch me now be a dog. Yet he persists in claiming that it is *justice* that he seeks, and adds now that he has sworn an oath to have his bond. Antonio gives up the attempt to speak, asking Solanio to desist too. He claims that Shylock seeks his life because "I oft deliver'd from his forfeitures / Many that have at times made moan to me" (22–23). In what we might call an effort to think well of himself, Antonio forgets or ignores the cruelty he has shown to Shylock—his cruelty to him as an enemy, one whose practices are vicious in his eyes and deserving of deep contempt. But he is bereft of hope. Against Solanio's comforting words that the Duke will not grant that the forfeiture of the agreement hold, Antonio points out that for the Duke to deny the

course of the law
...Will much impeach the justice of his state;
Since that the trade and profit of the city
Consisteth of all nations. (26–31)

In no other kind of republic would this situation have arisen. The Christian rulers of Venice have, we may say, taken the opportunity afforded by the Christian denigration of politics—of high political ends, which the Christian doctrine of two cities makes inevitable—to relegate the practice of virtue to a private sphere, for the sake of the only remaining public good: the city's wealth. In other words, Christian universalism, the universalism of love of members of all nations, has as a political consequence a cosmopolitanism centered on the pursuit of wealth. Recognizing that Venice has been thus reduced to the minimalist if strictly enforced dictates of commercial law, and that his case is therefore hopeless, Antonio can pray God only that Bassanio come to see him pay his debt (35–36). He is driven to seek confirmation or recognition of the nobility of his deeds in private, from his friend. As at Belmont, so in Venice, the nobility once sought in political life has been relegated to the private realm.

3.4: Portia Acts

At Belmont, Lorenzo praises Portia, telling her that if she knew how true a gentleman and how dear a lover of Bassanio is Antonio, she would be even prouder of her deed than "customary bounty can enforce you" (9). He attributes her actions to generosity, and believes (quite ridiculously) that she will be glad to learn how dear a lover of Bassanio is Antonio. Portia makes sufficiently clear in her reply that her deed is not done without attention to her own interests: "I never did repent for doing good" (10). And in this case, if Antonio is Bassanio's bosom friend, he must be like Bassanio, and so she is purchasing "the semblance of my soul / From out the state of hellish misery" (20–21). She purchases the semblance of her own soul. At the same time, of course, she is stopping Antonio from carrying out his noble deed on behalf of her husband, his beloved. She now pretends, to be sure, to be acting in a quiescent, humble way, prayerfully enduring what will come. She has, she declares, "toward heaven breathed a secret vow / To live in prayer and contemplation" at a nearby monastery until her lord's return (26–34). And she puts Lorenzo in charge of her household. But this is a wickedly humorous lie. She will in fact, disguised as a man, be rescuing her husband's friend from his hellish fate, rescuing Antonio from death for her husband's sake, and thus rescuing her husband from indebtedness or guilt for Antonio's deed. She will be acting both for her husband's happiness and her own, and will also save her husband's friend. She will thereby be garnering the debt, devotion, and allegiance of Bassanio. She acts for herself and her beloved, but with the semblance of pious devotion and legality.

Portia's plan—which she promises to tell Nerissa en route to Venice—is to send a letter, through Balthazar, to her cousin Dr. Bellario, from whom she expects in return court garments and notes. Bellario is a lawyer upon whom the Duke has relied in the past: through him Portia is acquainted with Venice's laws. She expects or perhaps already knows through Balthazar that the Duke has written to Bellario, and she intends to be representing herself as Balthazar, in court, with notes from Bellario (58–62)—though clearly Bellario's notes and Balthazar's own appearance in court could have done the trick. She and Nerissa, like the gold and silver caskets, will appear to be "accomplished with that we lack" (61–62). She will deceive, not out of vanity or a foolish estimate of her worth, but consciously, to achieve her own good. She will even have to lie within the lie—pretend on the road to be a bragging youth who has broken the hearts of honorable ladies. She cloaks her series of deceptions in the grand deception of quiescent Christian piety, prepared to outdo her Roman namesake in rescuing her troubled husband.

3.5: Belmont under Lorenzo

Launcelot, the play's only bridge between the Jewish and Christian households, for a second time makes the biblical doctrines of sin and damnation the object of comedy. He tells Jessica to be of good cheer, since she is damned, the sins of the fathers being visited upon their children. Her only way out is if her father isn't truly her father, that is, if her mother had been unfaithful, in which case, however, she is damned. Jessica replies that she will be saved through her husband, who has made her a Christian. Proving again that what moves him is his belly, Launcelot notes that "[t]his making of Christians will raise the price of hogs." Extending this jest, Jessica tells the entering Lorenzo that Launcelot says she is damned and has accused Lorenzo of being a bad member of the commonwealth for raising the price of pork. The jesting rests on the serious ground that good membership in the commercial commonwealth consists in concern for the price of commodities. The commercial commonwealth is not concerned with—nay, it is hindered by—religious ends, by attention to the immortal souls of its members. Lorenzo for his part promises to address only Launcelot's charge concerning the commonwealth (37–39, and cf. 2.4.33–37 with 2.6.51–57).

Lorenzo finds himself now, perhaps for the first time in his life, tasked with the responsibilities of an adult, and hence exasperated by Launcelot's series of punning replies to the orders he gives in his effort to run the household. "I pray / thee, understand a plain man in his plain meaning" (56–57). We are shown what would lead a Shylock to favor sobriety over such obesity of wit. Turning his attention at last to Jessica, Lorenzo asks her how she fares, but not waiting for an answer, asks her opinion of "the Lord Bassanio's wife." Her praise warrants our attention:

> Past all expressing. It is very meet
> The Lord Bassanio live an upright life,
> For, having such a blessing in his lady,
> He finds the joys of heaven here on earth,
> And if on earth he do not [merit] it, then
> In reason he should never come to heaven!
> Why, if two gods should play some heavenly match,
> And on the wager lay two earthly women,
> And Portia one, there must be something else
> Pawn'd with the other, for the poor rude world
> Hath not her fellow. (73–83)

Portia is a blessing so heavenly as to make heaven superfluous, and Bassanio meetly lives an "upright life" to deserve her. Such a life is, she implies, one of some self-denial, an eschewing of selfish pleasures so as to be worthy of the joy. But then Jessica's statement is incomplete, since anyone who finds his joy in this life is already rewarded: an ascetic life in a monastery would alone be called for. Moreover, to live such a life one must, as Jessica says, "merit it," that is, there cannot be the mere pretense of sacrifice, or else one will "in reason" not come to heaven. But how, then, can it be *sacrificial*, if it is to be rewarded in heaven? Is such a life not led precisely to benefit oneself eternally? The sacrifices of an upright life such as Jessica presents cannot then be sacrifices at all, but acts of long-range self-interest, a price to be paid. One could perhaps deserve eternal life by not seeking it, but Christianity calls one precisely to seek it. Her words inadvertently disclose the impossibility of becoming worthy of eternal life by self-sacrifice, since such sacrifice is not possible. It is perhaps in awareness of this, brought home by the fact that Bassanio already has his heavenly reward on earth, in Portia, that Jessica switches her argument to a pagan one: gambling, competing, that is, fighting, irrational gods would have trouble finding Portia's equal. Such gods would exist, however, at the cost of the moral order that promises eternal life. Might such reflections have moved Portia to abandon the faith of her father for the clear-sighted pursuit of her good in this life while, however, maintaining the appearance of upholding piety and the law? As we will see, she is much closer to Shylock and Antonio than to her Christian husband in her understanding of Venetian law.

As for Lorenzo, he fails to realize even the need to pay Jessica the compliment for which she is in part surely fishing: he gracelessly turns the praise of Portia into a praise of himself, and wants to feed his stomach before hearing more of it (83–90). He is indeed an excellent member of the commercial republic.

4.1: Portia at Court

The Duke of Venice opens the dramatic trial of Antonio lamenting Shylock's lack of mercy, finding him "incapable of pity" and "an inhuman wretch." But Shylock is, as we have seen, relying on the law to give him what he has been deprived of: dignity. His faith in a just God hangs in the balance. Antonio, by contrast, remains perfectly Stoic:

> I have heard
> Your grace hath ta'en great pains to qualify
> His rigorous course; but since he stands obdurate,
> And that no lawful means can carry me
> Out of his envy's reach, I do oppose
> My patience to his fury, and am arm'd
> To suffer, with a quietness of spirit,
> The very tyranny and rage of his. (6–13)

Antonio makes no pretense to care about the conversion of Shylock's soul to the true, heavenly goods; he makes no mention of enduring a wrong in order to awaken Shylock's conscience.[14] Patience is simply his own armor. Conversion, as we will see, he later demands simply as a punishment.

The Duke requests of Shylock, precisely as a Jew, a "gentle answer" to his query of whether he will proceed cruelly or show now "human gentleness and love." Shylock responds, however, that he is a man of his word; he has sworn an oath "by our holy Sabaoth" to have the pound of flesh, and warns of the city's punishment if he is denied: Venice will lose its charter of freedom (34–39). Free men keep their oaths. But free men also are expected to behave reasonably: why does he demand the pound of flesh? His answer is that he is like all men the slave of arbitrary, whimsical, capricious likes and dislikes. This is a tyrant's answer, but also an answer unanswerable by the laws of Venice or its modern cousin, the liberal state. It implies that there is no accounting for our opinions of noble and base, ugly and beautiful, repulsive and venerable, high and low; they are the product of blind passions to which we are subject; we have no choice over them and cannot be blamed for holding them; blame is attached only when we step outside the law to which we have consented, out of fear, to obey. Each of us should otherwise be left alone to pursue our whims, answerable to no one. "So can I give no reason, nor I will not, / More than a lodg'd hate and a certain loathing / I bear Antonio" (59–61). As Shylock tells Bassanio, who objects to the cruelty of the answer, "I am not bound to please thee with my answers" (65).

Venetian law is deliberately indifferent to questions of the right way of life, that is, to the ground of the quarrel, and so Shylock will stick to that law. He is surely aware that his own religion calls for mercy (see, e.g., Psalm 136), but exploits the law's freedom to do as he will within its confines.

Still, Bassanio seeks to engage him: "Do all men kill the things they do not love?" But Shylock's response is apt: "Hates any man the thing he would not kill?" Hatred drives him to kill. Bassanio presses him: "Every offense is not a hate at first." To this Shylock might well have noted that the offense in question goes back well beyond the three-month loan; he might again have recounted the years of abuse he has suffered at Antonio's hands. But this would open up the source of their dispute in the question of the right way of life. So a second time Shylock avoids that path: "Wouldst thou have a serpent sting thee twice?" He reduces Antonio's deeds, as he has his own, to a bestial level, and his requisite response to a matter of prudence. Antonio's resigned plea for Bassanio to desist appears to echo this reduction: Shylock does what he does, he avers, for the same reason the tides flow, the wolf eats the lamb, the mountain pines creak in the breeze. He blames the alleged necessity on Shylock's hard "Jewish heart" (70–83).

Shylock's fourth and final argument comes after he has firmly rejected Bassanio's offer of double the payment. The Duke asks him how he should hope for mercy, rendering none. The question reflects the level of commercial law that Shylock has so cleverly exploited: mercy is self-interested, a calculative prudence. Shylock is able to reject even this plea, however, through the law's low aim: "What judgment shall I dread, doing no wrong?" That he is not claiming here a perfection that frees him from fear of a demandingly high law, but stating merely that he acts within the low law of Venice, is made startlingly clear in the sequel, in which he reprimands the Venetians for their attempts to demand of him virtue that transcends the law. They know as well as he that slavery is wrong, that human beings are not asses and dogs and mules. Why, then, should he not tell them to liberate their slaves? To marry them to their heirs? To give them good things? Because they will respond (he says), "the slaves are ours," that is, we own them; they were dearly and legally purchased. So too with his pound of flesh: it is his. If not, "fie upon your law!" (89–103).

With this final argument Shylock implicitly admits that what he is demanding is just not in itself, at least in their eyes, but only by law. He exposes the Venetians' hypocrisy in demanding of him a virtue that goes beyond the law while they use the law to serve their interests. Not being a patsy, he will use the law as they do, and demands that it be binding. The law as he presents it is a tough, arbitrary laying down of how things are going to be. It is not always nor necessarily just; if it were, Venice would have no slaves. And if one begins challenging the law on the basis of a justice that is above the law, many wealthy and comfortable Venetians would suffer serious harm. The law quashes such challenges; that is its great virtue. And the Venetians know it: "I stand for judgment," as he says, and a little later, "I stand for law" (142). Nothing looms above the law in such a manner as to permit us to judge it. Rather, the law alone determines right and wrong, that is, it permits citizens to obtain what they take to be in their interests. Whether it is genuinely in their interest is, so far as the law is concerned, a nonquestion. On the basis of this proto-Hobbesian, Venetian understanding of law, Shylock rests his case.

Unfortunately for him, the Duke has sent for Bellario, and Portia, dressed as Bellario's boy Balthazar, will use this very understanding of the law to defeat him. Before she enters, Bassanio encourages Antonio by stating that Shylock shall have Bassanio's own flesh before he has a single drop of Antonio's blood. But the latter rejects this offer: "I am a tainted wether of the flock, / Meetest for death: the weakest kind of fruit / Drops earliest to the ground; and so let me" (114–116). If this seems vaguely Christian, Antonio dispels that appearance resoundingly in the words that follow: "You cannot better be employ'd, Bassanio, / Than to live still and write mine epitaph" (117–118). These proud words confirm Bassanio's earlier claim that Roman honor beats in Antonio's heart. They display a magnanimity that found its home, as we have seen, in ancient Rome,[15] and they show the first part of his response to bespeak nothing Christian but instead a readiness for death that has resulted from the loss of his material means and, more importantly, his loss of Bassanio to Portia—the enduring source of his sadness.

Christianity appears in fact only haplessly now in the figure of Gratiano, who again betrays his name with graceless and stupid railing. As Shylock whets his knife on the sole of his shoe, Gratiano blames him for his envy— his harsh desire to harm others. Gratiano raises again, that is, the question of motive, which, had he keener eyes, he would see has been skillfully shown by Shylock to be illicit. When Shylock shows his contempt for the youth's wit, Gratiano erupts with venom: " O, be thou damn'd, inexecrable dog!" And with justice seeming so absent from the proceedings, Gratiano screams that he is almost moved to waver in his faith: perhaps the pagan Pythagoras was right in claiming that the souls of beasts—dogs, wolves—enter human beings, as appears to be the case with Shylock. But Shylock reminds the raging youth that he stands for law (123–142).

This will now prove to be Shylock's undoing, at the clever hand of Portia. She is introduced by Bellario's letter as "a young doctor of Rome," a young body with an old head (153, 163–164) coming in the allegedly sick Bellario's stead. She grants immediately that law is on Shylock's side, and appeals therefore outside of it, to mercy, with her famous lines on its quality (184–205). She presents mercy not as something a sap would offer, but as a royal and even a divine virtue: if justice were done, no one would see salvation. And she appeals to the piety, common to Christian and Jew, that petitions God for mercy and that teaches "us" to be merciful (which finds expression in the *Pater Noster*). Yet as her concluding lines indicate, this whole appeal is a set-up:

I have spoke thus much
To mitigate the justice of thy plea,
Which if thou follow, this strict court of Venice
Must needs give sentence 'gainst the merchant there. (202–205)

Mercy alone is what stands between Shylock and the object of his desire. And Shylock, not unexpectedly, rebuffs her plea: "My deeds upon my head! I crave the law, / The penalty and forfeit of my bond" (206–207).

Portia's second attempt—a preparation, no less than the first, for Shylock's ultimate defeat—is begun by raising the question of payment. Bassanio offers now ten times the sum, as well as forfeit of his hands, his head, his heart, declaring that if this does not win, then it must be malice that bears down truth; justice is being defeated by malice. Is the law to support malice? If it does, Bassanio declares, then ignore the law: "To do a great right, do a little wrong, / And curb this cruel devil of his will" (216–217). His is a very tempting position—it is the gratifying premise, in fact, of many of our contemporary film dramas. It was likewise the position of Cassius, over and against the scolding of Brutus.[16] But Portia firmly opposes it:

It must not be; there is no power in Venice
Can alter a decree established.
'Twill be recorded for a precedent,
And many an error by the same example
Will rush into the state. It cannot be. (218–222)

She stands for unbending allegiance to the law. But unlike Brutus or, indeed, Julius Caesar, she does not do so on the republican ground that to allow anyone to stand outside the law would subvert the justice upon which the law stands.[17] Instead, her position bespeaks the *limits* of justice, the impossibility of it being attained in every case, and the consequent need for strong, unbending law. Hence Shylock, who fully shares this understanding, praises her exceedingly: "A Daniel come to judgment!" (223).[18] Portia again offers, though, a way out, bidding Shylock accept the offer of thrice the money. Shylock, apparently now believing that this is God's beloved Daniel, replies that he has an oath in heaven, and not for Venice will he lay perjury upon his soul (228–230). What we see now is the very opposite of the money-grubbing Jew portrayed by other playwrights: Shylock does *not* want the money, the ducats. His concern is for his soul, that is, his immortal soul, as his preceding reference to "Daniel" makes clear.[19]

With Shylock now devoted body and soul, as it were, to the law's execution, Portia announces that the bond is forfeit and hence the pound of flesh nearest the heart is lawfully Shylock's. Her final entreaty for mercy meets with a final rebuff of her, the "worthy judge." Antonio asks for a judgment, and Portia grants that the "intent and purpose of the law" corresponds to the stated penalty. Shylock can scarce contain his praise of Portia, and as he prepares the scales for the gruesome deed, she bids Antonio speak what he must believe to be his last words. They reflect his abiding stoicism and his abiding love for Bassanio. But they also finally address the matter of Bassanio's wife—not, however, in order to wish Bassanio happiness with her. Antonio's desire for his own abiding honor dominates his thoughts even here:

> But little; I am arm'd and well prepar'd.
> Give me your hand, Bassanio, fare you well.
> Grieve not that I am fall'n to this for you;
> For herein Fortune shows herself more kind
> Than is her custom. It is still her use
> To let the wretched man outlive his wealth,
> To view with hollow eye and wrinkled brow
> An age of poverty; from which ling'ring penance
> Of such misery doth she cut me off.
> Commend me to your honorable wife,
> Tell her the process of Antonio's end,
> Say how I lov'd you, speak me fair in death;
> And when the tale is told, bid her be judge
> Whether Bassanio had not once a love.
> Repent but you that you shall lose your friend,
> And he repents not that he pays your debt;
> For if the Jew do cut but deep enough,
> I'll pay it presently with all my heart. (264–281)

While he is prepared to die for Bassanio, Antonio offers him the comfort that it is a better fortune than to have miserably outlived his wealth. (He says nothing, in this would-be final speech, about God or the afterlife.) Yet this thought—that death is now a benefit to him—runs counter to the professed proof of his love for Bassanio: if death costs him nothing and is indeed a benefit, what great devotion is shown by it? In this conundrum, Antonio enacts a somewhat farcical version, appropriate to the commercial republic, of the problem attending the happy death that Brutus claims for himself, a death made happy by the public glory it bestows on him at the expense of the glory of his enemies.[20] A commercial republic affords no such opportunities. But it does still afford the opportunity for a noble death on behalf of one's friends. We are led to suspect that the true source of Antonio's wish to be relieved of life now is indeed manifest in the second half of the speech, where he commends himself to Portia and requests that Bassanio tell her the tale of Antonio's great devotional love. Bassanio's wooing of Portia has of course been the source not only of Antonio's enduring sadness but of the need of the loan from Shylock. His death would solve this problem, manifesting his great love while curing him of his sadness. But his request shows no concern for the effect that the triumphant, ultimate sacrifice he makes, as part of his vying love for Bassanio, will have on Portia's happiness. Nor can his deed be considered altogether friendly to Bassanio if, as he makes clear, it entails rendering him the mere writer of his epitaph, and the troubling loss of a beloved friend who died to pay his debt—as Portia had indeed perceived immediately upon hearing of it, and in her fear for what it would mean for her own happiness, has acted to overcome.

Portia's prudent fears are amply confirmed now by Bassanio's profession of his devotion to Antonio, as is the agreement we have observed between her and Shylock. Bassanio claims that he is prepared to "sacrifice" all that he has, including his "dear" wife, to deliver Antonio from Shylock. Portia immediately retorts: "Your wife would give you little thanks for that, / If she were by, to hear you make the offer" (288–289). She is clearly *not* prepared to be "sacrificed" for her husband's friend. After Nerissa has made a similar response to the similar profession of Gratiano (though one expressed in manifestly Christian terms), we hear a significant aside from Shylock: "These be the Christian husbands. I have a daughter; / Would any of the stock of Barrabas / Had been her husband rather than a Christian!" (295–297). Even a murderous Jew would not be prodigal and hence faithless in his love, as are Christians. Shylock is by far more aware of what it means to be a husband, and his agreement with Portia on law stems from this agreement, over and against Christian practice, from a recognition of the harsh truth about the exclusivity of devotional love and the harshness of the world to which it points. That Antonio has been from the opening of the play sad on account of his awareness of what Bassanio's love of Portia will mean to him bespeaks his agreement, too, with Portia and Shylock in this grave matter. Shylock's understanding of Venetian law has, accordingly, been one with these two Romans. We are thus shown the serious ground of Launcelot's equation of Judaism with paganism.

Having her own remarkably prescient thoughts publicly confirmed, Portia now springs her trap. She again proclaims that the court awards and the law gives a pound of flesh near Antonio's heart to Shylock. But, she adds, no drop of Christian blood shall be spilled, or his goods and life are confiscate to the state of Venice (305–312). Shylock asks if this is the law, and she ominously confirms that it is: you will see the act; you will have justice, more than you desire. Shylock, having many times praised her wisdom as a judge, is therefore now daunted: he requests instead of the flesh thrice the bond. Bassanio is prepared to give it, but Portia boldly persists: it is the flesh, or nothing, and only—she now adds—precisely one pound, or Shylock and his goods are confiscate. Shylock requests now only the principal, and again Bassanio is ready to grant it. But Portia denies it: Shylock has in open court refused mercy, she declares, so he will have justice rather than mercy. Shylock offers to go home, but Portia will not let him off: referring now to another law, proscribing an alien directly or indirectly seeking the life of a Venetian citizen, she declares half his goods confiscate to the state, and half to Antonio, and his life forfeit, if the Duke so demand it (313–363).

This remarkable defeat is carried out to the accompaniment of the vicious reaction of Gratiano, who screams nasty chants at Shylock. His low taunts (316, 322, 333, 340) reach a crescendo as Portia lowers the boom (369–374 and 379–381). While Gratiano's desire for the merciless death of Shylock is on display, this clearly is not what Portia has in mind. She can count, fortunately, on the mercy of the Duke, who pardons Shylock's life and reduces the state's forfeiture to a fine (368–372). Portia is careful to note that the reduction to a fine applies only to the state's half of his estate, not to Antonio's half. She has a plan, and its execution depends now on Antonio, whom she asks to render mercy. He complies: the half of Shylock's goods Shylock will have in use, and upon his death he will give them to Jessica and her husband, "the man who lately stole his daughter." (He readily and honestly admits that Lorenzo's deed was a *theft*.) But he demands in turn that Shylock now convert to Christianity as his punishment, and make a written gift of all he possesses to his "son" Lorenzo and to his daughter. He suspects—rightly—that Shylock will more readily accede to the care of his daughter than adhere to his faith. He recognizes the depth of Shylock's love of his own, and suspects that it will trump his religious scruples. Shylock agrees to this arrangement, but is obviously not simply content with it; he is "not well," he declares, in the last words we hear of him. Antonio for his part finds this compelled conversion merciful, and the final words spoken in court by the repulsive Gratiano make it appear so: he'd have had Shylock hanged (398–400).

Portia slips easily out of the Duke's dinner invitation, and then has a chance to test further, and more manifestly or enduringly, her husband's devotion, requesting of the grateful Bassanio the ring on his finger. He initially passes the test (426–445), but given what has said at the trial, this resolve clearly will not hold. Having offered "Balthazar" much, he is loath to deny Balthazar the one thing he has requested and claims he deserves. Bassanio has not seen and does not see what Portia and Shylock have seen: that there is a necessary limit to the objects of one's devotional love. What is at issue is summarized by Antonio's plea: "My Lord Bassanio, let him have the ring: / Let his deservings and my love withal / Be valued against your wife's commandment" (449–451). Bassanio is thus moved to show Antonio, who was prepared to die for him, that his love is, as he has publicly declared, truly reciprocated. Still pursuing her plan, Portia searches for the home of Shylock, to make official the agreement that will be "well welcome to Lorenzo" (4.2.4). She accepts Bassanio's ring from Gratiano, and Nerissa is careful to go to obtain from Gratiano the ring she had given him: it would be unpleasant, as they both know, if Gratiano kept his ring after Bassanio had given his over.

5.1: Portia Triumphant

Lorenzo, still acting lord of Belmont, exchanges words with Jessica about the lovely night, with its bright moon and sweet, gentle wind amid the quiet. They recount what lovers immortalized by poets have done "on such a night." Troilus discovered that Cressida is faithless, out in the Greek camp. This first example sets the tone, calling our attention to the depreciation of both politics and devotional love entailed in this tale—the comic portrayal of ancient heroism. Pyramus was, on the other hand, deceived by the appearance of the lion, and in mistaken grief for Thisbe, killed himself. Aeneas, contrastingly, left Dido behind at Carthage to found Rome: here in the middle example we are reminded of a jilted lover, but one jilted for the political, away from the supremacy of the household. The fourth example recounts how Medea, having made Jason's father young again, was then betrayed by Jason, who married the queen of Corinth instead of Medea. His ingratitude and infidelity were motivated by desire for a politically useful union. Fifth and finally, Lorenzo speaks of Jessica's "crime" (in leaving her father), and she of Lorenzo's dubious vows of fidelity to her. Keeping up the playfulness, Lorenzo claims to be slandered, but forgives her. A messenger, Stephano, arrives before things turn mushy, but not before we have seen that the couple's pagan models—none are Christian—have all been either faithless or deceived, their love ending in pain. Under Portia, at Belmont, things will be different.

Stephano claims that Portia and Nerissa have been praying at various roadside crosses, and promises that they will be arriving presently. We are thus emphatically reminded of Portia's lip service to the Christianity that has made ascendant the private realm over which she so deftly rules. But

Bassanio will soon be arriving too. Lorenzo therefore asks for preparations, especially music, to be made. He comments on the stars in a manner that is helpful in understanding the charming nature of Belmont: there is harmonious music of the "immortal souls" of the stars, he tells Jessica, but while ensconced in our mortal bodies we cannot hear it (60–65). In a subsequent long ode to music, Lorenzo argues that one who is unmoved by music's harmony, the concord of its sweet sounds, is not to be trusted. Music, as "the poet" (Ovid) intimates, moves even the stones and trees, changing the "nature" of the hard and of those filled with rage; it makes us for a time placid, soft, temperate, turning us to the high pleasures of love and harmony. It presents a temporary solution to the problems of discord, the chief cause of which is our mortal bodies and hence, one can say, whatever silences our understanding of what is always, or holds us back from knowledge.

We have summarized Lorenzo's reflections because they form such a sharp contrast to those of Portia that follow. She will achieve harmony and concord at Belmont, but she does not attempt to bring it about everywhere, even in Venice, nor does she consider doing so to be working in accord with a natural if imperceptible cosmic harmony. On the contrary, her initial reflections on the light in the darkness ahead indicate that she sees instead a fundamental and insurmountable disharmony in human affairs: "That light we see is burning in my hall. / How far that little candle throws his beams! / So shines a good deed in a naughty world" (89–91). Even and precisely if a good deed shines in it, the world is naughty. Nerissa then observes that when the moon shone, the candle's light was hidden. "So doth the greater glory," observes Portia, "dim the less" (93). None see the lesser glory when the greater shines; the lesser becomes at most a party to the service of someone else's greater glory. This theme of a fundamental disharmony in human affairs is continued in Portia's reflections on the music she hears: "Nothing is good, I see, without respect" (99), that is, without respect to something else. As she explains, music sounds sweeter at night than by the day, by dint of its isolation from all other sounds; it is "unattended." Like the isolated, sweet song of the nightingale, it would be less glorious during the day, in competition with other sounds (104–106). Shakespeare thus makes clear Portia's full awareness of the problematic, nonharmonious nature of the human quest for glory and, more generally, of the absence of a genuinely common good. Unlike Lorenzo, her stand-in at Belmont, she grasps the contradictory character of individuals' quest for fulfillment through glorious, noble deeds, deeds whose glory precludes others from obtaining their share of the noble. But Portia quickly hides this reflection from Nerissa in a pleasant conclusion, which makes all things

seem potentially harmonious: "How many things by season season'd are /
To their right praise and true perfection!" (107–108).
Portia, who claims to have been praying with Nerissa for their husbands'
health, instructs all of them to remain quiet about her absence. The evening at
this point mirrors Portia's present position: not bright, but merely luminous,
like "the daylight sick," when the sun is hidden. The entering Bassanio picks up
on Portia's comment about the sun and claims that they'd walk in light if she
were present. But her playful, punning response begins their discomfiture:

> Let me give light, but let me not be light,
> For a light wife doth make a heavy husband,
> And never be Bassanio so for me—
> But God sort all! You are welcome home, my lord. (129–132)

She will not be light (wanton) because she does not want a heavy (sad) husband. A clear-sightedness, again, directs her, even in love. She does not seek
mere physical pleasure, but for that reason is fully aware that love, like glory,
cannot be shared. And so it is again when she is introduced to Antonio, as
a man to whom Bassanio is "infinitely bound": "You should in all sense be
much bound to him. / For, as I hear, he was much bound for you" (136–137).
Her correction—not "infinitely" but "much" bound—is explained by her
broader point that his binding is due to reciprocal justice. And the correction
carries an implicit warning: she will be bound to Bassanio if he has indeed
been faithful to her. But has he been?
    That question is now raised as Nerissa reproaches Gratiano for giving
away her ring and for ignoring the significance of the oath that went with it:
"not for me, but for your vehement oaths / you should have been respective
and kept it" (155–156). If Gratiano is not a man of his word, she declares,
then perhaps he gave the ring to a woman. While Nerissa plays here with
the truth (159), the business of oaths is a serious one, as Portia now affirms.
Her Bassanio, she declares, would never give away the ring she gave him.
She thus makes Bassanio squirm; he knows now that he is in deep trouble.
And as she expects, Gratiano, ever the cretan, tries to get out of his trouble
by snitching on Bassanio: he has given away his ring! (179ff.). Not *the* ring?
asks Portia, and on hearing the answer, declares that Bassanio's false heart
"is void of truth," and she swears an oath—playfully, never to bed him until
he has the ring (190–191). But her play has the serious intent of teaching
her husband and his friend something of vital importance: fidelity to her,
first and foremost. Bassanio, naturally, defends himself on the ground of the
worth of the person to whom he gave the ring (192–202), and so the issue
of respective worth comes front and center.

Bassanio argues that if Portia knew to whom, for whom, for what, and how unwillingly he gave the ring, her displeasure would abate. But now the great Portia uncovers her greatness of soul, her magnanimity:

> If you had known the virtue of the ring,
> Or half her worthiness that gave the ring,
> Or your own honor to contain the ring,
> You would not then have parted with the ring. (199–202)

Here is raised the private realm's equivalent of the political or public realm's assertion of worthiness to rule, an assertion of who is "the abler," as Cassius had put it to Brutus, "to make conditions."[21] Portia, Bassanio must learn, is far more deserving of his honor and pledge of fidelity than anyone; he knows not half her worthiness. A reasonable *man* would be modest in demands, she adds, were Bassanio openly zealous in his devotion to her, and so she must believe that some *woman* has the ring. The dramatic irony is deep, and promises a happy conclusion, but Bassanio's trustworthiness is seriously at stake, as is the question of who deserves fidelity. He protests that he did the honorable thing (209ff.), thereby causing the problem to deepen.

For what Bassanio says in his defense is incontestably true: the ring went to a doctor of law,

> Even he that did uphold the very life
> Of my dear friend. What should I say, sweet lady?
> I was enforc'd to send it after him,
> I was beset with shame and courtesy,
> My honor would not let ingratitude
> So much besmear it. (214–219)

Antonio had requested that "Balthazar" be given the ring as requested; what kind of a friend, what kind of a man, would Bassanio be to deny this request of the honorable friend who had been willing to die for him, and of the man who had saved this very friend's life? Yet had he not sworn to Portia that he would never remove the ring, the symbol of his fidelity, until his death? There is in truth no way out for Bassanio that is not unjust. Having from the start anticipated this situation and having now brought it to a head, Portia makes clear to Bassanio that when he is torn in this way, by justice, fidelity to her must rule his soul; she must rule. Portia has, with Antonio, not only the virtues of an ancient Roman, but a clear grasp of the problem of republican virtue as we have seen it explored in *Julius Caesar*; this indeed is, as we have been led to suspect, the basis of her clear-sighted pursuit of what is good for her.

The situation she has brought about is, to be sure, a beautiful or poeticized one: she herself deserves both gratitude for saving Antonio and the fidelity of Bassanio; the contradiction in justice will be resolved by the revelation that Balthazar and Portia are one and the same person. And so all can be made well. But this most certainly is not always the case. And so before she resolves the problem, Portia prudently uses the situation to correct the underlying difficulty for her, that is, to reorder the friendship of Antonio and Bassanio. She ensures that Antonio will henceforth support Bassanio's fidelity to Portia. She first pretends that, since she suspects Bassanio has been sexually unfaithful to her, she will be unfaithful to Bassanio in return, will become "as liberal as you" (226). (Her choice of words reminds us that the question of who is deserving of devotion has been exacerbated in her husband by Christian liberality with respect to love.) Antonio is therefore compelled to speak up and declare himself the cause of the quarrel, which Portia's gracious reply ("you are welcome notwithstanding") quietly confirms (238–239). Bassanio asks for forgiveness for what he again calls an "enforced wrong," but an apology is not what Portia is after. She cuts him off in mid-sentence with an accusation of selfishness. He then swears an oath never more to break an oath with her. This of course is the problem, known well to any seducer of a married person: how can one any longer trust an oath-breaker? How can such a one retrieve his good name? In one way: if another honorable man should speak up for him as his surety. And so Antonio does (249–254), thereby giving Portia precisely what she has been seeking.

Antonio's new office is to ensure that Bassanio is ever faithful to Portia, that he "nevermore break faith advisedly" (i.e., intentionally), as Antonio astutely puts it (253), contradicting Bassanio's claim that his breach of faith was "enforced." Antonio recognizes that Bassanio made a decision for him over and against Portia, and submits himself now to being a true friend by serving Bassanio's fidelity to Portia. He also states that he would be dead now but for "him that had your husband's ring" (250). Portia thus has verbal evidence of Antonio's deep gratitude, for his very life, to "Balthazar." And so she begins to disclose her identity as "Balthazar" by giving the ring to Bassanio. But her identity is not made altogether clear before Gratiano again reveals his baseness: "What? Are we cuckolds ere we deserved it?" (265). That is, he expects at some time to deserve it. Portia finally rebukes him directly: "Speak not so grossly" (266), and we see who is now firmly in charge. She gives a letter from Bellario disclosing her identity and, able now to tell Antonio without qualification, "you are welcome" (273; contrast 139–141 and 239), she gives him a letter concerning his three ships, becoming thereby the source of his "life and living" (286). Finally, Nerissa discloses the solution of Lorenzo and Jessica's difficulty: Shylock's bequest of all of which he will die possessed. All gratitude and friendship now flow in Portia's direction. She has become the sun, dimming altogether the sacrifice Antonio was prepared to make for Bassanio.

The play had opened with Antonio's sadness and speculations about his ships; it closes with good news about his ships, delivered in such a way as to hide the new source of sadness for him, that is, his realization of being now and for the rest of his life second fiddle, a friend to Bassanio only and insofar as he ensures his fidelity to Portia. To be sure, this in a manner solves Antonio's problem, since he too is now devoted to Portia as to a goddess— one to whom he owes everything. But such subordination of one in whom "the ancient Roman honor" appears, to one in whom it appears more fully, is not an unmitigated blessing. His misfortune has provided her opportunity for greatness.

CHAPTER 4

KING LEAR: THE QUESTION OF DIVINE JUSTICE

*K*ing *Lear* explores the relations between love—be it filial, paternal, or erotic—and justice: our sense of worthiness, not only to be loved but to rule and be ruled. The most celebrated of Shakespeare's tragedies, it is also among the most difficult to interpret. The private affections of the king are bound up with his public rule, as are the private affections of everyone else in the play. And those affections, when unrequited or thwarted, appear to drive Lear to madness. But as Edgar notes, Lear's madness is mixed with reason (4.6.174–175). His experiences move him, owing to his depth and toughness of soul, to question what he has always taken for granted. And one important thing he has taken for granted is the existence of justice, human and divine. Moreover, in no play is "nature" more often referred to as a standard of human conduct, over and against both law or convention and the divine. More than in any other play Shakespeare ties the question of justice, of "deserving," to the question of the existence of gods, and it is reflection on precisely this question that drives Lear to madness, and then to an abortive recovery from it. We see political men and women act following both superficial and deep reflection on that question, and the political consequences of their doing so.

Act I

Kent and Gloucester, English earls, in the presence of the latter's bastard son Edmund, express their puzzlement about their King Lear's plans for the apportioning of his kingdom. The Duke of Albany (husband of Goneril) had seemed to both higher in Lear's affection than Cornwall (husband of Regan), but now Cornwall is equal to Albany. That the apportioning of the kingdom will be determined by the king's "affection" is taken for granted. If that affection is indeed won by the manifestation of genuine virtues becoming of a ruler, this arrangement might be sensible (though by no means optimal). But are Lear's two sons-in-law, like their wives, not capable of dissembling? And is it at all likely that Lear's affections are simply and altogether the result of a careful assessment of the worth of his sons-in-law to rule?

Before these questions come to the fore, and as a preparation for them, Shakespeare has Kent and Gloucester turn their attention to Edmund, who stands silently for a while as they discuss him. Kent inquires as to whether Edmund is Gloucester's son; Edmund (who knows Kent no more than Kent knows him) has been away from Lear's court for nine years, his education paid for by Gloucester. Kent almost (though not quite) says that there is no fault in Gloucester's adulterous conception of so "proper" an issue as he sees in Edmund. Gloucester then presents the law as having no effect on his affections for Edmund over and against the elder and legitimate son (Edgar):

> But I have a son, sir, by order of law, some year elder than this, who yet is no dearer in my account. Though this knave came something saucily to the world before he was sent for, yet was his mother fair, there was good sport at his making, and the whoreson must be acknowledg'd. (1.1.19–24)

This—the only statement that Edmund hears in the play from his father regarding affection and legitimacy—deprecates the law in favor of the beauty of the mother and the pleasure of the sexual act that produced the child. Edmund, as we will see, is listening carefully, and will follow the principle stated here by his father to its logical conclusion. He says in response to his introduction to Kent as Gloucester's honorable friend, and Kent's response that he must love him and sue to know him better, "Sir, I shall study deserving" (1.1.31). This statement tells us not only the theme of Edmund's reflections in the play, but also the theme of the play as a whole. Edmund professes that he will "study" worth or desert, that is, endeavor to prove himself worthy of Kent's affections, and he (and we) will be led to reflect on the question of what constitutes true worth or desert, desert by nature as opposed to mere law or convention.

★   ★   ★

Lear enters with his daughters and their husbands, and we learn that there is a third, youngest daughter, Cordelia; Lear's first words direct Gloucester to go and attend to Cordelia's two suitors, France and Burgundy. He then announces his plan to divide his kingdom into three parts, and offers two reasons for doing so. The first is personal: "To shake all cares and business from our age / Conferring them on younger strengths, while we / Unburthen'd crawl toward death" (1.1.39–41). The second is public-spirited: to prevent "future strife" over the kingdom. If Lear, approaching death, has come to see rule as a burden, he has not forgotten its desirability to younger, ambitious men. He assumes, however, that the rest he will now enjoy, through his children's care of the kingdom and hence of him, will not unduly impair their ambitions. He assumes, that is, that his elderly wish for rest, in the form that he will dictate, is a wish for something he deserves and therefore for something that will be accommodated by his (presumably just) sons-in-law. His plan thus appears to be incoherent; if his sons-in-law are as just as he assumes them to be, why would they need to be prevented from "future strife"? Or does Lear consider himself so very deserving that only the most monstrously ambitious would fail to protect his rest?

The questions become more pointed as Lear begins to enact a scene that he has prepared as a public justification of his division of the kingdom. Rather than divide it on the ground that Kent's and Gloucester's opening discussion has led us to expect, that is, on the basis of his respective "affections" for his sons-in-law, Lear professes to divide it on the basis of his daughters' respective love for *him*. He thus publicly if implicitly professes himself deserving of their love, and determined to allocate their respective shares of the kingdom on the basis of their capacity to recognize that desert and to articulate their consequent devotion to him. On this basis they will show that, above and beyond the affection he himself has for each by "nature," that is, as a daughter and perhaps also by age, they each "merit" the share of the kingdom that he will apportion to them (1.1.53).

Yet as the scene unfolds and each daughter is given a portion of the kingdom pictured on a map, we realize that the publicly professed ground of the apportionment is a mere pretense. Were it true, Lear could not possibly assign each daughter a portion (as he does) without having first heard each of them make her profession. Lear has, we therefore see, fully planned his apportionment: Goneril is scheduled to receive the northern portion, Regan the southern, and Cordelia the middle, where Lear himself intends to reside with his favorite daughter and her future French husband (Burgandy or, if not, "great" France—1.1.188–206), thereby providing a buffer between the two potentially contending daughters and their husbands.[1] The publicly professed ground of the apportionment hides this political ground, while providing a publicly professed complicity or agreement of the daughters in the apportionment.

For this plan to work, the daughters must be prepared to profess publicly their love of the King. This proves to be an easy task for Goneril and Regan, with the former professing Lear as dearer to her than any other good, and the latter professing herself an enemy to all other joys but him.

Their professions would be apt if expressed to a god. As her asides indicate, Cordelia is distraught by them. She loves Lear, and precisely for this reason cannot speak, since—we gather—the professions of her sisters are so transparently mercenary and overdone. She can, she concludes, show her true worthiness only by silence, risking thereby the loss of her dowry.

Having allotted to Goneril and Regan their portions, Lear makes clear his own preference for Cordelia ("our joy"), and that the middle portion—hers—is "more opulent" than either of the other two. But as Cordelia's asides have prepared us to anticipate, she must ruin Lear's scheme with her brutally frank speech. All she can say to win "more than her sisters" is "[n]othing," and, when pressed, she states, "I love your Majesty / According to my bond, no more and no less." Finally, she declares:

> Good my lord,
> You have begot me, bred me, lov'd me: I
> Return those duties back as are right fit,
> Obey you, love you, and most honor you.
> Why have my sisters husbands, if they say
> They love you all? Happily, when I shall wed,
> That lord whose hand must take my plight shall carry
> Half my love with him, half my care and duty.
> Sure I shall never marry like my sisters,
> [To love my father all]. (1.1.95–104)

While the first part of this speech might sound warm under other circumstances, in the light of her sisters' professions it must appear frosty. Cordelia is thus compelled to confront her sisters on their flattery: do they not have husbands? Is it not clear therefore that they dissemble in their professions of complete love of Lear? But she must thereby implicitly accuse her father of giving away two-thirds of his kingdom to rank flatterers. Finally, in her frankness Cordelia speaks of duties and bonds, that is, of the sacrificial *devotions* that genuine love entails, where her sisters, in anticipation of a reward, had pretended that their love was all joy. Cordelia is, as she says, "true" in her speech, but with devastating consequences.

For the publicly expressed truth is in this case so hurtful to Lear that he explodes in fury: "Let it be so: thy truth then be thy dow'r!" He swears an oath by Sun and Hecate, day and night, to disown Cordelia, declaring the most repulsive of human beings, the barbaric Scythians—cannibals of their own offspring—as close to him as she. The daughter who appears not to love him sufficiently is to him worse than worthless. Her apparent ingratitude to him—her seeming injustice—has utterly alienated her from Lear, from whom—he significantly adds—he had expected to receive something in return for what he has given her. "I lov'd her most, and thought to set my rest / On her kind nursery" (1.1.123–124). But does this not indicate that his own devotion has been, to some extent at least, less than wholly disinterested? Does Cordelia's profession of a fair and honest reciprocity for her father's devotions not therefore appear a more sensible sentiment than the fury of Lear at his daughter's failure to love him above all things? But does not *much or most* genuine love—including Cordelia's, who after all distinguishes the purity of her intentions from those of her sisters—entail a confusion on this score, a wish to be devotionally sacrificial and at the same time the expectation of reward for the alleged sacrifice? And is love not akin and more than akin to justice in this regard? Lear's conflation of his familial and filial affections with his political responsibilities and merits may be unique to pagan monarchy, but given the sense of "deserving" that political life and family life share, owing to the devotional love that is the lifeblood of each, the conflation is a natural one.

★ ★ ★

Lear's divestment of Cordelia of the portion of the kingdom he had reserved for her, and his complete disowning of her, move Kent to plead against his decision as "rash." The grounds of his plea are precisely his faithful and devout service to Lear: He speaks "plainly," telling Lear to keep not the hundred knights he proposes to keep but his whole kingdom, and he advises Lear that Cordelia loves him not least but more than her hollow-speaking sisters; Lear's decision, he advises, is hideously rash, even mad. The threat of death that Lear answers with does not silence Kent, whose life, as he movingly states, has been a pawn for Lear's, "To wage against thine enemies, ne'er fear'd to lose it, / Thy safety being motive" (1.1.155–157). Kent's words—especially in light of his subsequent deeds—remind us that the kind of devotion to which Goneril and Regan pay lip service has true, manly exemplars.

But Lear remains unmoved; he swears now "by Apollo," the avenging god, the god who brought the plague upon the Greeks at Troy for their mistreatment of his pious priest, Chryses (*Iliad* 1.10ff.). When Kent proclaims himself physician to Lear's "foul disease," and pleads again for the revoking of his gift to Goneril and Regan, Lear upbraids him as one who would seek to have him break the solemn oath he has sworn, "Which we durst never yet." To the pious and angry Lear, the supplications of Kent are traitorous. He banishes Kent, with an oath to Jupiter—king of the gods— and Kent departs with a pious affirmation, to Cordelia, of the justice of her speech. Lear's anger, and the demand for what he takes to be justice, have led him to affirm his faith in gods who would sustain it. But are there such gods? In the sequel, we will see the centrality of this question for Lear and the members of his court.

★   ★   ★

All that remains to be determined is the fate of Cordelia and her suitors. From Lear's exchange with Burgundy we learn that a deal has already been struck for Burgundy's politically motivated marriage to Cordelia: she, and therefore he, was to receive the middle portion of the kingdom. (Again we see Lear's political foresight: Burgundy, not the powerful France, would be the mediating power between the two sisters.) Is Burgundy still game, in the absence of the promised dowry? He respectfully declines: "Election makes not upon such conditions" (1.1.206). France—clearly Lear's second choice—now has his opportunity, and he takes it. Against Lear's counsel to turn his love a worthier way, he says that he cannot conceive, "on reason alone," that Cordelia, hitherto Lear's favorite, has done anything so monstrous as now to warrant Lear's disownment of her. This rational assessment of events moves Cordelia finally to explain the grounds of her position. She is glad, she states, not to have a tongue like her sisters', though "not to have it hath lost me in your liking." Her virtue, her incapacity to flatter, has lost her her father's love. Virtue is, tragically, unrewarded by Lear.

France is astounded that all that informs Lear's disowning of Cordelia is her being tongue-tied in flattery. He graciously asks Burgundy if he wants her, "herself a dowry," and Burgundy repeats that he will take her only if the former deal holds (1.1.244). But Lear again affirms that his oath is binding: "Nothing. I am sworn" (1.1.245); his obstinacy, which now intrudes explicitly upon his political design, is firmly tied to his faith in just gods who witness and uphold sworn oaths. France then claims her firmly to himself, as one beloved for her virtue. He redeems Cordelia's tragic plight, taking her as property thrown away; "Fair Cordelia, thou art most rich being poor" (1.1.249), he states, in agreement with Cordelia's self-assessment (1.1.230–233). He finds her virtue rich and true, entailing an authentic self-sacrifice that makes her worthy, to his delighted surprise, of his love. Lear leaves her to France as to her banishment.

★   ★   ★

At France's instruction, Cordelia bids farewell to her sisters, and through a paralepsis, we learn how much she in fact despises her sisters, and then they, her. Their chief fault, she suggests, is hypocrisy ("to your professed bosoms..."); she bids them love their father, wishing he were in a better place. "Prescribe us not our duties," Regan sharply replies to this proud and moralistic advice. Goneril is equally sharp: you deserve nothing, having scanted obedience; study how to please the one who in charity has taken you in. Cordelia then makes a prediction that the rest of the play indeed fulfills: "Time shall unfold what plighted cunning hides / Who covers faults, at last with shame derides" (1.1.280–281). This prediction (or hope) concludes the speech of a transformed Cordelia. She who was at the opening "poor Cordelia," seeing no way both to preserve her virtue and to flourish, has with France's rescue of her become a proud moralist, as confident in the power of justice as is her father. Whether her own fortunate experience in having her virtue rewarded warrants the confidence she here shows concerning the fate of moral faults—whether, that is, the world is such that each gets what he deserves, the unspoken assumption of all who are virtuous—will be unfolded through the remainder of the play.

But whether or not Cordelia is right to scold or warn her sisters in this way, the faults she sees in them are real. In striking contrast to Kent, neither of them has spoken a word in support of her, a fact the more damning in that both stand to profit from her banishment. Their hypocrisy is confirmed in the immediate sequel. Goneril, who has just blamed Cordelia, now confers with Regan concerning Lear's poor judgment in casting Cordelia off, ascribing it now to his age. Regan concurs, but adds that Lear has always lacked self-knowledge, and Goneril concurs that Lear's rashness is long-standing. It is difficult to know at this point whether theirs is a fair judgment of Lear, or the result of disgruntlement. In any event, anticipating that choleric old age can but add to Lear's distemper, they agree to find a means to deprive Lear of all authority, precipitating thereby his own angry study of "deserving."

★ ★ ★

Edmund opens the second scene with a soliloquy that begins with a praise of Nature, as a goddess, over and against custom and law, and he claims to serve her. We see immediately that he no less than Lear seeks divine or cosmic support for what he believes himself to deserve. And in an effort to escape the name "base" that attends his bastardy, he claims not only to have bodily dimensions as fit as those of his older brother, but to be the product of nature's true longings—those of "lusty stealth"—over and against those of husband and wife, which are merely legitimate, "dull," and "stale." Edmund seems somehow aware, however, that nature is not a goddess or may even be indifferent to considerations of worth or desert: his speech ends with a prayer not to Nature but to "gods" that they may "stand up for bastards" (1.2.22), as he moves to deprive his brother of his title.

Edmund succeeds in tricking both his father Gloucester and his brother Edgar, with the pretense of "virtue" (1.2.45), that is, by appearing to desire his brother's good more than his own. As part of the deception of his father he puts into Edgar's mouth something that would seem to belong in his own:

> I have heard him oft
> maintain it to be fit that, sons at perfect age and fathers
> declin'd, the father should be as ward to the son, and
> the son manage his revenue. (1.2.71–74; cf. 2–6)

This statement of what we might call the naturally fitting over the conventionally fitting horrifies Gloucester, who hears in it an echo of the rebellious letter Edmund has penned and forged as Edgar's (1.2.46–54). Edgar's alleged plot to kill Gloucester may be "unnatural," as Gloucester first calls it (1.2.76), especially given that his father "so tenderly and entirely loves him" (1.2.96–97), but this reported opinion concerning the fitting relation of old fathers and sons in their prime surely conforms with nature—as even Gloucester himself implies. He is troubled, after all, by Lear's banishment of Kent (1.1.23 and 116–117), who had stood up for Cordelia, and troubled even by Lear's treatment of Cordelia, which he declares to be against nature or her "bias" (1.2.110–111). And if Lear is wrong and Cordelia right, then unthinking subjection to an aged father is wrong. Nature, at least, doesn't support such subjection.

In his confusion and his horror, Gloucester turns (as had Casca in *Julius Caesar*) to a direct criticism of philosophic wisdom, "wisdom of nature" (and its necessities), and now presents recent, unusual motions of heavenly bodies (eclipses) as linked to the unusual, disordered actions of human beings.

> These late eclipses in the sun and moon portend no good to us. Though the wisdom of nature can reason it thus and thus, yet nature finds itself scourg'd by the sequent effects. Love cools, friendship falls off, brothers divide: in cities, mutinies; in countries, discord; in palaces, treason; and the bond crack'd 'twixt son and father. This villain of mine comes under the prediction; there's son against father: the King falls from bias of nature; there's father against child. We have seen the best of our time. Machinations, hollowness, treachery, and all ruinous disorders follow us disquietly to our graves. (1.2.103–112)

To Gloucester's mind, the deeds of Edgar and Lear have been preceded by heavenly portents of them, indications that suggest a whole world out of order. The portents disclose themselves as such when seen in the light of the human events that follow them. In that light, the *natural* explanation of the eclipses, that is, as events that are rare but explicable as caused by necessities unrelated to and indifferent to human events, appears deficient. The natural explanation fails, according to Gloucester, to take into account the unusual, disordered human deeds as "sequent effects," that is, as evidence of a linked human decline. That decline therefore calls into question the wisdom of seeing a nature to things at all. The very concept "nature" is, Gloucester states, "scourged" by these effects—devastated, chastised, and perhaps even punished. What had seemed like nature, that is, reliable, predictable necessities in the heavens and predictable inclinations ("biases") in humans, now appears to be a merely temporary order and regularity, subordinate to some other, hidden powers. These are either by their "effects" seen to be bent on skewing the human world toward evil, or—more likely—they wish through eclipses to warn good men like Gloucester of an imminent moral decline in human affairs. He is led to proclaim the conservative's motto: "We have seen the best of our time." The moral decline has begun, portended by forces that exceed the wisdom of those who claim there is an indifferent nature manifested in astronomical bodies and their motions. Gloucester is thus moved to turn from nature to supernatural forces in an effort to explain the disappointment of his hopes in man. Not surprisingly, he will later appeal in his misery to "kind gods" and avenging gods (cf. 3.7.35, 70, 92).

When Gloucester departs, Edmund scoffs at his father's statement on eclipses and human disorders. But his rebuttal is very peculiar. It notably lacks any defense of "the wisdom of nature," that is, of science or philosophy, which Gloucester had attacked. It presents instead a remarkable defense of human moral responsibility. Edmund begins by taking Gloucester's speech as a perfect example of how men blame their bad fortune on heavenly bodies rather than on themselves and their own deficiencies: "This is the excellent foppery of the world, / that when we are sick in fortune—often the surfeits of our own behavior—we make guilty of our disasters the sun, the moon, and the stars" (1.2.118–121). But if our behavior is in truth the cause of our misfortunes, as he suggests, what is the cause of our behavior? With a subtle shift—from speaking of purported causes of bad fortune to speaking of purported causes of vice, defects, or evil-doing—Edmund insists that those behaviors are *free* of causes, of necessities:

> we make guilty of our disasters
> the sun, the moon, and the stars, as if we were
> villains on necessity, fools by heavenly compulsion,
> knaves, thieves, and treachers by spherical pre-
> dominance; drunkards, liars, and adulterers by an enforc'd
> obedience of planetary influence; and all that we
> are evil in, by a divine thrusting on. An admirable

evasion of whoremaster man, to lay his goatish disposition on the charge of a star! My father compounded
with my mother under the Dragon's tail, and my
nativity was under Ursa Major, so that it follows,
I am rough and lecherous. [Fut,] I should have been
That I am, had the maidenl'est star in the firmament
Twinkled on my bastardizing. (1.2.120–133)

Edmund's recapitulation of his father's argument states much more clearly than his father had that heavenly bodies or "divine thrusting on" are causes of human evils (which Gloucester had indeed suggested—but only suggested—by calling the disorders "sequent effects"). Against this recapitulation, Edmund would have us blame ourselves, that is, he emphatically claims that we are free to be both foolish and vicious; neither crimes nor foolish mistakes are necessitated. Strikingly, he here no longer praises his adulterous conception as superior to the "stale" mating of husband and wife, but treats adultery as "evil," one of those deeds from which men would exculpate themselves by reference to compulsion. He even suggests that Gloucester has merely been attempting to excuse his own adulterous actions, even though Gloucester has *not* been doing so, even implicitly; Gloucester has spoken of a general decline that has only recently begun, since the eclipses.

Edmund's denunciation of his father's speech is thus revealingly problematic. He offers a moral critique of astrology, by whose doctrines heavenly bodies are alleged to determine human inclinations and deeds, but he altogether misses the fact that his father had pitted the understanding of eclipses as "portents" against the alternative of seeing them as the work of nature, that is, necessitated regularities discernible by reason. Gloucester had implied against that philosophic alternative that there is a power behind the motions of bodies, evident in eclipses followed by disordered human acts, and he had suggested or at least left open the possibility that those powers were now punishing ("scourging") man. Edmund's neglect of this fact, and his fierce focus on the issue of freedom versus compulsion, shows him to be much closer to his father's understanding than he knows. That focus seems tied, moreover, to his preoccupation with his bastardy (see also his addition of "nuptial breaches" to his father's list of effects of eclipses at 2.2.148)—to a desire to escape from any necessary limits to worthiness that bastardy might impose upon him. Just as his rebellion has included an appeal to gods for help, and a claim to serve Nature as his "goddess," so it includes a dogged assertion of the fundamental tenet of the moral life: moral freedom. He sees "evil" no differently than do those around him, but he wishes to consider himself free to do it, or fully responsible for it, so that he may deserve whatever his actions bring him.

Just how Edmund can understand the doing of "evil" as somehow worthy of desert becomes clearer in the sequel, in which he succeeds in deceiving his brother and then blames Edgar's "foolish honesty." Edmund implies that those with wit or intelligence, especially in the capacity to deceive the honest, should rule:

> A credulous father and a brother noble,
> Whose nature is so far from doing harms
> That he suspects none; on whose foolish honesty
> My practices ride easy. I see the business.
> Let me, if not by birth, have lands by wit:
> All with me's meet that I can fashion fit. (1.2.179–184)

In rebellion against customary or lawful deserving, Edmund acts on the principle that honesty is foolish and wit is deserving; the law supports honesty, whereas whatever Edmund can make *appear* fit by his fashioning of it—as he has begun to do against the honest Edgar—is to him "meet."

★   ★   ★

Goneril's expectation of trouble from her father proves to be sound. But the source of that trouble is not, as she would have it, the flaws of a Lear entering into his dotage. Lear's attempt to retain his kingly prerogatives and trappings (including above all his hundred knights) while ceding his power and preeminence to his two daughters and their husbands (cf.1.1.130–139) results in the conflict of political authority that Goneril had anticipated. One of them must rule; who will it be? Lear has struck Oswald, Goneril's gentleman, for "the chiding of his Fool" (1.3.1). Perhaps Oswald deserved Lear's blows; the Fool after all offers Lear wise counsels that he may not otherwise receive, counsels that include a questioning of the wisdom of investing Goneril with political authority (cf. 1.4.95–188). This might have moved Oswald, in fidelity to his Goneril, to chide the Fool. Was it right or wrong of him, then, to do so? The determination of who rules must, Goneril sees, be settled if political order is to be maintained.

> By day and night he wrongs me, every hour
> He flashes into one gross crime or other
> That sets us all at odds. I'll not endure it.
> His knights grow riotous, and himself upbraids us
> On every trifle. (1.3.3–7)

Lear's attempt to retain his prerogatives threatens to result (and will, in fact, result) in civil war. Whatever he does contrary to Goneril's rule is a wrong to her, and hence a crime. The failure of Lear's planned apportionment of the kingdom and his treatment of Kent and Cordelia are doubtless weighing on him and perhaps setting him on edge. Or is it Goneril who is being thin-skinned? In any event, Goneril's solution to the difficulty is to bring the question of rule to a head by an entrapment, or passive provocation, that will drive Lear to Regan, with whom she has conspired:

> When he returns from hunting,
> I will not speak with him; say I am sick.
> If you come slack of former services,
> You shall do well; the fault of it I'll answer...
> Put on what weary negligence you please,
> You and your fellows; I'd have it come to question.
> If he distaste it, let him to my sister,
> Whose mind and mine I know in that are one,
> [Not to be overrul'd. Idle old man,
> That still would manage those authorities
> That he hath given away!] (1.3.7–18)

Lear and his men are to be moved, by this planned negligence and coldness, to his angry upbraiding of Goneril. It is clear, then, that the alleged crimes and wrongs have not yet risen to a level that would pose a threat to the order of Goneril's realm. Her excuse is that Lear's elderly decline will move them in that direction ("Old fools are babes again" [1.3.19]), and eschewing the flatteries that could have smoothed things over with Lear, she turns instead to provocation. Her impatience to rule her realm unimpeded—that is, without the requisite kindness and deference to her aging father—ignites the anger that will move Lear toward madness.

But Lear has his scheming defenders too. Kent, who like Cordelia had prided himself on a loving frankness—on seeming to be no other than he is—now borrows a page from the deceiving sisters; he is disguised, but "with good intent" (1.4.2).

> Now, banish'd Kent,
> If thou canst serve where thou dost stand condemn'd,
> So may it come, thy master, whom thou lov'st,
> Shall find thee full of labors. (1.4.4–7)

As much as any Christian would subsequently be, Kent remains a good and faithful servant to his lord even when banished for having dared to disobey by acting on his own understanding of good and evil. He recommends himself to Lear's service as one who professes "to serve him truly that will put me in trust, to love him that is honest, to converse with him that is wise and says little, to fear judgment, to fight when I cannot choose" (1.4.13–17; see also 31–35). He professes to have the virtues not of a ruler but of a servant, which he indeed proves in the course of the play: he will eventually follow Lear to the grave rather than accept rule when it is offered to him.

Kent's first deed in his new position is to trip up Oswald—which moves Lear to say "I'll love thee"—and then drive him away (1.4.86–94). Kent has just heard of the "abatement of kindness" toward Lear and his men on the part of Goneril (which had, perhaps necessarily, begun even before her explicit orders) and he has witnessed firsthand Oswald's failing respect for Lear; he proves his fidelity in this situation. But his siding with Lear over Goneril and her men is shown to have a reason that goes beyond blind fidelity: his master Lear is shown in this scene to be self-reflective and self-deprecating, and so worthy of Kent's allegiance. Lear states that he had blamed the "faint neglect" of him of late on his own "jealous curiosity" rather than on any deliberate intention to be unkind; he is quite aware that he can be misled in his perceptions of respect for himself and so had guarded himself against it. And he had on his own well noted his Fool's despondency at Cordelia's departure (1.4.67–71, 75). He is, finally, quite patient with his Fool, who calls the faithful Kent a fool for taking the side of one who is out of favor, and Lear a fool for having given away his lands and title and cleft his crown in two. It is Goneril, in fact, who proves unable to bear the Fool's barbs (1.4.95–201). Lear is manifestly different from the obstreperous and thin-skinned old man that Goneril paints him to be.

But Goneril now makes the concluding move in her scheme, driving Lear to become her image of him. His knights, of whose conduct she has told Lear, continue their carping and quarreling, she claims, and so she concludes that the conduct is sanctioned by Lear, especially in light of what he "too late have spoken and done." (Lear has, then, reproved his knights, but too slowly for Goneril.) Her care for the state makes it necessary, she declares, to censure and redress the fault. Lear can scarce believe his ears—that it is his daughter who speaks, or he who hears it. Calling this reaction similar to Lear's "other new pranks," Goneril now accuses his knights of debauchery, "Epicureanism and lust," and orders him to cut his retinue to a few old familiar men, or she will do it herself. "Degenerate bastard," declares Lear, as he orders his horses saddled so that he can set out for Regan, "I'll not trouble thee; / Yet have I left a daughter" (1.4.253–254). Goneril answers this response by accusing Lear himself of criminal insolence and negligence: "You strike my people, / And your disorder'd rabble make servants of their betters" (1.4.255–256). The question of who rules has, as she intended, now come to the surface.

Lear's pain at Goneril's words is exacerbated by the entrance of Albany, whose confused silence moves Lear to curse the monstrous ingratitude of his daughter. Albany can only counsel patience, prompting Lear to defend

his knights from Goneril's charge and to express, for the first time, regret
at his treatment of Cordelia. The knights are "men of choice," that is, his
choice, he asserts, and to question their worth is to question his. Cordelia
never went nearly so far.

> O most small fault,
> How ugly didst thou in Cordelia show!
> Which, like an engine, wrench'd my frame of nature
> From the fix'd place; drew from my heart all love,
> And added to the gall. O Lear, Lear, Lear!
> Beat at this gate, that let thy folly in
> And thy dear judgment out! (1.4.266–272)

But this self-blame and regret of the loss of his steady or hitherto fixed
"nature" is expressed together with an increasingly harsh blame of Goneril.
Albany's pathetic plea of guiltlessness and ignorance of the cause of Lear's
trouble merely prompts Lear to send up a hateful prayer, a plea for a curse
upon Goneril. He now prays to the same deity whom Edmund had claimed
to serve: "Nature…dear goddess" (1.4.275). His plea is for a divine punishment of her—barrenness, or sorrow-inducing children—for her ingratitude.
And his curses increase when he discovers that Goneril has already cut his
retinue in half (1.4.293). For the first time, he weeps, but then reflects that
his other daughter is sure to comfort him with vengeance upon Goneril:
"she'll flay thy wolvish visage," and he will be restored to kingship, regain
his dignity. The hope that Regan will do all this moves Lear to stop praying; he turns to the divine when human means to obtain what he thinks he
deserves appear to be unavailable.

Lear's final departure prompts Goneril, in conference with Albany, to lay
out her defense of cutting the force of knights in half. She had originally
counseled the pious, objecting Albany ("Now gods that we adore," Albany
had asked, "whereof comes this?") to remain ignorant of her business with
Lear, and to simply "let [Lear's] disposition have that scope / as dotage gives it"
(1.4.290–293). She claims now to have acted out of fear for her and Albany's
safety. But Albany's response—"you may fear too far"—moves her to disclose
what we have been led to suspect: little or no harm has yet come from Lear's
men: "Safer," she retorts, "than to trust too far. / Let me still take away the
harms I fear, / Not fear still to be taken. I know his heart" (1.4.328–330).
Her actions have, she here admits, been preemptive, and after sending off a
letter to Regan, she blames Albany for being womanly (of "milky gentleness") and unwise in the matter. Poor Albany, in his dutiful love of Goneril
(cf. 1.4.311–312) can at this point do no more than warn lamely and vaguely
of consequences.

The first act closes with Lear sending Kent with letters of his own to Gloucester's estate and setting out to meet Regan, remorsefully blaming himself, for a second time, for having wronged Cordelia. His Fool blames him, however, for failure to look out for his own interests, and warns that Regan will act as has Goneril. Lear, who does not want such a world as his Fool articulates—where self-interest should guide one—worries that he will "forget" his "nature," and says another prayer: "O, let me not be mad, not mad, sweet heaven! / Keep me in temper, I would not be mad" (1.5.46–47). His second reference to his nature as a thing fixed or true is thus followed by a prayer to "heaven" as a source of strength in maintaining it; "heaven," that is, the gods, not nature, are the source of his direction. His treatment at Goneril's hands threatens, he fears, to overturn his sanity, which has hitherto rested on the assumption—identical to that of Cordelia—that he would receive what he believes himself to deserve. Lear has never studied deserving, but is about to be compelled to do so.

Act II

Edgar falls victim to Edmund's scheme; to his ruin he trustingly follows Edmund's instructions to flee. Their father, too, is taken in by Edmund's pretense to have countered, in a sword fight, Edgar's alleged plan of patricide. Edmund claims to have proffered dire warnings about the gods' thunderous punishments and to have made other virtuous entreaties against the planned patricide. He is careful to include in his account the claim that Edgar boasted that his word would be above suspicion against the word of a bastard, so that Gloucester now promises to work the means to make this "loyal and natural boy" legally capable of inheriting his brother's place. With Gloucester thus taken in, the duping of Regan and Goneril, who arrive as guests, is an easy second step, as Edmund had foreseen; none could accuse Gloucester's report of being motivated by unjust or selfish designs. The gullible and hence heartbroken Gloucester need but tell what he has heard to the suspicious and vengeful Regan and Cornwall, and Edmund's way is won: Edmund has to Cornwall's mind, by his virtue and obedience, proven himself deserving of his and Regan's deepest trust (2.1.113–114). Regan and Cornwall are unsure of what to do with Lear, however; they have received letters from both Goneril and Lear, and seek Gloucester's advice. It is quite possible at this point, despite Goneril's confidence in her sister's agreement on what to do with Lear, that Cornwall and Regan will take up Lear's cause, that is, side with Albany and avert the civil war that is already being rumored (cf. 2.1.6–13).

In the light of those rumors, it is less puzzling than it would otherwise be that Kent, arrived at Gloucester's estate, picks a fight with Oswald, using the longest and most amusing list of scurrilous epitaphs in all the plays. Kent means to encourage a war between Cornwall and Albany. He opposes Oswald in the name of honesty, independence, courage, humility, depth of attachment, and loyalty to the royal Lear. And as had Edmund, so Kent here draws a distinction between nature and law or convention: "Nature disclaims in thee: a tailor made thee," he taunts Oswald (2.2.55). But to Kent, following nature means being brave, strong, honest, and true. Oswald certainly bears out Kent's accusations, not only screaming for help but telling the arriving Regan and Cornwall that he has spared Kent's life owing to his old age (2.2.62–63).Yet Kent is here indeed, as he is charged with being, a ruffian, and in his attempt to defend his angry treatment he cannot (or will not) provide Cornwall with a good reason for his antipathy to Oswald. He says that he simply dislikes Oswald's face, and accuses him of being a dog (i.e., unthinkingly and servilely loyal). Cornwall is therefore moved to suspect some design beneath Kent's apparent plainness, and so should we. He orders Kent thrown into the stocks, and Regan commands that he be kept there all night.The manifest political effect of Kent's action is to confirm the reports, brought by Oswald, of the riotous behavior of Lear's men. And this is precisely Kent's intent. It moves Cornwall to believe Goneril's rather than Lear's letters—to believe, that is, that there is good reason for Goneril's actions against Lear (2.2.139–140). It thereby prevents Cornwall from judging the situation as had Albany, and so sets up the occasion for Cordelia's return, with French troops, to effect the restoration of Lear. Kent has, in fact a letter from Cordelia (2.2.165–170), and even eschews the pitying Gloucester's offer to intercede on Kent's behalf. Kent's heart is, it seems, as much with Cordelia as with Lear, and would have Lear's redemption effected through her.

★   ★   ★

Edgar, hitherto so honest and guileless (though as contemptuous of astrology as Edmund—cf. 1.2.138–151), now shows resourcefulness in necessity. He takes on the appearance of a mad beggar from Bedlam. He knows that he has lost what was his by convention or law, and—seeing for the first time the fragile character of convention, its deceptive character—he now exploits conventional appearances, to save himself (2.3).

   Lear, meanwhile, has found the disguised Kent in the stocks, and immediately blames Cornwall and Regan: his outrage and his oath to avenge it set the scene. His Fool gives him more Machiavellian advice (2.4.46–55), but then, strikingly, the Fool changes his tune: he will not be "wise," he declares, but a fool, that is, loyal to Lear (2.4.82–84). Lear demands to speak with Cornwall, but when he fails to appear, Lear attempts to excuse him:

> may be he is not well:
> Infirmity doth still neglect all office
> Whereto our health is bound; we are not ourselves
> When nature, being oppress'd, commands the mind
> To suffer with the body. I'll forbear. (2.4.105–109)

Lear—again displaying an empathetic patience—equates Cornwall's "nature" with his body, and contrasts it with his "mind," which is weaker and hence, while ordinarily free to perform its duties, succumbs with the body to sickness. Lear's forgiving disposition is reversed, however, when he remembers Kent in the stocks (2.4.112):

> Death on my state! wherefore
> Should he sit here? This act persuades me
> That this remotion of the Duke and her
> Is practice only. (2.4.112–115)

Lear's reaction rests, however, on Kent's account of how he came into the stocks, which is far from complete and rather air-brushed (cf. 2.4.40–42). Lear's anger is rising in him, but—like Odysseus—he orders his rising heart down (2.4.121–122; cf. *Odyssey* 20.18). Hoping again for comfort from Regan, he forgets the injustice to Kent (2.4.132–133). But Regan accuses him of not valuing Goneril's worth, of not realizing that Goneril is a dutiful, obliging daughter who has cut off Lear's riotous followers for a "good end." She concludes (echoing Edmund's words) that Lear is old and should be ruled, and that he should ask Goneril's forgiveness for his injustice. Lear mocks this request, and again calls down divine vengeance on Goneril for her ingratitude (2.4.162–164), thereby confirming in Regan's mind what the two sisters had called Lear's rashness (2.4.169).

In his hope that Regan's "tender-hefted nature" (2.4.171) is different from Goneril's, Lear claims that he will never curse her, who is tender, knows the duties of nature, the bond of childhood, and gratitude. But she is unmoved. And so he again remembers Kent (2.4.182, 188–189). When his hope for comfort from Regan fails, that is, he attends to injustice and demands its rectification. Goneril's entry moves Lear to pray again to heaven; he vows that he would rather bear necessity than go back to Goneril. But this vow, and his apparent forgiveness of Goneril, is spoken only with the hope of staying, he and his hundred knights, with Regan (2.4.225–231). When Regan reduces them to twenty-five, on the same grounds that Goneril had halved them, Lear decides to return to Goneril, who had offered fifty (2.4.255); he will settle. But the two of them then question why Lear needs even a single one (2.4.263), and driven almost to despair, he explains, in his famous speech:

> O, reason not the need! our basest beggars
> Are in the poorest thing superfluous.
> Allow not nature more than nature needs,
> Man's life is cheap as beast's. Thou art a lady;
> If only to go warm were gorgeous,
> Why, nature needs not what thou gorgeous wear'st,
> Which scarcely keeps thee warm. But for true need—(2.4.264–270)

Our natural needs are small, and superfluities are a manifestation of worth, over and against mere natural needs, the restricted meeting of which would make man's life "cheap as beast's." The natural is in the first place the bodily; genuine human worth exceeds nature's cheap needs. Gorgeous clothing reflects rank even at the expense of or in defiance of natural needs like warmth.

But even in making this case Lear comes close to sounding like a beggar to his hard-hearted daughters, and so interrupts himself to address a prayer to the gods:

> You heavens, give me that patience, patience I need!
> You see me here, you gods, a poor old man,
> As full of grief as age, wretched in both.
> If it be you that stirs these daughters' hearts
> Against their father, fool me not so much
> To bear it tamely; touch me with noble anger,
> And let not women's weapons, water-drops,
> Stain my man's cheeks! No, you unnatural hags,
> I will have such revenges on you both
> That all the world shall—I will do such things—
> What they are yet I know not, but they shall be
> The terrors of the earth! You think I'll weep:
> No, I'll not weep.
> I have full cause of weeping, but this heart
> Shall break into a hundred thousand flaws
> Or ere I'll weep. O Fool, I shall go mad! (2.4.271–286)

Lear prays to the gods for a noble anger as a weapon against what has happened, a manly alternative to weeping. To weep would be to admit that man's life is indeed cheap as a beast's. To bear tamely what has happened would be to be fooled by the gods into thinking he has no dignity, or that we aren't really more than beasts. It would be permitting himself to be moved by the despairing thought that no gods can come to one's aid. Lear wishes to stand against that thought, in the name of human dignity, worth, rank-ordering. He would avenge himself on those who would reduce his dignity to the level of beast, but to be capable of exacting such vengeance, he in his present, frustrating powerlessness needs gods who control the "terrors of the earth."

Why, though, does Lear, who is on the verge of weeping and has full cause to weep, apostrophize the Fool, who has been telling him that he should not have given up his power? Something is now troubling Lear that extends beyond his angry desire for vengeance. The gods may, as he hopes, bring revenge—but why did they permit this to happen in the first place? Why would they delude him, or stir his daughters' hearts? Are they gods at all? Or is the Fool perhaps correct that one should be guided not by a sense of dignity or deserving, sanctioned by gods, but by interests, provident for oneself rather than assuming divine providence?

Regan, with the agreement of Goneril and Cornwall, orders that the doors be locked, in fear that Lear's retinue of knights might attack. Albany is absent.

Act III

One of Lear's gentlemen reports to Kent the whereabouts and state of Lear, who is not only exposed to the night's harsh elements but "contending" with them, and "strives in his little world of man to outscorn / The to-and-fro-conflicting wind and rain," alone but for the Fool's company (3.1.4–17). Kent, now thick in conspiracy with Cordelia and France, trusts the gentleman with intelligence gathered from servants concerning the abiding split between Albany and Cornwall, and sends the gentleman to the secret French forces—including Cordelia—at Dover, to carry news of "how unnatural and bemadding sorrow / The King hath cause to [com] plain" (3.1.38–39).

We then see and hear for ourselves what has been reported of Lear, as Shakespeare takes the daring step of presenting a raging king on a heath during a terrible storm. Lear implores the winds to blow, thunder and lightning to "crack Nature's molds," to destroy that which "makes ungrateful man" (3.2.1–8). His anger at the ingratitude of his daughters has now grown to anger at ungrateful man, and a call for the elements to be used for divine destruction. Yet seeing his enslavement to the elements of the storm, "A poor, infirm, weak, and despis'd old man," he calls them "servile ministers" of his "two pernicious daughters" (3.2.21–22), and then resolves to be patient and quiet.

Kent, finding Lear, declares this the worst night he has ever seen, one that man's nature cannot endure. His words spark Lear to speak again, now in reflection on the storm, with an explicit appeal to the gods:

> Let the great gods,
> That keep this dreadful pudder o'er our heads
> Find out their enemies now. Tremble, thou wretch
> That hast within thee undivulged crimes
> Unwhipt of justice! Hide thee, thou bloody hand;
> Thou perjur'd, and thou simular of virtue
> That art incestuous! Caitiff, to pieces shake,
> That under covert and convenient seeming
> Has practic'd on man's life! Close pent-up guilts,
> Rive your concealing continents, and cry
> These dreadful summoners grace. I am a man
> More sinn'd against than sinning. (3.2.49–60)

The storm is, Lear now holds, directed not only against ingratitude, and is not on the side of his daughters; it is directed against the simulators of virtue, the secretly guilty; safety resides in true virtue, which renders one worthy of the just gods' favor. And so Lear fears not the elements, since he is a man "more sinn'd against than sinning." Still, he accepts Kent's offer to go to a hovel, being cold. Hearing that Kent's entreaties at the house have been denied, he again expresses doubts about his sanity: "My wits begin to turn" (3.2.67).

Gloucester, meanwhile, seeks to help Lear with the assistance of Edmund, who pretends to agree with his father that the daughters' treatment of Lear is "unnatural" (3.3.1–2). He also discloses to Edmund the location of a letter he has received from the French forces come to avenge Lear. But to Edmund, his father's courtesy to Lear—forbidden by the daughters—and the hidden letter are "a fair deserving" (3.3.23), that is, a good means to gain a reward for himself. Edmund has been studying deserving, and having concluded that the justice that would hold him back is merely conventional, he simulates virtue once again and betrays his father, in order to take his place. That is, Edmund means to advance yet again by means of the very thing for which Lear has just called for divine punishment. Will the gods punish him?

Back on the heath, Kent tells Lear that the open night is a tyranny (i.e., not any instrument of divine justice), and "too rough / For nature to endure" (3.4.2–3). But Lear will not enter the hovel. He is still too troubled to feel, as Kent does, the storm's effect on his skin: "this tempest in my mind / Doth from my senses take all feeling else, / Save what beats there—filial ingratitude" (3.4.12–14). He is again torn between weeping at

the thought of having been shut out on such a night, and a determination
to endure, manfully eschewing self-pity and seeking instead his daughters'
punishment:

> Is it not as this mouth should tear this hand
> For lifting food to't? But I will punish home.
> No, I will weep no more. In such a night
> To shut me out? Pour on, I will endure.
> In such a night as this? O Regan, Goneril!
> Your old kind father, whose frank heart gave all—
> O, that way madness lies, let me shun that!
> No more of that. (3.4.15–22)

Lear would steer away from the grief-inducing and—as he for a second
time states—madness-inducing reflection on his heart's having "given all"
only to be rewarded with ingratitude. He is openly determined instead—
against this reflection—to pray and then sleep (3.4.27). Does he sense—and
recoil from—the contradiction between the claim to have "given all," that
is, sacrificed his good, and the expectation to have been rewarded for it—a
contradiction that could indeed point to the absence of just gods to whom
one could pray?

Before entering the hovel, Lear certainly takes a significant step away
from the angry demand for dignity that had characterized his "O, reason
not the need" speech. He insists that the Fool, "[y]ou houseless poverty,"
enter the hovel first, and then reflects on others in like condition:

> Poor naked wretches, wheresoe'er you are,
> That bide the pelting of this pitiless storm,
> How shall your houseless heads and unfed sides,
> Your [loop'd] and window'd raggedness, defend you
> From seasons such as these? O, I have ta'en
> Too little care of this! Take physic, pomp,
> Expose thyself to feel what wretches feel,
> That thou mayst shake the superflux to them,
> And show the heavens more just. (3.4.28–36)

This is the pivotal point, for Lear and for the play. Reflecting on the plight
of the poorest, Lear chastises himself for his negligence of them; his own
exposure to the experience of neediness now turns him away from the
sentiments of self-pity or anger that it had hitherto provoked, and toward a
desire to better manifest the heavens' justice. The outward trappings of his
dignity or rank appear no longer as a necessary confirmation of his worth
but as mere pomp, an impediment to justice, something to be shed for

justice's sake. Yet this new reflection entails of course a recognition that the heavens are in need of being shown "more just," that is, that as things stand, divine justice does not appear to be operative in the world. Those who would benefit from the shaking of the "superflux" are after all as likely as Lear to be "more sinn'd against than sinning." Why have their pathetic cries not been heard by the just gods upon whom Lear has called in his misery? Could just gods be absent from the world? From this point until Lear's attempt to cheer Cordelia as he and she are led off to prison, Lear says no more of divine justice, but turns in another direction: toward understanding natural necessities and "unaccomodated" man.

He is set firmly on that course by his encounter with Edgar, disguised as Poor Tom of Bedlam, who emerges from the hovel. Did he, Lear asks, come to be this way through giving all to his daughters? When Tom responds with complaints about the "foul fiend" leading him astray and vexing him, Lear repeats his question, and calls down a curse of plagues on Tom's daughters. Kent's statement that Tom has no daughters prompts harsh words from Lear: "Death, traitor! nothing could have subdu'd nature / To such a lowness but his unkind daughters" (3.4.70–71). Lear's empathy is quite absurdly complete; the self-same experience as his must have caused Tom's lowliness; Lear's isn't a unique case but an exemplary one. But Tom, after some brief nonsense, recites some (of the biblical) commandments: "Take heed o' th' foul fiend. Obey they parents, keep thy word's justice, swear not, commit not with man's sworn spouse, set not thy sweet heart on proud array. Tom's a-cold" (3.4.80–83). He claims, that is, to be suffering for his sins.

Lear's interest is now piqued; he asks Tom what he has been, and Tom responds with a litany of sins—of pride, lust, false oaths, lust again, wine, more lust, falsehood, bloodiness, sloth, greed, cruelty, preying. The deadly sins move in the direction of the bestial, and Tom advises all to steer clear of them, that is, he suggests that his present fate is a punishment for these sins. Now given what we have seen of Lear on the heath, we might have expected him to have remarked here that Tom has indeed been justly punished. But his response moves in the opposite direction: "Thou wert better in a grave than to answer with thy uncover'd body this extremity of the skies" (3.4.101–102). Where Lear had formerly presented his own virtue or innocence of sin as a protection against the storm, he here presents Tom's lack of physical protection as the only real concern. One could say of course that given Tom's professed litany of sins or vices, he has nothing else upon which to rely than the physical, but then with so many vices, how did he survive the divine vengeance of the heavens? Or is not the absence of the divine what Lear is pointing to by the nonpious or technical phrase "extremity of the skies"?

Lear now turns to a contemplation, followed by an imitation, of the naked Tom:

> Is man no more than this? Consider him well. Thou ow'st the worm no silk, the beast no hide, the sheep no wool, the cat no perfume. Ha? here's three on's are sophisticated. Thou art the thing itself: unaccommodated man is no more but such a poor, bare, fork'd animal as thou art. Off, off, you lendings! Come, unbutton here. (3.4.102–109)

Lear tears off his clothes, the very symbols of convention, to become like Tom "the thing itself: unaccommodated man." He has hitherto sought to obtain the conventions, procured by human arts, as symbols of his worth, at the same time that he has sought the gods' support for his dignity. He now seeks to be without them, and suggests that they belong to the beasts from whom man has artfully stolen them. Neither a beneficent Nature nor providential gods but *poverty*, lack of accommodation, is, he has now concluded, the true situation of man; that poverty is the very cause of arts and inventions through which man escapes his natural condition and adorns his life with the trappings of dignity. Man has been driven, spurred by harsh nature, to rescue himself from his naturally impoverished condition through labor and the arts.[2] His natural needs are not easily met, nor his life sustained by divine care. What had seemed repulsive to Lear in the light of his belief in providential gods appears now, with that belief slipping, as the reasonable truth. His faith in the gods had caused him to be dissatisfied with and to reject as absurd what reason now shows him to be true.

Gloucester's arrival, and his offer to bring Lear—in defiance of the sisters' orders—back to the house where a fire and food await, cannot move Lear from his single-minded pursuit of the consequences of his newly gained insight. "First let me talk with this philosopher. What," he asks this unaccommodated man, "is the cause of thunder?" (3.4.154–155) Lear's belief—that thunder is the work of "the great gods" (3.1.49–51)—is now replaced by an inquiry into a cause, a necessity. Kent pleads with Lear to go into the house with Gloucester, but Lear persists: "I'll talk a word with this same learned Theban." He asks Tom what his study is, and Tom replies "How to prevent the fiend, and to kill vermin" (3.4.157–159), that is, his study is justice, the means—as he has been suggesting—to avoid suffering a bad fate. Lear asks to have a word with him in private. Kent asks Gloucester to implore Lear again, since his "wits begin t'unsettle," and Gloucester empathizes: the grief Lear has suffered at the hands of his daughters is like his own grief at Edgar's betrayal of his love, which "hath craz'd my wits." Yet this gracious response actually brings out the differences rather than the similarities between Gloucester and Lear. Gloucester has a "natural" son (cf. 2.1.84) who has taken the conventional place of his beloved Edgar; Lear has himself banished his most beloved daughter, and been left to the elements by the other two. Gloucester considers Lear's present condition to represent a turning away from the grief-inducing truth about his daughters (cf. 4.6.279–283), but Lear's grief at their hands has in fact now deepened into a questioning of the gods and inquiry into nature, with the assistance of Gloucester's (disguised) legitimate son. No such questioning has yet begun for Gloucester; when it does, it will take the form of suicidal despair, and the disguised Edgar will then act to restore his father's faith in the gods. (The grounds for that despair are laid in the next scene, in which Edmund discloses Gloucester's treason and persuades Cornwall that he acts for the good of the realm despite his sense of filial obligation [3.5].) Lear's manic pursuit of answers to the questions in which he is engaged leads him to insist again on the company of Tom, the "noble philosopher," "my philosopher," "good Athenian" (3.4.172–180), and so all are compelled to enter the hovel with them, in which Lear will continue his philosophic inquiries with a "trial" of Regan and Goneril.

Lear "arraigns" his daughters, in absentia, with the help of the Fool, making Tom the "learned judge." Goneril is to be tried first, but she quickly escapes. What Lear says next indicates that both will in fact "escape" any guilt: "Then let them anatomize Regan; see what breeds about her heart. Is there any cause in nature that make these hard hearts?" (3.6.76–78). The discovery of any physical cause of Regan's hard-heartedness, the cause that Lear now seeks, would exculpate her; it would deprive justice of its ground, the moral freedom that it needs (and on which Edmund had been so insistent). The trial over, Lear falls asleep, and through Gloucester's intercession he is moved on a litter to Dover and the French troops. The next time we see him, in recovery from his ordeal—the tempest of his mind—he will still be contrasting nature with art, admitting that rain and thunder do not do his bidding (4.6.86–105), and have become a king who pardons all injustices, especially those of a sexual nature (4.6.108–131); he will go so far as to suggest that there is no justice: "None does offend, none, I say none" (4.6.149–172, esp. 168).

★   ★   ★

While Lear is moving away from an angry demand for vengeance and belief in the gods who would support it, Cornwall begins, in the name of vengeance, the most horrific deed in the play. He orders Gloucester arrested and tried for treason, for which Regan recommends hanging,

Goneril, blinding. Cornwall sends Goneril to Albany with a letter inform-
ing him of the French troops' landing. He also sends with her Edmund,
who is to advise Albany of the need for speedy preparations against the
French; he considers the vengeance to be taken upon Gloucester "not fit
for" Edmund's beholding. In light of what follows it is worth noting that
Cornwall is not insensitive to what (in his ignorance of Edmund) is fitting,
nor should we overlook the fact that Gloucester is indeed guilty of treason.
He was in fact captured on his way to Dover with some 35 knights, where
he was to meet up with the French forces. Gloucester's fidelity to Lear
against the extraordinarily harsh and devious treatment of him at the hands
of his daughters is surely meant to have our sympathy, and more of it is
won in this scene. But this should not blind us to the fact that he is, legally,
a traitor, nor to the importance of this fact for the course of Cornwall's
actions. Yet Cornwall discloses in a brief exchange with Regan a crucial,
tyrannical disposition:

> Though well we may not pass upon his life
> Without the form of justice, yet our power
> Shall do a court'sy to our wrath, which men
> May blame, but not control. (3.7.24–27)

Cornwall would have his desire for vengeance unchecked by the limits
imposed by law, which to him are mere forms; he will go through the
motions. He justifies his vengeance on the ground that it is compelled
and hence uncontrollable. But if human beings can be so compelled
against what is just, then his own wrath—which rests on the assumption
of Gloucester's moral freedom—has dubious grounds. So too does Regan's
charge of Gloucester with ingratitude (3.7.28) seem remarkably bereft of
self-knowledge. Lear's recent "madness" (especially his desire to find the
physical cause or necessity of his daughters' ingratitude) appears, in light of
this confusion or incoherence, to be remarkably sane.

Gloucester, who calls Cornwall and Regan his "friends," understand-
ably seeks to hide his activities from them. The servants are slack in the
sad task of binding old Gloucester's arms, prompting the ragingly angry
Regan, who has already called Gloucester an "ingrateful fox," to yell "Hard,
hard. O filthy traitor!" She insults his dignity by cruelly plucking his beard,
moving Gloucester to swear by the "kind gods" for her wickedness against
her host. But—thanks to Edmund—Regan and Cornwall have the damning evidence of the letter. Gloucester at first claims that the letter is from
a neutral, but this of course cannot be. Besides, Gloucester admits that he
has conveyed "the lunatic king," as Regan calls Lear, to Dover, and she asks

him why, but does not wait for an answer, bent as she is on excoriating his defiance of her authority: "Wherefore to Dover? Wast thou not charg'd at peril—" Cornwall must intervene in order to get Gloucester's answer to the first question.

That answer calls their rule into question as cruel and unjust: whatever Lear did, Gloucester argues, he did not deserve such treatment as they have accorded him in the storm. Against their cruelty, Gloucester vows to "see winged vengeance overtake such children" (3.7.66). But Cornwall homes in cruelly on the verb: "See't shalt thou never," and he stamps out one of Gloucester's eyes. Gloucester's piteous plea for help against this new cruelty includes a plea to the gods (3.7.69–70), which Regan answers with the demand that the other eye be put out. No gods arrive. But one of Cornwall's long-serving men is moved by the horrific spectacle to disobey him, calling on him to hold his hand. The servant claims to act (as had Kent to Lear) not in rebellion but in genuinely faithful service, that is, out of loyalty to his lord's true good, and that true good is justice. Regan answers the claim by calling the servant a "dog"—which the servant proudly rejects. Regan then slays the servant from behind, but not before the servant's fatal wounding of Cornwall, whose last act is to gouge out Gloucester's remaining eye.

As he does so, Gloucester cries out for Edmund's help ("Edmund, enkindle all the sparks of nature, / to quit this horrid act") prompting Regan to disclose that Edmund is the very source of their information: "Thou call'st on him that hates thee…Who is too good to pity thee." Regan is not amoral; to her, goodness consists of unflinching devotion to the realm she rules over, over and against "nature's" bond of kinship. If Lear confused justice and filial devotion, Regan moves in the opposite direction, severing them. Gloucester is thus made to see the truth about his sons just as he loses his eyesight, and asks the "kind gods" to forgive him for the abuse of Edgar. The remaining servants—who had lacked the bravery to defy their cruel lord—realize that at issue in these events is the status of justice human and divine: should monstrous wickedness like that of Cornwall and Regan go unpunished—should these rulers instead flourish—the just will turn wicked. They turn their attentions to caring for the blinded Gloucester, and decide to draft mad Tom of Bedlam to serve as Gloucester's eyes; by doing so, they would in their ignorance prepare the very restoration of just rulers that they seek (3.7.83–107).

Act IV

In his final words on the heath Edgar, as poor Tom, had, reflecting on the plight of the king, observed the salubrious effect of witnessing tragedy, that is, its lightening of humans' grief. His own grief lightened, he had resolved to disclose himself at the right time in order to prove his guiltlessness and be reconciled with his father (3.6.102–115). He continues that hopeful theme as we see him again: those of high station live ever flattered and in fear of being secretly despised, while for the lowliest like himself there is hope, since there is nowhere to go but up. But the sight of his blinded father, accompanied by a faithful old servant, compels him to revise this thought considerably:

> My father, parti-eye'd? World, world, O world!
> But that thy strange mutations make us hate thee,
> Life would not yield to age. (4.1.9–12)

This newest grief moves Edgar to declare that we learn to hate the world and wish it gone by the time we are old, otherwise life—a kind of force— would not yield to age; we would remain young. But he does not despair, and in a play in which there is endless seeming, Edgar will soon perform the most remarkable of deceits in order to rescue his despairing father.

Hearing Gloucester confess his own foolishness to the faithful old servant, and his request to touch Edgar before he dies, Edgar suffers yet deeper grief: "O gods! Who is't can say, 'I am at the worst?' / I am worse than e'er I was… And worse I may be yet: the worst is not / So long as we can say, 'This is the worst'" (4.1.24–27). Life promises endless grief. He cannot yet disclose who he is and thereby grant the one thing his father craves, the one thing that would grant him a last measure of joy. The pathos is deepened as we learn that Gloucester, while with mad poor Tom the night before, had thought of Edgar, but his then-ignorant mind was unfriendly to him. We are reminded that Gloucester was unable, seeing, to recognize the naked Tom as his son; Edgar was in his mind a clothed nobleman; seeing Tom had caused Gloucester, he now relates, to think man a worm. He was, moreover, as he has just told the old man, one who stumbled when he saw, unable to recognize the soul of Edgar for what it was, that is, taken in by Edmund's exploitation of appearances. Reminded now of his former memory of a mistakenly judged Edgar, Gloucester is driven to a dark thought: "As flies to wanton boys are we to th' gods, / They kill us for their sport" (4.1.36–37). We are, as Plato's Athenian Stranger puts it in the *Laws* (709a1–3; cf. 644d7–e4 and 803c4–5) the playthings of the gods, insignificant toys. Hearing this, Edgar regrets that he must remain poor Tom, compelled to "play fool to sorrow" and bring anger rather than comfort to himself and others.

At Gloucester's order his old servant leaves, but will "for ancient love," as Gloucester bids him, bring clothing for Tom on the way to Dover. Edgar has trouble maintaining his act any longer. "And yet I must" (4.1.54); and so he does. Gloucester offers Edgar his purse, and in his abiding ignorance proffers an explanation that is in all ways mistaken: "Here, take this purse, thou whom the heav'ns' plagues / Have humbled to all strokes. That I am wretched / Makes thee the happier" (4.1.64–66). Gloucester seems to mean that in his wretchedness, he has compassion for one similarly humbled by the heavens, and so Tom benefits, receiving his money. But his money would be Edgar's anyway. Another meaning, unintended by Gloucester, would be the thought that Edgar had expressed on the heath (3.6.102–115), that is, the beneficial witnessing of the tragic sufferings of the great. But Edgar, whose own plight was lightened by witnessing that of Lear, can gain no relief from witnessing his father's humiliation and suffering. He may nonetheless find in his father's words the beginning of a way to save him.

For Gloucester has now reinterpreted his suffering and the gods' role in it. The heavens do not use him as a plaything, but have humbled both Tom and him for the sake of justice:

> Heavens, deal so still!
> Let the superfluous and lust-dieted man,
> That slaves your ordinance, that will not see
> Because he does not feel, feel your pow'r quickly;
> So distribution should undo excess,
> And each man have enough. (4.1.66–71)

Gloucester now presents his own blinded plight as a manifestation of divine justice, which would have the surfeited, who eschew divine law in pursuit of their own pleasures, feel the power of the gods so that they might feel the sufferings of others, as he now does. As had Lear, Gloucester calls for the shaking off of superfluities and their distribution to those who do not have enough. But Lear had chided himself for scanting the needy and thereby failing to manifest the justice of the heavens; his thought had not shown the restoration of a faith in divine justice, but had been the beginning of his questioning of it, which he then pursued relentlessly, to the discovery and emulation of "unaccommodated man." Gloucester is, by contrast, moved to despair of his late-gotten wisdom: punished, he asks Tom to bring him to the brim of Dover's cliff, from which place "I shall no leading need" (4.1.78). Edgar, here listening carefully to his father's despairing piety, will there cure him.

★   ★   ★

The cause of the much rumored disagreement between Albany and Cornwall, as well as the disaffection of Goneril with her husband and

love of Edmund, now comes to sight. Albany had haltingly objected to
Goneril's initial treatment of Lear, or what he knew of it, out of a dutiful
love of her (cf. 1.4.311–312). But he is, as Oswald now reports to Goneril
and Edmund, a man "chang'd." Goneril's treatment of Lear, of which he
has intelligence (cf. 4.2.29–50), has disaffected him. "I told him," reports
Oswald,

> of the army that was landed;
> He smil'd at it. I told him you were coming;
> His answer was "The worse." Of Gloucester's treachery
> And of the loyal service of his son,
> When I inform'd him, then he call'd me sot,
> And told me I had turn'd the wrong side out. (4.2.4–9)

Goneril, mistakenly but honestly, explains this to Edmund (in Oswald's
presence) as "the cowish terror of his spirit / That dares not undertake;
he'll not feel wrongs / Which tie him to an answer" (4.2.12–15). She and
Edmund have already been conspiring to act without and against Albany,
and so she sends Edmund back to Cornwall rather than have him deliver
Cornwall's messages to Albany. She will herself, she suggests, take on the
man's part, and then, kissing Edmund and placing her necklace on him,
promises him the full conception of their plan, if he would dare on his own
behalf. "Yours," he replies, "in the ranks of death" (4.2.26). To such a man,
Goneril exclaims, are a woman's services due.

Albany enters and declares Goneril "not worth the dust which the
rude wind / Blows in your face" (4.2.30–31). She has, he explains, by her
behavior toward Lear shown herself of unbounded wickedness. Who so
condemns her origins must, like a branch broken from a tree, wither and
be burnt up. The truest and most vital affections of nature, he implies, are
likewise the most basic and fundamental: if she treats her own father so
poorly, her nature "cannot be bordered certain in itself." Goneril expresses
contempt for what she chides as sermonizing, which moves Albany to
declare her sense of wisdom and goodness that of the "wild," the degenerate, the barbarous. As had Gloucester, he declares her treatment of Lear,
"gracious old man," to be worse than what beasts would accord him. And
like Cornwall's servants, he fears the result of the delay of divine justice:

> If that heavens do not their visible spirits
> Send quickly down to tame these vild offenses,
> It will come,
> Humanity must perforce prey on itself,
> Like monsters of the deep. (4.2.46–50

Will Albany, then, take the side of Lear in the imminent battle?

Goneril declares him a "milk-liver'd man," lacking a sense of honor, unable to distinguish what should be borne and what opposed, and foolishly pitying those who are "punish'd / Ere they have done their mischief." For a second time she asserts the wisdom of a preemptive strike, a punishment before the crime, and calls Albany a "moral fool," one who is wondering why France threatens the state rather than taking up arms, as he should, against France. She implies that Albany thinks they should (like Gloucester, or Macduff) blame themselves—their treatment of Lear—for the sufferings that threaten, rather than manfully calling those that would inflict those sufferings "wrong." Manliness, to her as to Lady Macbeth, consists in a capacity to defend oneself against all insults and harms. And since it does, then preemptive action is altogether appropriate. Unlike Brutus, Goneril does not need to talk herself by any "fashioning" pretense into a preemptive strike. Moral limits are for fools. Albany is thus proven right: Goneril's actions know no bounds, and her thinking would indeed lead to a limitless war of all against all.

To Albany, loyalty, like charity, begins at home. If the natural subpolitical institution, the family, is not upheld, with reverence for age and ancestor as something natural—if loyalty to the state is divorced from natural filial affection, which both Lear and Gloucester have sought—and instead a fierce defense of an individual's own good takes precedence, the result will be action uncurbed by limits. And to Albany, those limits are what Gloucester had called "heavens' ordinance." His hope in the gods and their swift vengeance is confirmed with a messenger's report of Cornwall's death at the hands of the servant, in defense of Gloucester; "This shows you are above, / You justicers, that these our nether crimes / So speedily can venge!" (4.2.78–79)—a thought that requires that he overlook, in his regard for Gloucester, the death of the just servant.

Goneril is utterly unmoved by Albany's declared faith in divine justice. Her concerns remain ambitiously focused on securing Edmund. She remarks, in an aside on the news of Cornwall's death,

> One way I like this well.
> But being widow, and my Gloucester with her,
> May all the building in my fancy pluck
> Upon my hateful life. Another way,
> The news is not so tart. (4.2.82–87)

The other way entails, of course, the murdering of Regan and the assumption of the throne of England with Edmund. Albany again seems correct: The means to which Goneril will resort in service to her ambitions are limitless.

The scene concludes with Albany hearing from the messenger that Edmund knew of the wickedness that was to occur and left the house to permit it.

Albany vows to live to thank Gloucester for the love he has shown Lear, and to avenge his eyes. He is, contrary to Goneril's claim, clearly not milk-livered. He acts—as he believes the gods do—to avenge a wrong to another rather than slights against himself. But can he bring himself to join a rebellion?

★ ★ ★

The question of loyalty to the state versus loyalty to one's wife and her father persists in scene three: Kent learns from one of Lear's gentlemen that the King of France, constrained by a "fear and danger" to his state at home, has suddenly returned to France, leaving the Marshal of France in charge of his forces (4.3.1–8). The king had come in response to the imprecations of his wife Cordelia, who wished to rescue her father from his sufferings (cf. 4.4.25–29). His absence certainly cannot help the cause of his troops. Kent is not alarmed, however. He is for his part intent on learning in what way his own letter has moved Cordelia. Passion, the gentleman reports, seemed to be king, but Cordelia was queen over it (i.e., publicly controlled herself). The gentleman then offers a report, of irresistible beauty, of how Cordelia was moved by the letter:

> Not to a rage, patience and sorrow [strove]
> Who should express her goodliest. You have seen
> Sunshine and rain at once; her smiles and tears
> Were like a better way: those happy smilets
> That play'd on her ripe lip [seem'd] not to know
> What guests were in her eyes, which, parted thence,
> As pearls from diamonds dropp'd. In brief,
> Sorrow would be a rarity most beloved,
> If all could so become it. (4.3.16–24)

In Kent's response to this tearful reaction we witness his deep love of Cordelia. To the extent that his letter has provoked Cordelia's pity for Lear, Kent has simultaneously induced in her gratitude for himself as Lear's faithful, comforting servant in his hour of need. For this reason Kent wishes to know precisely why Cordelia was crying, and so we learn the contents of the letter:

> Faith, once or twice she heav'd the name of "father"
> Pantingly forth, as if it press'd her heart;
> Cried, "Sisters, sisters! Shame of ladies, sisters!
> Kent! Father! Sisters! What, i' th' storm? i' th' night?
> Let pity not be believ'd." There she shook
> The holy water from her heavenly eyes,
> And, clamor-moistened, then away she started
> To deal with grief alone. (4.3.25–32)

Kent—whose letter has told Cordelia of the storm, and his role in protecting Lear from the fate her sisters brought upon him—is as devoted to her as
any Christian saint will be to Mary. And Cordelia will indeed subsequently
utter words to Kent that she would not allow herself to speak to her father
(at least after her sisters' flattery of him): "O thou good Kent, how shall I live
and work / To match thy goodness? My life will be too short, / And every
measure fail me" (4.7.1–3). While this good and faithful servant—whose
deeds require that there be evils to be overcome—will respond that "[t]o be
acknowledg'd...is to be o'erpaid" (4.7.4), he clearly desires his deeds to be
acknowledged by his beloved mistress. He wishes to be thought deserving
of her love.

Lear is, Kent tells the gentleman, sometimes aware of what is afoot, but
is too "ashamed" of his unkindness to Cordelia to meet with her. Shame,
"burning shame"—not guilt before the gods—moves Lear. He will eventually ask forgiveness from Cordelia (4.7.83; 5.3.10–11) but unlike Gloucester,
he never once asks it of the gods. In the meantime, a tearful Cordelia seeks
him out; he has, she reports—and as befits his return to "unaccommodated
man"—bedecked himself in the flowers of weeds that grow amid "our sustaining corn" (4.4.6). She orders a hundred soldiers to seek him out, as a
doctor assures her that herbs will assist the repose that nature prescribes as a
nurse for his illness. After so great a tempest in his mind, Lear indeed needs
sleep. In her filial affection Cordelia permits herself here another exaggera-
tion that she had not at the play's opening: "He that helps him take all my
outward worth" (4.3.10).

★   ★   ★

Oswald has let Regan know that he has a letter from Goneril for Edmund,
and Regan seeks to counter what she knows is her sister's love-letter with
one of her own. Goneril's letter—which Oswald dutifully keeps from
Regan's hands—will prove to be crucial to the outcome of the play, as
the letters soon fall into Edgar's hands. That occurs when Oswald, following the order he here receives from Regan to kill Gloucester, makes an
attempt on Gloucester's life. Regan's reason for this order is that pity for
Gloucester moves "all hearts against us" (4.5.9–11). Were Gloucester dead,
his suffering would end, and hence there would be no pity for him. She is
also fearful that Edmund, in pity of his father's misery, might kill himself.
The man she believes Edmund to be, whom she loves, is by no means the
true Edmund.

Before Oswald can find Gloucester, however, Edgar performs on him his
great deceit, one that is in its intention the opposite of Edmund's deceits and
is much more like that of a Prospero—or a Shakespeare. He and Gloucester

are now arrived at Dover, and Edgar, by painting an imaginary scene of high cliffs for his blind father, convinces him that they are on the precipice. "Why I do trifle thus with his despair," he declares in an aside, "Is done to cure it" (4.6.32–33). Here, we may say, is the poet's justification for writing tragedy, filling our imaginations with things salutary but untrue. Gloucester kneels and prays to the "mighty gods," renouncing this world because in opposing the gods' wills further, his nature, hateful to them, would burn itself out. While he does not question their strict justice, he finds himself unable any longer to bear their justice. Only hope in just gods who remit sins and (piteously) offer redemption from them would make continuance of life bearable. After Gloucester "jumps," Edgar pretends to be below on the shore and to have watched Gloucester fall or rather fly like a bird from the top of the cliff. "Thy life's a miracle," he declares (4.6.55). Gloucester is disappointed; he had hoped (like Cassius) to find in death a means to "beguile the tyrant's rage, and frustrate his proud will" (4.6.63–64). Does he refer to god? Edgar educates him other-wise, moving him to see his salvation as a miraculous escape from demons. He does so much as Prospero will seek to educate those under his providence—not, however, through manifest enchantment but rather through exploitation of his father's blindness.

> Upon the crown o' th' cliff, what thing was that
> Which parted from you? ...
> As I stood here below, methought his eyes
> Were two full moons; he had a thousand noses,
> Horns welk'd and waved like the [enridged] sea.
> It was some fiend; therefore, thou happy father,
> Think that the clearest gods, who make them honors
> Of men's impossibilities, have preserved thee. (4.6.67–74)

These words work as a tonic on Gloucester:

> I do remember now. Henceforth I'll bear
> Affliction till it do cry out itself
> "Enough, enough," and die. That thing you speak of,
> I took it for a man; often 'twould say,
> "The fiend, the fiend!"—he led me to that place. (4.6.75–80)

Gloucester will now bear affliction until it kills him. And this has been Edgar's design—to give him hope in providential, redeeming, miracle-working gods. Through the yarn he spins, Edgar teaches his father a version, a pious version, of the virtue that he himself possesses in its solid, clear-sighted, wide-awake form: endurance of necessary sufferings, without the demands for a better world that lead either to anger or to despair. Seeing the great difficulty in the attainment of such virtue, Edgar is able to provide the means to a gentler, more hopeful version of it, through his great deceit.

Given the wisdom Edgar has displayed in saving his father, it is not surprising that he finds the flower-crowned Lear, who now enters, both mad and—in Lear's speech on justice from which we have previously quoted—full of "[r]eason in madness" (4.6.175). Lear rejects laws and justice as mere pretense, especially laws relating to sexuality; he rejects marriage, or the illegality of adultery, and is moved to reduce human sexuality to that of beasts; he denies that lust is shameful in fact, that shame or the demand for modesty and chastity is anything but a hiding of lusty desires. Still, this thought in the end repulses him. He resolves that he will not love, after recognizing his own mortality (4.6.133–139). He then instructs the blind Gloucester against any faith in justice. Knowing firsthand the immunity from scrutiny that "robes and furr'd gowns" bestow, or how gold plates sin so that against it "the strong arm of justice breaks," he declares that none offends (4.6.164–166). Who believes in justice "seems to see things thou dost not" (4.6.171–172). And like Edgar, Lear counsels Gloucester to be patient, calling the world "this great stage of fools" (4.6.183). Cordelia's men find Lear and he thinks himself a prisoner; he calls himself "the natural fool [i.e., plaything] of fortune," that is, *not* of the gods (4.6.191; contrast 4.1.36–37), and runs off. And in marked contrast to his pious father's prayer that the "ever-gentle gods" let him die only when they please, Edgar states that he himself is "a poor man, made tame to fortune's blows, / Who, by the art of known and feeling sorrows, / Am pregnant to good pity" (4.6.221–223). He and Lear are one in seeing fortune, not the gods, behind their fate and their pity.

But now Oswald happens upon them, intent to kill Gloucester and claim the prize that Regan has put on his traitorous head. Edgar is reluctantly compelled to take Oswald's life—he has contempt for Oswald's villainous fidelity to Goneril, but is altogether lacking in any desire to be his executioner. He then takes the letters that Oswald had with his dying words bid him deliver to "Edmund Earl of Gloucester." Just as Edmund had found Gloucester's letter from the French conspirators to be "a fair deserving," the means to make him deserving of reward (cf. 3.3.23), Edgar expects that the letters to Edmund "[m]ay be my friends." He fights the scruple that would stop him from opening them with the argument that Edmund and Oswald are after all his mortal enemies. He is disturbed to learn of Goneril's desire to have Edmund murder Albany and take his warm place in bed with her, as her new husband, but this news does, of course, make the letter his friend. He takes the time to bury Oswald, despite his being no more than "the post[man] unsanctified of murtherous lechers," and resolves to disclose Goneril's letter to Albany when the time is right. But when is that time?

The act closes with Cordelia, as we have seen, thanking Kent profusely for his service (4.7.1–3). She trusts that "kind gods" will cure "this great breach in his abused nature" (4.7.13–16); Cordelia is as pious as Gloucester and Albany. In Lear's presence she upbraids her sisters for their lack of pity of him, and he agrees. He is recovering; as the doctor says, "The great rage, / ...is killed in him," and he asks her to forgive him (4.7.77–84). He is fully aware, that is, of the foolishness of his actions toward Cordelia, and regrets the harm they have done her.

Act V

As the battle between the French and English forces is about to commence, Edmund, serving in Cornwall's stead, expresses doubts about Albany's reliability; he fears Albany's "self-reproving." Regan takes this as an opening to speak of Albany's wife Goneril. "But have you," she asks Edmund directly, "never found my brother's way / To the forfended place?" He denies it on his honor, and she pleads that he not be familiar with Goneril, whom she "never shall endure." Both of the sisters want Edmund, and we could almost say that both deserve him. Goneril, arriving with Albany, declares in an aside that she would prefer to lose the battle than to have Regan "loosen him and me." This amazing sentiment—the loss of the battle means, after all, French rule over Goneril and over all of England—does not so much confirm Albany's thesis that loyalty must begin at home as it bespeaks Goneril's deep affection for Edmund and jealous hatred of Regan (5.1.1–19).

Albany declares to Edmund that the reported reason for the war is "the rigors of our state," which have "forced" those who come with the King and his daughter "to cry out." And he makes it clear that he agrees with this report. In a perfect summary of his position he states that "where I could not be honest, / I never yet was valiant." Unlike Edmund, whose valor is in his own behalf, Albany can be brave only when the cause is just. But Albany now faces in his justice a serious conundrum. If, as he has claimed, loyalty begins at home, with filial devotions, and other devotions follow from that, what does one do when the security of the state ceases to be consistent with filial devotion? The question of whether he can join the forces of the rebellion must now be answered. He attempts to resolve it in this way:

> For this business,
> It touches us as France invades our land,
> Not bolds the King, with others whom, I fear,
> Most just and heavy causes make oppose. (5.1.24–27)

He will fight France as France who "invades our land"; he will not fight France who comes to support King Lear along with others who join with France owing to the "just and heavy causes" they have against the present rulers. But this is one and the same France (as the beloved and ambitious Caesar whom Brutus slew was one and the same man). France invades the land of England on behalf of the just; Albany would fight him in self-defense, or to keep the land of England free of foreign domination, but recognizes that the invader comes not to enslave but to liberate. Albany cannot be faithful, and hence just, to his wife and sister-in-law and their state and at the same time faithful to the justice that he recognizes and in whose name France has come (5.1.20–27). He here sidesteps rather than confront that contradiction.

Edmund declares that Albany "speaks nobly," but we know from Edmund's soliloquy at the end of this scene ("my state / Stands on me to defend, not to debate") that this is a pretense. His courage remains of the self-defending sort that causes Regan and Goneril to swoon over him. His single-mindedness in pursuit of his own good is indeed a solution of sorts to the problem that Albany resolves only through a false distinction between two kings of France. Yet it suffers from the divisive barbarism that, as Albany had noted, follows in its train. Even here, while Regan and Goneril put an end to Albany's questioning of the justice of their deeds, they are in secret division over Edmund. "Combine together 'gainst the enemy," Goneril states, dismissing the matter of their injustice against Lear as an internal one—she who has just told herself that the internal matter of not losing Edmund matters more to her than losing the battle. She wishes to stay with Edmund rather than depart with Regan, and notices Regan's effort to keep her from him (5.1.28–37).

Edgar, still disguised as a peasant, delivers to Albany Goneril's letter (5.1.40–50; cf. 155–161), and requests, if victory is Albany's, to have a trumpet call a champion who will (in battle) prove its contents true. But Edmund's machinations go beyond even what this letter confirms; his agenda is full of murders. He now discloses, in soliloquy, that he has indeed sworn his love to both jealous sisters and therefore has a need to have one of them murdered. He will make use of Albany in the battle, before murdering him in the way Goneril devises (though he will not necessarily then chose Goneril over Regan). And he will thwart Albany's intention to show mercy to Lear and Cordelia after the battle by murdering them as well. All this to defend his state.

★   ★   ★

Edgar, back with his father but still disguised, must leave him for the battle, but promises to return (5.2). He tells Gloucester to "pray that the right may thrive," that is, he continues his encouragement of piety in his father. But if Gloucester prays, the prayers go unanswered: the battle is lost, Lear and Cordelia taken prisoner, and Edgar commands that they must leave. But the bad news has returned Gloucester to his funk: "A man may rot even here." Edgar will have none of this. Compelled by the urgency of a retreat, he rebukes Gloucester: "What, in ill thoughts again? Men must endure / Their going hence even as their coming hither, / Ripeness is all. Come on." We thus receive a clear statement of the resignation that informs Edgar's actions, a pious version of which he has been imparting to his father. "Ripeness is all": being ready to die when the time comes, but not giving up before then. Gloucester, interestingly, concurs with it, but in a manner that indicates that he is prepared to rot right there: "And that's true too." That is, what he and Edgar have said are both true; he now considers himself ripe for death. The difference between the two is that Edgar's resignation entails no despair. Death he will accept only when the time comes; he will not jump into the grave.

In the victorious English camp (5.3) Edmund orders the captured Lear and Cordelia under guard until the others can sentence them. Cordelia expresses her sorrow for the "oppressed king." But Lear, content to be with Cordelia, offers a hearty reply:

> Come let's away to prison:
> We two alone will sing like birds i' th' cage;
> When thou dost ask me blessing, I'll kneel down
> And ask of thee forgiveness. So we'll live
> And pray, and sing, and tell old tales, and laugh
> At gilded butterflies, and hear poor rogues
> Talk of court news; and we'll talk with them too—
> Who loses and who wins; who's in, who's out—
> And take upon 's the mystery of things
> As if we were God's spies; and we'll wear out,
> In a wall'd prison, packs and sects of great ones,
> That ebb and flow by th' moon...
> Upon such sacrifices, my Cordelia,
> The gods themselves throw incense. Have I caught thee?
> He that parts us shall bring a brand from heaven,
> And fire us hence like foxes. Wipe thine eyes;
> The good-years shall devour them, flesh and fell,
> Ere they shall make us weep! We'll see 'em starv'd first. (5.3.8–25)

Lear is content to pray and sing and tell old tales with Cordelia; political life is reduced now in his eyes to that of "gilded butterflies," the cynical business of "who's in, who's out," to be observed like a sport. Lear has a great distance from it as he contemplates or imagines life in prison with Cordelia. Prison is no prison at all but a relief from empty political life, an opportunity to take up "the mystery of things / As if we were God's spies." The "as if" is crucial: the monotheism that Lear expresses here is accompanied by a disposition to human affairs that is usually associated most closely with Epicureanism, watching them all from a distance, and the reference is quickly replaced by a reference to "gods." And Lear is offering all of this, of course, in part as a consolation to Cordelia, who is weeping over his fall and their joint plight. "Wipe thine eyes," he tells her, and presents their plight as a "sacred sacrifice," something upon which the gods themselves throw incense. He offers the hope that only a "brand from heaven" could part them, smoking them out like foxes. They will outlast all their enemies, who shall never make them weep. He expects, and leads Cordelia to expect, that they will be exempt from all political sufferings.

But it is not to be so; withdrawal to prison cannot save them. Edmund immediately plans, with an ambitious captain, to carry out their murder, winning him over with Machiavellian advice concerning the need for adaptability, or the changeability of justice (5.3.26–34; cf. *Prince* 25). The captain justifies his murderous obedience by claiming that he is no mere horse or mule but will do "man's work" and be rewarded (5.3.38–40). Edmund's rule, we see, would be such as to make dutiful adherence to justice appear altogether burdensome in the light of prospective advancement.

Edmund is not to rule, however. Albany arrives with Regan and Goneril, and his greeting of Edmund is carefully measured: "Sir, you have show'd to-day your valiant strain, / And fortune led you well" (5.3.39–40; cf. 103). He implies that Edmund has but one virtue, valor, and even this he retracts by claiming that mere chance led him to victory. The reason for his coolness begins to be apparent when he requests the captives of Edmund "to use them / As we shall find their merits and our safety / May equally determine." The old issue of who is to rule returns; Albany will not have Edmund making the determination of what is to be done, but will make it himself, on the grounds of the prisoners' merits and "our safety." Continuing to negotiate the conundrum of having opposed the just cause of Lear, he here divorces the king's and Cordelia's merits from the rebellion.

But Edmund now attempts to take charge, stating his own judgment of what was fit to do with Lear and Cordelia: imprisonment under guard. He offers two reasons. The first is to protect against the possibility that Lear's age and title will turn the soldiers against them. He does not suggest that Lear himself has sought to bring this about, but that conventions—Lear's age and title—will charm the "common bosom" and could turn them against them, which "do command them." Edmund thereby begins his coming out. With—as he thinks—Cordelia's and Lear's death sealed, the two sisters on his side, and he the victor in the battle, he believes he holds all the cards, and so he does not hesitate to draw a distinction between his commanding sentiments and those that would move the common people. The second reason he offers for keeping Lear and Cordelia imprisoned and under guard is that they will appear tomorrow or later, "when you shall hold your session." The public explanation he gives for the delay is of course fully honorable: post battle is no time to decide on their fate. We sweat and we bleed, are in sorrow, and the quarrel needs to cool off. He defies Albany's stated desire to have Lear and Cordelia handed over with an appeal for propriety and moderation.

Albany, equipped with Goneril's letter, firmly if politely rejects this defiance. "Sir, by your patience, / I hold you but a subject of this war, / not as a brother," that is, as neither equal nor kin (5.3.59–61). If as seems likely his intention here is to provoke not only Edmund but the sisters, he succeeds. Regan now enters the lists in Edmund's behalf, to be crossed by Goneril, not against Edmund but against Regan speaking so hotly for Edmund. Regan claims that Edmund acted on her behalf, leading her troops, her powers, and hence is indeed "brother" to Albany. Goneril wishes Edmund's accomplishments to stand alone rather than to stand for Regan's. ("Yours," we recall Edmund telling Goneril, "in the ranks of death.") Goneril, who has already poisoned Regan (cf. 5.3.96), now taunts her: "if he should marry you," she exclaims, Edmund would be fully invested with Regan's privileges. "Jesters," Regan retorts, "often prove prophets." The vicious cat fight would continue but for the fact that the poison now begins to affect Regan, who turns from answering Goneril to proclaiming Edmund to all the world her lord and master, to dispose of her and her rule as he wishes. Goneril, taken aback, asks Regan "Mean you to enjoy him?," and her reaction gives Albany the confirmation he wishes of Goneril's affection for Edmund.

Albany brings the matter now to a head: "The let-alone lies not in your good will." Edmund reprimands him: "Nor in thine, lord." But this final, direct defiance of Albany's authority moves him to a harsh reply: "Half-blooded fellow, yes." With the poison further weakening Regan, she would have an official proclamation of Edmund's title, but Albany now gracefully but firmly discloses his information:

> Edmund, I arrest thee
> On capital treason, and in thy [attaint],
> This gilded serpent [Goneril]. For your claim, fair [sister],
> I bar it in the interest of my wife;
> 'Tis she is sub-contracted to this lord,
> And I, her husband, contradict your banes.
> If you will marry, make your loves to me,
> My lady is bespoke. (5.3.82–89)

Goneril keeps up her well-bred contempt, taunting Albany's statement as "[a]n enterlude!" But all is deadly serious from here out; Albany calls for the trumpet to summon the prover of treason, as Regan is dying of the poison. If the prover does not come forth, Albany declares, throwing down his glove, he himself will fight. Edmund accepts the challenge, still firmly denying that he is a traitor.

★ ★ ★

Edgar appears in response to the trumpet's call. And in response to the Herald's request for his name, his quality, and why he has answered the summons, he declares his name lost by treason, his quality "noble," and his reason for coming to encounter Edmund with his sword. As had Albany, Edgar declares Edmund's single virtue to be valor, despite which and despite his recent victory by fortune, he is a traitor,

> False to thy gods, thy brother, and thy father,
> Conspirant 'gainst this high illustrious prince,
> And from th' extremest upward of thy head
> To the descent and dust below thy foot,
> A most toad-spotted traitor. (5.3.135–139)

Edgar presents himself as proving the gods' justice. In his reply, Edmund does something very foolish:

> In wisdom I should ask thy name,
> But since thy outside looks so fair and warlike,
> And that thy tongue some say of breeding breathes;
> What safe and nicely I might well delay
> By rule of knighthood, I disdain and spurn.
> Back do I toss these treasons to thy head,
> With the hell-hated lie o'erwhelm thy heart,
> Which for they yet glance by, and scarcely bruise,
> This sword of mine shall give them instant way
> Where they shall rest for ever. Trumpets, Speak! (5.3.142–151)

Edmund was not bound to fight, Edgar having failed to disclose his name. Shakespeare drives the point home by having Goneril repeat it, after Edmund has fallen:

> This is practice [trickery], Gloucester [i.e., Edmund].
> By th' law of war thou wast not bound to answer
> An unknown opposite. Thou art not vanquished,
> But cozen'd and beguil'd. (5.3.152–154)

The naming of Edgar would, moreover, have resulted in his immediate arrest. The question then is: why did Edmund not demand it?

The answer appears, it seems, in Edgar's charge that Edmund is false to his gods. Edmund, we recall, serves the goddess "Nature," and in her service is not bounded by law or convention, which he merely exploits to fashion things "fit." By law, by the conventions of knighthood, he could ask the name of the challenger, but he eschews it, relying instead on what he himself can perceive and judge: by his looks and speech, the challenger is noble, and that is sufficient for him. Edmund is as it were proving—certainly to himself—that he is not simply false, but consistently directed by, and true to, his goddess, Nature. She, not the laws of men, binds him. Edgar took a risk in coming as he did, but he has guessed rightly that Edmund would act as he did. For Edgar too, as we have seen and will soon see again, grasps as well as Edmund the great gulf between what is by nature and by convention.

Albany now reproaches Goneril, who is swooning over the wounded Edmund, very harshly: "Shut your mouth, dame, / Or with this paper shall I stopple it. Hold, sir.— / Thou worse than any name, read thine own evil" (3.5.155–157). The letter, she knows, discloses her treachery, but when asked if she knows the letter, she replies with brazen defiance: "Say if I do, the laws are mine, not thine; / Who can arraign me for't?" (5.3.159–160). She is indeed a perfect match for Edmund; she implies her freedom from laws, which are there to serve her interest, not bind her. Albany judges her response "most monstrous," and it does seem sufficiently tyrannical to have settled her guilt. Yet Albany asks again if she knows the letter. She replies, with her final, defiant words on stage, "Ask me not what I know." Fearing her suicide, Albany commands someone to go after her and "govern" her. Intriguingly, no one exits.

Edmund, dying, confesses now to all that he has been charged with and "much more," as "the time will bring out." But far from showing remorse for any of it, he remains to this point still intent that his plans against Lear and Cordelia succeed, as his reference to "time" especially indicates (contrast 245–248). He does *not* seek forgiveness but offers instead to forgive his successful opponent, "if thou'rt noble." Edgar thereupon proclaims both his identity and that the gods are just:

Let's exchange charity.
I am no less in blood than thou art, Edmund;
If more, the more th' hast wrong'd me.
My name is Edgar, and thy father's son.
The gods are just, and of our pleasant vices
Make instruments to plague us:
The dark and vicious place where thee he got
Cost him his eyes. (5.3.167–174)

Edmund professes his agreement with this profession of divine justice: "Th' hast spoken right, 'tis true. / The wheel is come full circle, I am here." But the evidence that each presents for divine justice is remarkably thin. We are supposed to believe that Gloucester's blinding by Cornwall in the last year of his life is explained by the fact that he conceived Edmund in the dark! Nor is Edmund's claim concerning "the wheel" (of fortune) particularly pious.

Our doubts on this score are deepened when, after Albany has exchanged friendly words with Edgar, the latter explains where he hid himself and how he knew the miseries of his father.

> By nursing them, my lord. List a brief tale
> And when 'tis told, O that my heart would burst!
> The bloody proclamation to escape,
> That follow'd me so near (O, our lives' sweetness!
> That we the pain of death would hourly die
> Rather than die at once!), taught me to shift
> Into a madman's rags, t'assume a semblance
> That very dogs disdain'd; and in this habit
> Met I my father with his bleeding rings,
> Their precious stones new lost; became his guide,
> Led him, begg'd for him, sav'd him from despair;
> Never (O fault!) reveal'd myself unto him,
> Until some half hour past, when I was arm'd.
> Not sure, though hoping, of this good success,
> I ask'd his blessing, and from first to last
> Told him our pilgrimage. But his flaw'd heart
> (Alack, too weak the conflict to support!)
> 'Twixt two extremes of passion, joy and grief,
> Burst smilingly. (5.3.182–200)

This "tale" is such as to disclose to the reader, who knows the longer version, that the profession of faith in divine justice that Edgar has just made is a pretense. Edgar could not be moved to pity his father's blindness—as he makes clear he did—if he thought that blindness was a condign punishment for his adulterous conception of Edmund "in the dark." Moreover, Edgar says nothing here about how he met and slew Oswald and came thereby upon the letters, by pure chance; without those letters, Edmund, not Edgar, would have succeeded, "the wheel" not have turned. Edgar does state that he saved his father from despair, but he does not say how; we recall that the means was the invention for his father of the miracle at Dover, that is, by deceiving him into thinking that he was in the hands of providential gods. And why *did* Edgar not reveal his identity to his father before a half hour ago? He waited, he implies, until he was "armed" and ready for combat. That is, he did not and does not make the mistake of thinking that, with justice on his side, victory will be his—that justice without arms is sufficient—the mistake of Macduff and the characteristic mistake of believers in divine justice, one that he himself had made with Edmund early in the play. Finally, Gloucester's "flaw'd heart" was, according to Edgar, "too weak the conflict to support." The conflict he mentions is between the passions of "joy and grief," but might it not also have been between appearance and reality—between the divine providence he had been taught by Edgar and the human providence that Edgar was now disclosing to him?

Edgar has been reflecting, since the beginning of his flight from Edmund's machinations against him, on life and death. This speech is no exception, and the final words of the play will be his, on the same subject. Here, he declares parenthetically, "O, our lives' sweetness! / That we the pain of death would hourly die / Rather than die at once!" So sweet is life that we cling to it, though we hourly die the pain of death—in our griefs. Death is feared not as painful but as the unwelcome end of life's sweetness. Yet as this suggests, and as his formulation upon seeing his blind father for the first time had suggested, the sweetness eventually fades: "O world! But that thy strange mutations make us hate thee, / Life would not yield to age." We come, he implies, eventually to hate the world, and so life yields to age. Life comes to its end through a series of disappointments and griefs, which make life give up. This is consistent with Edgar's resignation, but it seems to discount, to some extent, the natural aging and failure of the human body. It is in any case very far removed from any hope in divine providence.

Edmund claims to be moved, by the tale of their father's suffering and Edgar's attempt to relieve it, to "perchance do good" (5.3.200–201). Yet instead of doing good—with precious time, as he knows, passing—he bids Edgar speak on, noting that he has more to say. Albany pleads with Edgar not to do so, since what he has already heard is woe enough. Yet Edgar speaks on—fully aware that griefs kill, that only one who loves sorrow would wish to hear more, and even as he is about to tell now yet another tale of how grief weakens men! He relates how Kent found him, in clamor of his father's death, and how, learning the truth that poor Tom was the disguised Edgar, broke into loud tears and recounted a piteous tale of himself and Lear, "which, in recounting, / His grief grew puissant and the strings of life / Began to crack." In telling this tale Edgar is compelled to refer to the fact that Kent, "having seen me in my worst estate, / Shunn'd my abhorr'd society" (5.3.205–219). He had omitted in his first tale any mention of his interaction with Kent and Lear on the heath; he alludes to it here indirectly, and we are reminded of the central theme of Lear's encounter with poor Tom, that is, Lear's discovery of natural man stripped of conventions. And

Kent, we are reminded here, ultimately takes his bearings, as did Gloucester, from convention. Like Gloucester, Kent is weakened by the recounting of truth. His recent approach to Edgar was made only when Edgar was fitted in armor for combat. Convention usually hides from men like Kent and Gloucester the awful truth about nature, by which Edgar takes his bearings. Edgar and Edmund share an insight into nature, it seems, and unlike those around them, draw some kind of strength from it, a capacity to hear and endure sorrowful news, expecting no trouble-free world nor, in the case of Edgar, any assistance from any divine beings whatsoever.

★   ★   ★

Albany, the political moderate who has an enduring faith in divine justice, continues to preside over the scene. He now receives the news of his wife's suicide and her confession of having poisoned Regan, and Edmund is moved to confess that he was indeed contracted in marriage to both of them. Albany's reaction to this news is quite remarkable: "Produce the bodies, be they alive or dead. / This judgment of the heavens, that makes us tremble, / Touches us not with pity" (5.3.231–233). The absence of pity in the genuinely pious Albany, in the face of what he believes to be a divine punishment, confirms our suspicion of Edgar's mere pretense to such a belief, in the case of Gloucester's blindness and more generally.

Albany immediately turns to Kent, apologizing for scanting courtesy to him. Kent has come to bid "my king and master aye good night." This reminder of Lear finally moves Albany to demand of Edmund the king's and Cordelia's whereabouts, and as the bodies of Regan and Goneril are brought out, a transformed Edmund at last relents from his final machination:

> Yet Edmund was belov'd!
> The one the other poisoned for my sake,
> And after slew herself…
> I pant for life. Some good I mean to do,
> Despite of mine own nature. Quickly send
> (Be brief in it) to th' castle, for my writ
> Is on the life of Lear and on Cordelia.
> Nay, send in time. (5.3.240–248)

Edmund now realizes that in spite of his "nature," to which he now clearly attributes the crimes he has committed, he was beloved. Only the grim deaths of Regan and Goneril bring this home to him, or rather, Goneril's willingness to poison her sister, for his sake, and kill herself in despair of having him. Her willingness to do such deeds—her defiance of the most sacred laws—convinces Edmund that he was genuinely loved and not merely used.

His sense of deserving confirmed at last by these horrific deeds, he does a good deed.

Albany, who had neglected the "great thing" of Lear and Cordelia, now shows still more absence of mind. He tells Edgar to run to the castle, but neglects to ask Edmund who was given the office of carrying out the deed. Edgar, ever with presence of mind, asks this of Edmund, as well as for a token of his reversal of the order. Free of conventions himself, Edgar is most attentive to their place even in the most urgent affairs.

But it is all for naught, as Albany's final prayer, "the gods defend her," goes unanswered. Lear carries the dead or dying Cordelia onto the stage. His words are pathetic and contradictory, as he moves between knowledge and hope:

> Howl, howl, howl! O, [you] are men of stones!
> Had I your tongues and eyes, I'ld use them so
> That heaven's vault should crack. She's gone for ever!
> I know when one is dead, and when one lives;
> She's dead as earth. Lend me a looking-glass,
> If that her breath will mist or stain the stone,
> Why then she lives. (5.3.258–264)

He laments her, "gone forever," as he blames the rest for not howling as he would. He knows she is dead, but hope moves him to seek evidence that she lives. The three principal witnesses of the scene react tellingly to it. Kent wonders if this is the promised end of the world, to which Edgar replies, "Or image of that horror?" suggesting perhaps that it is an image of one's own death that would end the world for oneself. Albany asks for that end to come; it is to him too harsh a world to be allowed to continue to exist. Using not a mirror but a feather, Lear thinks he sees it move, and his hope returns. This, he declares, would redeem all sorrows. But it is not to be.

Kent now seeks Lear's recognition and acknowledgment of his deeds, but Lear's concern is with the dead Cordelia. The rest are "murderers, traitors all." Lear again fancies he hears her speak, "gentle and low." All then learn of Lear's final, moving act for Cordelia: "I killed the slave that was a-hanging thee." Public recognition of this deed turns Lear's mind away from Cordelia and to his once vigorous and noble past, when such deeds were many, and then to his old age, and thence to Kent, who remains intent on Lear's recognition of him. After Kent speaks of Fortune's love and hatred of them both, Lear does recognize him. But Kent is intent that Lear realize it was he, disguised as Caius, who lately tended to him. Lear, surprisingly, declares Caius "dead and rotten." Kent sets him straight, and Lear declares him "welcome."

But Kent, playing on the word's literal meaning, replies that none are "well come" here; "All's cheerless, dark, and deadly." He then reports to Lear the news of Regan and Goneril's deaths, both of which, he suggests, were suicides. Lear agrees that they have foredone themselves or are desperately dead, dead in despair—in the very way that Edmund and Goneril had hoped to frame Cordelia's murder (cf. 5.3.255). And despair does seem to be what destroyed Goneril, at least, who saw no hope of continued joy without Edmund. Both were in the end weak, as Edgar might say, against life's buffets and adversities. Edgar appears to agree with Albany that it is now vain to present themselves to Lear ("Very bootless," he replies), but the reason, in Edgar's mind, may be not (as Albany thinks) that Lear does not know what he says, but rather that Lear's life must end, that the loss of Cordelia must prove too much even for him, crushing the happiness that he had begun to experience and thus his life.

Albany, hearing the news of Edmund's death, dismisses it as a "trifle here." What would have been for Albany another confirmation of divine justice is contemned as a trifle, as the overwhelming grief of Cordelia's death and its effect on the aged, daunted Lear consumes his attention. Albany now does all he can, as he thinks, to bring comfort to the political realm, by turning over his power to Lear, and calling for Edgar and Kent to have "such additions to your honors" as they have "more than merited." He is intent to the end that the deserving receive "the cup of their deservings"—friend and foe (5.3.297–305). We are thus reminded of the confusion of his position; it is not clear whether Kent, Edgar, and Lear, who have just participated in a rebellion, are the foes of whom he speaks; the rest, certainly, are dead. There is in any event a sharp contrast between what he would effect, the rewarding of the virtuous, and the action of the gods. Cordelia, the leader of the fight to avenge the injustices against Lear, is dead, and her death will now kill Lear. Kent, too—as he himself is about to say—will soon die. Where are the wages of virtue?

Lear's final words make this question hard to ignore:

> And my poor fool is hang'd! No, no, no life!
> Why should a dog, a horse, a rat, have life,
> And thou no breath at all? Thou'lt come no more,
> Never, never, never, never, never.
> Pray you undo this button. Thank you, sir.
> Do you see this? Look on her! Look her lips,
> Look there, look there! (5.3.305–312)

The finality of Cordelia's death moves him to wonder—to his very end he wonders—why beasts should have this strange thing, life, while she has it not. Desert appears to have nothing to do with human fate.

The tired and half-broken Kent calls for Lear's heart to break, and he must curtly suppress Edgar's effort to encourage Lear to "look up," that is, away from Cordelia's lips, which do not move. "Vex not his ghost. O, let him pass, he hates him / That would upon the rack of this tough world / Stretch him out longer." Edgar, offering no lamentation, matter-of-factly acknowledges Kent's point: "He is gone indeed." And Kent responds in kind. "The wonder is he hath endur'd so long, / He but usurp'd his life." Albany is by contrast focused on the grief, the woe, of the event. He now offers the state to Kent and to Edgar. But Kent announces his own impending death. "I have a journey, sir, shortly to go: / My master calls me, I must not say no." Faithful to the end, Kent takes Lear's death as his own call to die, with an implied hope of serving him in the hereafter. That hope sustains his devotion to service.

Edgar, who will now rule, closes the play with words that show some indulgence of the need to speak griefs freely.

> The weight of this sad time we must obey,
> Speak what we feel, not what we ought to say:
> The oldest hath borne most; we that are young
> Shall never see so much, nor live so long. (5.3.324–27)

He who has said so often in the play not what he feels but what he "ought" to say—especially in the matter of the gods' providence—and has fought against deadly despair, sees the need now to allow genuine human feelings their expression, weighed down as all are by the "sad times." Like *Macbeth's* Malcolm, Edgar would now have grief given its full expression, avoiding what for most would be a mere unhealthy pretense of a stiff upper lip. But his final lines are paradoxical. The sad time will, he indicates, make his life and that of other youths shorter; he seems to suggest a general decline in the ability to bear up, or perhaps suggests that still greater sorrows await his generation. His true position seems to be that the sufferings he and other youths have borne have come too early, been too much to sustain the sweetness of life and hence the desire for it. He, in any event, will now rule. He alone has been able to bear up, even if it has cost his life some years. Having such a clear-sighted ruler, who knows what is required to sustain the moral hopes and expectations of his people, provides some hope to an ending otherwise marked by gloom.

King Lear presents us with the attempt of a thoughtful and remarkably resilient former king whose experiences drive him to an active denial of divine law and move him, through the "tempest" of his mind, in the direction of an understanding of "unaccommodated" man, man as he is by nature and without any of the artful conventions that support the belief in providential gods. Though he considers this path "madness," and while it does tax his wits beyond what they can bear, it leads him to what might have been a more serene life of greater acceptance of nature's necessities but for the death of his beloved daughter. Edgar, who benefits from an observation of Lear's experience and with the benefit of a more youthful and supple soul, is the better able to endure suffering himself and to provide a salutary, hopeful, pious version of the truth to his father and then to his future subjects. In *The Tempest*, to which we now turn, Shakespeare presents us with the educational project of Prospero, who lost his rule of Milan through his philosophic study of the liberal arts and who endeavors, on behalf of his daughter and himself, poetically to educate those who come under his rule in the manner that Edmund educates his father—in divine providence. But that education is, as we will see, informed by a hard-won awareness of the true place of human beings in an indifferent universe that must vanish as completely as Prospero's poetic apparitions.

CHAPTER 5

THE TEMPEST: A PHILOSOPHER-POET EDUCATING CITIZENS

*T*he *Tempest* is the only play of Shakespeare named after a natural phenomenon, but the phenomenon turns out to be not natural at all.
Like most everything else in the play, from beginning to end, the tempest
is brought about in accordance with a single character's plan and deeds.
In this the play most resembles the Platonic dialogues, though its central
character, Prospero, who indeed spent a great deal of time studying "the
liberal arts" instead of ruling Milan, does not engage in Socratic dialectic.
His situation is such that his efforts are wholly bent on his and his daughter's return to an Italy from which they have been exiled, and the securing
of a promising marriage of his daughter to the heir apparent to Naples,
whose king has, in league with Prospero's brother, usurped Prospero's
rule of Milan. To achieve this end, Prospero must engage in the education
of the many different characters in the play; the question of what is the
best, and the best means to achieve, moral and political education is thus
one of the two great themes of the play. The other is the related question
of who should rule, which is posed loudly and clearly in the dramatic
opening and informs every subsequent scene. The play's magical quality
is accounted for by powers that Prospero has by some accident acquired
and which he renounces at the successful conclusion of what he calls his
"project" (5.1.1; cf. Epilogue, 12). But whatever the source of those powers, his use of them is determined by his wisdom, which includes knowledge of the prerequisites and means of the moral education of human
beings. That wisdom turns out to be incomplete, however, and finds its
necessary complement through the observation of the actions of his (nonhuman) slave, Caliban. In the Epilogue, we are prompted to reflect on the
relation between the "project" of the philosopher poet Prospero and that

of Shakespeare himself, in his education of both citizens and potential philosophers.

★ ★ ★

Act I

The play opens with a stunningly dramatic portrayal of the ancient metaphor of the ship of state. In the middle of a tempest, the ship's master gives orders to the boatswain ("Speak to the mariners") to prepare them for the swift execution of oft-rehearsed routines, to which the boatswain then directs them. ("Take in the topsail. Tend to th' / master's whistle.") Knowledge—of winds, forces of resistance, ballast, and so on—is clearly needed to guide the ship through the storm. This knowledge, based on necessities, is genuine and so uncontroversial that it is conveyed not by speech but by the master's whistle—by mere voice, technical and apolitical. The master's whistle calls into action procedures of the sailors' art based on this knowledge, directed through an accepted rank ordering ("Here master; what cheer?") and enjoined through appeal to the urgency of the moment ("Fall to 't, / yarely, or we run ourselves around").

As the mariners' procedures are being executed, two political rulers, Alonso the King of Naples and Antonio the Duke of Milan, appear on deck. In their fear of the storm they demand to learn from the boatswain the master's whereabouts, and order the boatswain to urge his men to action. They aren't obeyed; they aren't even merely ignored. To their shock and anger, they are told to keep quiet and stay out of the way. The storm's urgency has usurped their authority. "I pray now keep below," the boatswain first tells the rulers, who do not even realize that the master is already whistling his commands ("Do you not hear him?"). With the persistence of Antonio's entreaties, the boatswain grows more impatient. "You mar our labors…you do assist the storm" (1.1.11–14). The storm is the common, manifest enemy, and the ship's salvation against it is in the hands of knowers; all others are an obstruction. Were the storm human, the boatswain's words would amount to a charge of treason against the royal party. But Gonzalo, a member of Alonso's council, orders the boatswain to be patient. "When the sea is," replies the boatswain harshly. "Hence! What cares these roarers for the name of king? To cabin! silence! trouble us not!" The forces of nature are indifferent to what, in their fiercest face, becomes a mere name, "king." The boatswain is compelled to follow the storm in its indifference to that name, treating royalty like so many unruly youth.

Gonzalo's final advice to the boatswain, "Good, yet remember whom thou hast aboard," moves the boatswain to make the question of rule of the ship, and hence of what guides his own deeds, crystal clear:

> None that I more love than myself. You are
> a councillor; if you can command these elements

to silence, and work the peace of the present, we will
not hand a rope more. Use your authority. If you cannot, give thanks you have liv'd so long, and make
yourself ready in your cabin for the mischance of
the hour, if it so hap.—Cheerly good hearts!—Out of
our way, I say. (1.1.19–27)

The boatswain (who, pressed like the others by the storm, does not speak
in verse) not only repeats the point that the elements do not honor human
authority; he now directly challenges Gonzalo to use his authority to "work
the peace of the present." Only if Gonzalo can succeed will the boatswain
stop his activity and that of his men. The boatswain's defiant "we" stands
in contrast to the royal "we"; he employs the pronoun in order to include
his mariners (whom he briefly apostrophizes again). Attentive to his duties,
which are dictated by the master's art, the boatswain's concern in executing
them is frankly for himself; he is indifferent to the worth or dignity of the
rulers to whom he is expected loyally to devote himself. And he views the
storm as a matter of fortune, not as a thing divinely sent. Gonzalo sees in
such speech grounds for hanging ("his complexion is perfect gallows").

The situation of the boatswain is an extreme and dramatic version of
one that we are all likely to have experienced when compelled by urgent or
extreme need to set aside deference to alleged lawful superiors (or to law), to
civil speech, to manners, or to correct form, as inconsequential niceties. Living
in a liberal democracy, we will even tend to relish the lowly, hard-working
boatswain's defiant disposition as he gives the clueless, boastful royalty a piece
of his mind. But the issue that is being presented runs deeper than one of
exculpatory necessities and the foolishness of monarchy. The ship is after all
being run as a monarchy, with the master ruling the boatswain who in turn
rules the sailors. The master is a parallel monarch, with his own chain of command, a man who in this situation must have unimpeded command. The king
of Naples for his part knows this; he stays below when ordered, praying with
his son the prince (1.1.53); when the others return to the deck to dispute rule
again, with the king's brother Sebastian and Antonio hurling vicious epitaphs
for insubordination at the boatswain, he ignores them (1.1.40–46, 56–58). The
issue as Shakespeare presents it is one of who should rule, with knowledge or
science being in this situation the clear title. Is there, he compels us to ask, in
normal circumstances a political art or science that a ruler should possess as
title to rule? Is ruling a technical activity in the way that sailing is? Or is something else required? Are the objections raised by the royal party simply absurd,
or do they reflect a sensible demand for deference to lawful authority that is
lost or questioned only at great risk?

The question is further urged upon us by a number of peculiarities in the
opening scene. The first is the thick use of "good," a word that appears five

times, with different intents. In an extreme situation like this, what is good is or should be obvious: the urgent. But it is not usually so obvious, and fights over what is genuinely good characterize political life everywhere. And even if grasping what is good were not difficult and hence contentious, the particular content of the good would vary with time and place. Gonzalo's final words in the scene, for example, express a willingness in this situation to exchange "a thousand furlongs of sea for an acre of barren ground" (1.1.65–66), and in general the urgent can displace the more inherently desirable. Chance, too, which the boatswain twice mentions, can disrupt our settled plans to obtain what we consider good. Finally, the science or art of ruling a ship is subordinate rather than architectonic; where the well-run ship is headed or should be headed, in accordance with what is good or best, or whether humans should even use ships at all, does not belong to that art.

The related question of humans' final destination is raised in the mariners' cry "All lost! To prayers, to prayers!," and in both Gonzalo's injunction that they join the king and his son in prayers and in his penultimate exclamation that "the wills above be done!" (1.1.51–53). These statements contrast markedly with the disposition of Antonio, who blames the failings of others for the plight of them all and who, following Sebastian's suggestion, takes his leave of the king before the ship goes down (1.1.40–64). Is there, then, a willing god to whom one should pray? Gonzalo clearly believes so: he repeatedly claims that the boatswain's deserved fate—hanging—affords hope that they will all be saved (1.1.28–33, 46–48, 58–60). His hope is that justice will prevail; if it does not, "our case is miserable." But justice can prevail only if they can survive the storm to hang the boatswain, which—as the boatswain has made clear—it is not in Gonzalo's authority to ensure, but which is determined, in Gonzalo's words, by "the wills above."

But if there are gods, what do they ask of us? The insults hurled at the boatswain—that he is blasphemous, uncharitable, a whoreson, insolent, a drunkard—all name vices; are the corresponding virtues—pious reverence, charity, chastity, respectfulness, sobriety—what the gods ask of us? Do they make one worthy of the respect of human beings? Worthy of rule? The disposition that these virtues bespeak, the disposition to serve others—the just intention—would seem to be as crucial to what we want in a ruler as the art or science possessed by the master and boatswain. But does the architectonic knowledge or science that the political ruler needs support these devotional virtues, this just intention?

Whoever is to rule well must clearly have some wisdom, some compelling answers, to these questions. But even if such wisdom is clearly called for, other questions remain. Where might one obtain such wisdom? And if the boatswain encounters such fierce opposition to his rule in this crisis situation, what kind of opposition can be expected even to a wise ruler, in peaceful times? Is ruling worth the effort of overcoming such opposition? Is it something that the wise—assuming they are available—would find desirable? Do the wise wish at all to rule the ship of state?

★ ★ ★

These questions prepare us for the play's longest scene (1.2) where we meet Prospero, the man whose magic has brought all of the action about, and his daughter Miranda; his nonhuman subjects Ariel and Caliban; and then Ferdinand the son of the King of Naples. Miranda suspects that her father's "art" may be behind the terrible storm, whose effects have caused her to suffer in pity for the doubtless "noble creature" and "poor souls" that have perished in the shipwreck. Were she "any God of power," she states, she'd have sunk the sea to save them. Concern for a small, observed, precious part would have caused her to destroy the whole. Were she a powerful God, she would be a manifestly foolish one, because a too pitying one. Prospero implies that he has indeed brought it about, but he attempts to calm her pity. "Be collected, / No more amazement. Tell your piteous heart / There's no harm done." When she persists in her woe, he repeats "No harm." He is executing a plan, and while she is not privy to it (or, as we will see, to very much else that he has done in his life), he tells her that it is all done in care "of thee my dear one, thee my daughter" (1.2.17). His affection seems as narrow as her pity, but it is broader in its attention to potential collateral damage: "No harm."

The assurance of "no harm" accords with Prospero's name: he will make things prosper or bring about good. And while his deeds will entail dealing with enemies, he intends no harm to them either. His words could thus remind one of the conclusion to which Socrates moves Polemarchus in Plato's *Republic* (335b–e): the just man harms no one, not even his enemies. Whatever Socrates's purpose might have been in driving Polemarchus to that remarkable conclusion, it reflects his serious position that punitive justice ought to be good for the one suffering it rather than a means of exacting retribution or gratifying an angry desire for vengeance. And Prospero is, as his daughter will say of him, remarkably free of anger (1.2.496–499, 4.1.144–445), even if he will occasionally see the need to feign it. He chides Miranda not for having compassion, which he considers a "virtue" (1.2.27), but for its misplaced object in this particular case. He has by his art, he assures her, "so safely ordered" the terrible spectacle of the shipwreck

> that there is no soul—
> No, not so much perdition as an hair
> Betid to any creature in the vessel
> Which thou heardst cry, which thou saw'st sink. (1.2.29–32; cf. Luke 21:18)

If his powers are godlike, as Miranda has suggested, he is like a beneficent, mild-tempered providential god, who despite the evidence of his daughter's eyes has ordered all things by his art away from harm and toward the good. At the peak of that good is not worship of himself, however, but instead the welfare of his beloved daughter, who is "a third of mine own life, / Or that for which I live" (4.1.3–4). If Prospero is, Shakespeare would seem to have us think, an excellent ruler, he rules—remarkably—without the punitive spirit that had characterized the king's party on the ship, and—perhaps relatedly—without any reverence for "the wills above." He rules, in fact, to achieve at least one aspect of his own good.

Prospero has, however, kept Miranda ignorant not only of his present design but of herself ("who / Art ignorant of what thou art") and of his own former greatness (1.2.17–18). She professes to be remarkably without curiosity on this score, content with the life or with the father that she knows (1.2.19–22). "The hour's now come," however, for Prospero to teach her, and so he removes his "magic garment...my art" (1.2.24–25). He will put it back on soon, but only after he has taught Miranda something about herself. But why only now? We can discern the answer from what she now learns. Prospero used to be the Duke of Milan, until his brother Antonio usurped the throne in alliance with the king of Naples, "an enemy inveterate" to Prospero; they sent Prospero off on a leaky boat with Miranda, in which the two of them came to this island. Prospero may have forborne from disclosing this tale hitherto because it is too horrific for the tender heart of Miranda; he perhaps wished her to remain altogether ignorant of such evils. She must hear of them now, however, for she is about to be rescued, brought back to Italy and made a crown princess. She certainly shows herself still too piteous and even naïve as he tells the tale (see 1.2.116, 118–120, 132–135, 150–152). Yet she also shows awareness of evil ("Wherefore did they not / That hour destroy us?"), of which Prospero approves ("Well demanded, wench"), and she wonders how the two of them came ashore at all (1.2.138, 59). She is not simply innocent of evil, nor has Prospero endeavored to keep her so. Perhaps then, he withheld this story from her hitherto simply because he did not know if they would ever be saved, and wished not to destroy—by making her cognizant of what she had lost and thereby, perhaps, bitter about it—that portion of happiness that Miranda had on the island. As it is, she remembers when as a three-year old she had four or five women-in-waiting (1.2.41–47). In either case, Prospero has shown care to protect her from knowledge of what could disturb her contentment. And his careful education of her, to her great profit (1.2.171–174), has included inculcation of belief in "Providence divine" or "Heavens above" (1.2.159, 174) though when he puts his magic robe back on he speaks instead of "Bountiful Fortune" as responsible for the "accident" that has brought near the island his enemies (1.2.169 s.d,

Collier ms.; 177–179). Prospero is in the habit of withholding the truth from
Miranda, and substituting beneficent falsehoods, for what he takes to be her
own good. As we will see, this also characterizes his education of everyone
else in the play. But Miranda must now learn of their past in Milan, where Prospero was
once Duke. His explanation of how he came to lose his rule through his
brother's machinations includes, however, telling indications that Prospero's
own studies made it easy for Antonio to usurp his title:

> My brother and thy uncle, call'd Antonio—
> I pray thee mark me—that a brother should
> Be so perfidious!—he whom next thyself
> Of all the world I lov'd, and to him put
> The manage of my state, as at that time
> Through all the signories it was the first,
> And Prospero the prime duke, being so reputed
> In dignity, and for the liberal arts
> Without a parallel; those being all my study,
> The government I cast upon my brother,
> And to my state grew stranger, being transported
> And rapt in secret studies...
> I, thus neglecting worldly ends, all dedicated
> To closeness and the bettering of my mind
> With that which, but being so retir'd
> O'er-priz'd all popular rate...
> [And Antonio] needs will be
> Absolute Milan—me (poor man) my library
> Was dukedom large enough. (1.2.66–77, 89–92, 108–110)

Prospero preferred to the practice of his rule over Milan the education of
his mind in the liberal arts through the study of books. And he still does:
when Gonzalo fitted the boat of his exile with provisions, "Knowing I lov'd
my books," relates Prospero, "he furnish'd me / From mine own library with
volumes that / I prize above my dukedom" (1.2.166–168). The final verb is
in the present tense. Prospero prizes what since Plato's *Republic* (521d–536e)
have been called the "liberal arts," the study becoming a genuinely free human
being and whose study prepares one for the philosophic life. He is what Plato's
Socrates called a "philosopher king," and since—as Socrates himself makes
abundantly clear—the two parts of that term stand in contradiction with one
another, he had to move toward one or the other. He was moved toward the
first rather than the second. In pursuit of the philosophic life—of the good,
the improvement, of his mind—he lost his titular rule; the more he learned,
the less devoted he became to the care of his people. His brother's perfidy was

only the concluding act of this drama; the greater part was Prospero's progressive loss of his interest in ruling.

★   ★   ★

But marooned on the island with his daughter—who sustained his determination in the face of their plight (1.2.152–158)—he was compelled to rule, becoming "schoolmaster" to Miranda (and master over Ariel and Caliban). And there are actions that he must now take immediately, with the help of Ariel, if he is to bring the two of them back to Italy. Donning his magic robe (of whose source we have not yet heard) he puts Miranda to sleep, and calls Ariel, his pagan servant sprite who has been the executor of the tempest, or of its appearance to everyone's minds, and who reports that all are safe. The sailors have all been put into a deep sleep, he reports, and the rest of the ships have gone on to Naples, thinking the king's ship lost (1.2.187–218). Ariel has performed faithfully and well.

But a quarrel arises between Ariel and Prospero. Its source is Ariel's desire for his liberty. His cheerful service is, we now learn, compelled, and Prospero has promised him imminent freedom (1.2.245–249). Perhaps having learned from his experience the necessity of harshness, Prospero calls Ariel "malignant thing" and "my slave" (1.2.257, 270), and reminds Ariel—who according to Prospero is forgetful—of the torment from which he freed him. We thus come to know a little bit about the source of Prospero's magical powers, that is, how he came to have Ariel and other spirits subject to himself. Ariel had been the servant of Sycorax, a witch who had formerly ruled the island, but Ariel was "too delicate to act her earthy and abhorr'd commands." She therefore imprisoned him in a cloven pine tree for a dozen years, and in the meantime died, leaving only her "freckled whelp, hag-born" son Caliban on the island. Prospero freed Ariel from the torment with his "art" (1.2.291); he does not say how he came upon it, though Caliban, who could not speak, much less read, when Prospero met him, may well have been the source of the book from which Prospero learned magic. (Caliban knows that the magic is from "books," though he does not realize that it is from a single book—see 3.2.89–95 and 5.1.57 with 3.1.94; he was certainly the source of many other good things on the island for Prospero—see 1.2.331–374, 2.2.148–173, 3.2.42–53, 89–103). Perhaps it is not only Ariel who forgets the sources of his salvation. In any event, Prospero for his own purposes now keeps Ariel temporarily enslaved, moving him with a mixture of carrot and stick. Ariel—who has been promised his freedom and can rule himself—clearly does not in any conventional sense deserve to be enslaved.

As for Prospero's other slave, Caliban, who is now ruled simply by the stick, Prospero did once entrust him with freedom, lodging him in his

cave, until he attempted to rape Miranda—an act for which he still shows
no remorse whatsoever. "O ho, O ho, would't been done!," he exclaims
shamelessly. "Thou didst prevent me; I had peopled else / This isle with
Calibans" (1.2.349–51). Miranda, too, is harsh with him. She had, she says,
out of pity (what else in Miranda?) taught Caliban to speak. Why Prospero,
her only teacher, considers Caliban a slave is clear from Miranda's judgment: "Abhorred slave, / Which any print of goodness wilt not take, /
Being capable of all ill!" (1.2.351–53). As in the case of his brother, so in
the case of Caliban, Prospero was, it seems, too trusting, and Caliban appears
incapable of remorse. These two facts seem to account for Prospero's per-
sistently harsh attitude to Caliban, his conviction that Caliban simply has
a bad nature that no nurture can overcome (cf. 4.1.87–90). Caliban in
any event now obeys Prospero out of fear of the power of his "art," that
is, the power that the enslavement of Ariel has made available to Prospero
(1.2.373). Where Ariel had been previously enslaved and imprisoned and
is now promised his imminent freedom, Caliban had freedom, but has
through his deeds lost it. Shakespeare thus poses to us the question: by
what acts or manifest virtues do we deserve freedom or enslavement? Can
we deserve either? This is a particular form of the question we have seen
in all four previous plays: by what virtues does one deserves to rule, even
over oneself?

★   ★   ★

Alonzo's son Ferdinand is, in accordance with Prospero's plan and through
Ariel's faithful service, now lured into the presence of Prospero and Miranda.
He fancies the alluring songs of Ariel to be sweet music for a god, music that
comforted him when he was weeping over what he takes to be the cruel fate
of his beloved, drowned father, and that now includes songs of him. Seeing
Ferdinand, Miranda takes him for a spirit, then "[a] thing divine, for nothing
natural / I ever saw so noble" (1.2.419). (The aged Prospero must look quite
different.) Despite Prospero's insistence that this man "eats, sleeps, and hath
such senses / As we have," and would but for his grief, "beauty's canker," be
called a "goodly person," she persists in taking him for a god. Ferdinand for
his part takes Miranda to be a goddess (1.2.423), which is more impressive,
since Ferdinand has seen many beautiful women. In this context Ferdinand
unconsciously utters a revealing pun on her name ("O you wonder!"
cf. 3.1.36–37: "Admired Miranda"). Upon discovering that Miranda is not
married, and that she speaks his language, and after seeing her expressions of
pity for him and her appeal to Prospero for gentleness, Ferdinand proposes
to make her queen of Naples, that is, to marry her, on two conditions: if she
be a virgin and if "her affection [be] not gone forth" (1.2.448–449).

Prospero must at this point intervene. The magical powers at his disposal have brought the couple together, but now a naturally magical desire, over which he neither has nor wishes control—love—has begun its work. As his asides indicate (1.2.420–422, 439–443, 451–453, 491–500), he is deeply pleased with this result. The two lovers are in the thrall of one another. Prospero (and we) therefore witness the curious behavior of lovers submitting themselves to one another, vowing perpetual fealty. What is this power of love that it has such an effect? It entails the promise of happiness and, as with Ariel's submission to Prospero, the fear of terrible unhappiness. And just as Ariel must prove himself worthy of his freedom, so the lovers wish to prove themselves worthy in each other's eyes. They can do so by sacrifice of all other things to the joyful presence of their beloved. So Ferdinand expresses himself willing to be imprisoned if he can but see Miranda once a day (1.2.487–493). This is precisely what Prospero had wished, and the imprisonment of Ferdinand will test whether he means it, making the winning of Miranda a thing difficult. Love quickly makes, in other words, the assumption of a moral freedom, a capacity to give up one's own good for the sake of what is perceived to be a transcendent, pure good, and Prospero now makes use of that assumption. What Prospero promises Ariel is a freedom of a different kind: "Thou shalt be as free / As mountain winds, but then exactly do / All points of my command."

Not spirits like Ariel, to be sure, but human beings, at least serious ones, have this peculiar sense, born it seems of erotic longing, that their happiness can and must be deserved. Prospero counts on it, and proves to be correct in his direction of it. But is there any genuine foundation for this sense? If a just god rules over the world, as does a beloved over her lover, there is. But what if instead an indifferent nature orders the whole? Does nature even make quite clear who deserves our devotion and who does not? Prospero, for his part, does not think it does: he has to test Ferdinand, and even make the object of Ferdinand's love—Miranda— seem more desirable for being difficult to obtain; he must artificially make her something to be earned by labors. Miranda, however, does think that nature makes her distinctions of worthiness plain: "There's nothing ill can dwell in such a temple," she says of Ferdinand. "If the ill spirit have so fair a house, / Good things will strive to dwell with't" (1.2.458–460). Her optimism concerning nature's manifestations of worthiness through looks is obviously ill-founded. But Miranda is so moved by Ferdinand that she would disobey her wise father's orders (2.467ff.). Prospero must even warn that if she persists, she will make him hate her. And she does indeed require this rebuke. As Prospero tells her, "Foolish wench, / To th' most of men this is a Caliban, / And they to him are angels" (1.2.41–82); what does she know of men? The same could, however, be said of most loves, which can blind lovers to all but their beloved as surely as the island has blinded Miranda to all other men.

Act II

In the second act we meet up again with king Alonso and his men, and then with servants (Stephano and Trinculo) who were aboard the ship. Prospero does not appear in this act, though he is as vigilant of his plan as Ariel is in his execution of it. Gonzalo, the honest and faithful councillor, attempts to cheer up his king, looking for the silver lining in their dark cloud, while Sebastian and Antonio make sport of his efforts. Gonzalo is genuinely pleased with the island. Unlike the lord Adrian, who finds it uninhabitable, Gonzalo claims that "here is everything advantageous to life" (2.1.50). He is genuinely dazzled by the verdant nature of the place, while Sebastian and Antonio think he is "missing the truth totally" (1.2.58), that is, that they are all stranded on an island desert of human beings. But the apparently Pollyannish Gonzalo notices, as they had not, that their clothes are fresh. He is not just the chipper old fool that Sebastian and Antonio account him; he notices genuinely good and wondrous things. He also knows his mythology and history, recounting that Dido, queen of Carthage, was widowed—by her Phoenician husband Sychaeus, thereafter by her lover Aeneas—and that Tunis is the modern-day Carthage.

Still, Gonzalo does make a persistent diplomatic mistake here, thrice reminding Alonso of the marriage of his daughter Claribel to the king of Tunis. Since Tunis is directly across the Mediterranean and just south of Naples, that marriage appears to have been strictly political; like his taking of Milan, it is part of Alonso's grand design to secure the whole of Italy under his rule. Gonzalo brings up Claribel's marriage in a hapless effort to cheer the king: we're safe, and your daughter is successfully married. Count your blessings; things could have been much worse. But Alonso is in no mood to hear it: "You cram these words into mine ears against / The stomach of my sense. Would I had never / Married my daughter there!" (2.1.107–109). Had Alonso not gone to Tunis, his son Ferdinand, the heir of Naples and Milan, would still live. His plan is in tatters, his dear son perished, and despite the lord Francisco's claim to have seen Ferdinand swim safe to shore, Alonso is too remorseful to be hopeful. Ferdinand's death is an accident, but one that would not, he is clearly thinking, have occurred had he himself not overreached. His brother Sebastian now drives the point home: you are to blame; we begged you to marry her to a European, and she begged you, and even considered disobeying you, but you did not listen. You have lost your son; you are to blame (2.1.110–128).

Alonso's despair makes no sense, of course, unless he takes the storm as a divine punishment. He could otherwise oppose Sebastian's argument with the retort that Sebastian makes it with the benefit of hindsight: did Sebastian oppose the marriage on the ground that if it took place, they would all be tempest-tossed on their return voyage from Tunis, with Fernando drowned? If not, what grounds does he now have for blaming Alonso? But Alonso makes no such rebuttal. He holds indeed that he is to blame somehow. We thus see the other side of the love-induced desire to be esteemed worthy or deserving of happiness: remorse when our happiness is not attained. When told that the fault is his own, he replies, "So is the dear'st o' th' loss" (2.1.136). He feels, in short, that he is being punished. As we will see, this sentiment of remorse will make him amenable to a certain kind of education by Prospero.

Gonzalo agrees that Alonso is to blame, declaring what Sebastian speaks to be "the truth," even if it lacks "some gentleness" (2.1.138), that is, even if this is the wrong time to say it. But Gonzalo now attempts to divert the king from his remorse, addressing the question of rule over the island, and thereby giving us his vision of the best regime or commonwealth (2.1.148–168). It would, he indicates, include the absence of business or trade, of magistrates, of letters or learning, of riches or poverty, of slaves or servants, of vineyards (of permanent land use by a single party), of metal, corn, wine, oil, work, or occupation. All men would be idle, and women too, but innocent and pure. Sebastian and Antonio point out the problem with his scheme: how does one legislate such anarchy? If Gonzalo were to lay the scheme down, then he would be the ruler.

Gonzalo's vision is communist but not Marxist; it entails a renouncing rather than an embracing of the conquest of nature, or technology, which, Marx would later argue, was helping to rescue whole populations from the idiocy of rural life. Gonzalo counts, as Marx will not, on a bounteous "nature" to bring forth all that humans need (2.2.16–65). If the provision of bounteous goods for all is indeed simply a matter of redistribution, Gonzalo's vision might be sensible. But is it? Nature surely does not, without human art, provide abundance. Moreover, even if it did, humans want more than to be idle and have their basic needs met. The "treasons and felonies" that Gonzalo would banish are committed not, as he assumes, simply from need but also out of ambition for more. Human love or erotic longing is for something more than the useful, and it engenders (as we have seen) ambitious sentiments of worth, and hence of rank ordering and pairing off. Competition, jealousies, vengeances, hatreds could be eliminated only at the price of eliminating such longing, and with it most of the moral life of man. However snide their criticisms, Sebastian and Antonio are much more sober and thoughtful with respect to surpassing the "golden age" of which Gonzalo speaks than is he, and his faith in the existence of such an age, as we have seen in other plays, goes hand in hand with his moral hopes that the world we have is the result of moral failings rather than the unplanned results of an unthinking nature.

Gonzalo's vision of a perfect commonwealth certainly fails to move Alonso, and provokes such ridicule from Antonio and Sebastian as even to make Gonzalo come close to losing his composure. But Ariel puts him and all the others, except Sebastian and Antonio, to sleep, and we see vividly the kind of ambition that Gonzalo's vision had neglected. Antonio now persuades Sebastian to do as he has done: murder his brother and take over the kingdom. Antonio effects his persuasion with a simple argument: your hope of rule is in your brother's death. Sebastian's only counterargument concerns the very thing that has been affecting the king: "But, for your conscience?" Does it not trouble Antonio for his having usurped his brother's rule? "I feel not / This deity in my bosom," Antonio replies coolly. "Twenty consciences, / That stand 'twixt me and Milan, candied be they, / And melt ere they molest!" (2.1.275–280). The conscience, he suggests, is something that itself leads to belief in a divinity, and he spells out his conscience-less reasoning:

> Here lies your brother,
> No better than the earth he lies upon,
> If he were that which now he's like—that's dead,
> Whom I with this obedient steel, three inches of it,
> Can lay to bed for ever; whiles you, doing thus,
> To the perpetual wink for aye might put
> This ancient morsel, this Sir Prudence, who
> Should not upbraid our course. For all the rest,
> They'll take suggestion as a cat laps milk;
> They'll tell the clock to any business that
> We say befits the hour. (2.1.280–289)

To kill Alonso would be to render him no more than earth; he in truth lacks the dignity that Gonzalo ("Sir Prudence") believes him to have. And persuasive speech will easily silence all criticism. Sebastian agrees to the ruthlessly bold plan. He and Antonio are human beings of a quite different sort than Alonso or Gonzalo. Antonio has no conscience, and hence no reverence for the divine nor respect for the human, and he would have the same be true of Sebastian. Their deed would be done without attention to desert and hence without guilt.

But before they can strike, Ariel awakens Gonzalo, who immediately comes to the king's aid. Prospero had foreseen—indeed, provided the chance for—this conspiracy. It was a test, and Antonio and Sebastian have failed it. No longer is Prospero amazed—as he had claimed to Miranda to be—by the perfidy of brothers; he rather anticipates it, and his "art," as Ariel states, had disclosed it to him (2.1.297–299). As for Gonzalo's gallant saving of Alonso, it is likewise something Prospero expected. But it is the kind of noble deed that Gonzalo's imagined commonwealth would render impossible, since that commonwealth would eliminate the need for moral virtue. The conspirators are able to hide their design at the last minute, and will await another opportunity, as the party goes in search now of Ferdinand, since Alonso proves to be still hopeful that his son is alive (2.1.300–325).

★   ★   ★

Another conspiracy, of a much more comical variety though with equally deadly intent, is underway on another part of the island (2.2). Caliban is busy gathering wood, grousing about the afflictions that Prospero sets upon him, as he says, "for every trifle." He certainly has a miserable enough life to welcome the arrival to it of two of the nobles' servants, Trinculo and Stephano. Caliban first mistakes the former for one of Prospero's spirits, and lays down flat, so as to be unnoticed. Fearing a storm, Trinculo ducks under Caliban's cloak. The tipsy Stephano then mistakes the two of them for a four-legged beast, and looks to take it back home to sell as an oddity. He then gets Caliban drunk. The liquor induces Caliban to take Stephano to be a god, whom he would serve (2.2.115–116, 125–126, 148–149). He appears—at least when drunk—to be in need of a god, a master, someone to whom to bow. The bowing does not arise out of a calculation of his own relative powerlessness against Prospero (cf. 5.1.295–298); it rather bespeaks a genuine awe or reverence of the novel experience of potent liquor and of him who has provided it. His service to Stephano will prove to be both faithful and prudent, and such as to move Prospero to reappraise his harsh judgment of him.

Act III

At Prospero's orders Ferdinand is undergoing the labor that will make his love seem deserved and make Miranda seem to be a being who must be deserved, available only to one who would serve even in a debased office in order to be with her. He hauls wood, a job that is inherently base or odious, as he and Miranda call it. It requires only brawn, not skill, and even animals have brawn. However necessary, it borders on the bestial. Labor is not inherently good—*pace* the Christian or (subsequently) Marxist teaching. All that makes it good for Ferdinand is the thought of performing it for the sake of Miranda, who appears the more gentle to him as her father appears harsh. Miranda, he knows, weeps over his plight, which clearly delights Ferdinand for the affection it betrays for him. (He thinks he deserves better than the task of hauling wood, and enjoys the thought that she too thinks he deserves better. We recall Kent's pleasure at the tears of Cordelia.)

Miranda enters, and shows the depth of her sentiments and how such sentiments turn in noble hearts to personifying poetry: "When this burns," she says of a log, "'Twill weep for having wearied you" (3.1.18–19). She manifests the tendency of longing to invest the inanimate world with an awareness and a purposefulness that enhances the beloved's significance, just as Lear's thwarted love had moved him to address the winds and lightning on the heath. Her father (who is stealthily watching the scene) is, she mentions, busy for three hours "at study" (which remains, we thus learn, not uncommon for him). Ferdinand should therefore rest. She offers to do the work herself, which he will of course not allow; he should rather break his back than have her undergo such dishonor. Would he have such sentiments if she scorned him? We'll never know. For now, infected as she is (in Prospero's words), she is moved to requite Ferdinand's professions of affection.

Prospero had forbidden Miranda to mention her name to a stranger, in regard for her modesty. But when Ferdinand asks for it, "Chiefly that I might set it in my prayers," she complies: "Miranda—O my father, / I have broke your hest to say so" (3.1.37–38). Ferdinand then woos her, telling her that unlike other women he has liked for their several virtues, she has all the virtues, so that there is no defect to quarrel with noble grace in her. Her response is frank: she knows no one of her sex but herself, nor more men than Ferdinand and her own "dear father"; she is "skilless" of how features are abroad. (We are reminded that Prospero has had to be both father and mother to her.) She will nevertheless respond to his admiring words in kind:

> but by my modesty
> (The jewel in my dower), I would not wish
> Any companion in the world but you;
> Nor can imagination form a shape,
> Besides yourself, to like of. But I prattle
> Something too wildly, and my father's precepts
> I therein do forget. (2.1.53–59)

While she is not altogether uncomposed or forward, Miranda appears to honor her father's precepts in the breach. Still, we gain some understanding of the aim of her father's careful education of her from these precepts. With respect to her relations with eligible young men, the education aimed above all at the cultivation of modesty, a virtue little supported in our day and sometimes even excoriated as an instrument of oppression. We have therefore to make a special effort to understand Shakespeare's sympathetic portrayal of it. It is not a philosophic but a moral virtue. Its opposite, immodesty, would encourage being indiscriminate, needy of the affection of others, and hence prodigal with one's favors. It would bespeak a lack of self-respect, a desperate need to arouse the attentions and passions of everyone and anyone rather than reserving oneself for the most deserving. It would cheapen one's worth, thereby lessening the attentions of those who would make stable, affectionate spouses.

Modesty is also a requirement of civilization; humans require a much longer time to be nurtured than any other animal, and a high human life requires a long time indeed, throughout puberty and adolescence. For unlike other animals, we need judgment to guide our lives, a faculty that is liable to go awry especially in adolescence. We learn it from our parents, whom we can trust to guide us, but which they cannot provide without some permanence to their relations. Binding them to each other permanently rather than briefly is the virtue of fidelity, supported by public vows. The act of reproduction is, after all, given to animals, and if sex is easily available anywhere, with no responsibilities attached, then men and women (but especially men) have less reason to make their relations permanent. Sexual modesty, a "bashful cunning," as Miranda calls it (3.1.81) was thus once what women would teach other women for the sake of their self-respect and for their indirect, civilization-preserving rule over men. As we will see in the fourth act, Prospero attempts to inculcate chastity, the close kin of modesty, in Ferdinand and Miranda both, by means of a play put on through his art.

Here Miranda's love overcomes her modesty, to the delight of Prospero. Her spoken admiration of Ferdinand moves Ferdinand to declare to her his "soul's" speech:

> The very instant that I saw you, did
> My heart fly to your service, there resides,
> To make me slave to it, and for your sake
> Am I this patient log-man.(3.1.64–67)

Miranda then asks, quite forwardly, whether he loves her, and he calls heaven and earth to witness that he truly does, "Beyond all limit of what else I' th' world, / Do love, prize, honor you." This profession prompts her, in the name of "plain and holy innocence," to declare

> I am your wife, if you will marry me;
> If not, I'll die your maid. To be your fellow

> You may deny me, but I'll be your servant,
> whether you will or no. (3.1.83–86)

And Ferdinand expresses himself in turn "humble ever," and her husband "with a heart as willing / As bondage e'er of freedom" (3.1.63–90). Since they have been speaking of their willing enslavement to one another, this final line brings out the paradox of their affections; they are devoted and ready to sacrifice—but with the hope of joyful self-fulfillment *such as one finds in a slave's longing for freedom.* Looking on the exchange, Prospero can rejoice "At nothing...more" (3.1.93–94).

★   ★   ★

Prospero has "much business" to attend to, but he does so unaware of what is developing between Caliban, Stephano, and Trinculo (3.2). That the "slave" Caliban might turn his chance meeting with these two into an attempt at his own liberation was something to which Prospero had given no thought. And Caliban will now through his deeds and speeches demonstrate to us, as he will eventually to Prospero, that no more than any rational being does he deserve to be enslaved. He senses that Trinculo, who expresses doubts about Caliban's serving abilities, is not as valiant as Stephano, and so he will not serve him; he thinks Trinculo belongs on his level, under Stephano. He objects to being mocked by Trinculo, and demands that Stephano punish Trinculo appropriately; he has a sense of his dignity or worth—that he deserves to be treated in a certain way—and expects his ruler to mete out rewards and punishments in accord with proper worth. (This is one of the burdens of rule that Prospero did not wish to bear in Milan.) He has a clear sense, that is, of distributive and punitive justice.

Still more impressive is Caliban's manifest ability to hatch a conspiracy against Prospero. He tells Stephano and Trinculo—not for the first time; he is clearly intent on this matter—that through sorcery Prospero cheated him out of the island, which was his. He invites Stephano now to dare to avenge the "tyrant" Prospero and become lord over the island. Caliban is choosing his ruler, on the basis of his perception of justice. This and his plan manifest the capacity for political judgment or prudence that belongs to a free human being. He will himself even forego lordship over the island, serving the "noble lord" Stephano, and he proposes a plan to kill Prospero while he sleeps. Ariel, who now comes upon them, attempts to disrupt the conspiracy with ventriloquized charges of lying, but the result is only that Trinculo receives, at the request and to the delight of Caliban, more blows from Stephano. Caliban even wishes to rise now into second place in the pecking order, offering to beat Trinculo after Stephano is finished. He suggests multiple ways to kill Prospero in his sleep, but thrice repeats the need to seize his books and (eventually) "burn" them, which would, of course, also liberate Caliban from any sorcery by his new master.

Finally, Caliban shows how capable he in fact is of suppressing his own sexual longings, as he recommends Miranda to Stephano:

> And that most deeply to consider is
> The beauty of his daughter. He himself
> Calls her a nonpareil. I never saw a woman
> But only Sycorax my dam and she;
> But she as far surpasseth Sycorax
> As great'st does least. (3.2.98–103)

In thus spelling out the greatest allurement of overthrowing Prospero, Caliban makes clear that he himself was moved to his attempted rape of her not only by a desire to have "peopled...this island with Calibans" but—like Ferdinand—by Miranda's beauty. "She will become thy bed, I warrant, / And bring thee forth brave brood" (3.2.104–105). This persuades Stephano, at last, to accept Caliban's plan; he wishes to become king of the isle and have Miranda as his queen, with Caliban and Trinculo as his viceroys. (Trinculo, having previously been demoted, now accepts the offer gratefully.)

Ariel has heard the whole business, and will report it now to Prospero (3.2.115), but not before he has led the three off with a song, which at first frightens Trinculo ("O, forgive me my sins!") and Stephano, but not Caliban, who allays their fears:

> Be not afeared, the isle is full of noises,
> Sounds, and sweet airs, that give delight and hurt not.
> Sometimes a thousand twangling instruments
> Will hum about mine ears; and sometimes voices,
> That if I then had wak'd after long sleep,
> Will make me sleep again, and then in dreaming,
> The clouds methought would open, and show riches
> Ready to drop upon me, that when I wak'd
> I cried to dream again. (3.2.135–143)

Caliban's beautiful description of the beautiful music gives us yet more evidence that he was not meant to be enslaved. But it likewise shows us that his life is not so miserable under the despotism of Prospero. Still, Caliban seeks liberation from his enslavement. The final display of his abilities comes in his warning to Stephano that he will not come into rule of this enchanted island unless he destroys Prospero. Caliban is very clear-sighted about what must be done to the "tyrant," and will prove still more so in the actual attempt, from which both he and Prospero will learn something of each other.

* * *

The business to which Prospero had to attend, when overlooking the sideshow (and in the event, comic) conspiracy of Stephano, Trinculo, and Caliban, is the education of the royal party, whose members have been searching the island for Ferdinand (3.3). Gonzalo cannot go on in the search; Alonso too is exhausted; and Sebastian and Antonio continue to plot against the king. Prospero's plan for the educative redemption of his enemies is at this point taken up in earnest. He, "on top, invisible," directs his spirits to play enchanting music and then to display the apparition of a feast, served by strangely shaped beings, for the fatigued and famished party. The apparition moves everyone, as Prospero intended, to affirm the opinion that there are indeed wonders in the world. That is, their faith in such wonders returns, and their appetites, too, are whetted. But as they move toward the food to eat it, Ariel descends upon it, amid thunder and lightning, as a harpy, and the feast vanishes. He then admonishes Alonso, Antonio, and Sebastian concerning their need for repentance:

> You are three men of sin, whom Destiny
> That hath to instrument this lower world
> And what is in't, the never-surfeited sea
> Hath caus'd to belch up you; and on this island
> Where man doth not inhabit—you 'mongst men
> Being most unfit to live. I have made you mad;
> And even with such-like valor men hang and drown
> Their proper selves. (3.3.53–60)

They draw their swords, but Ariel assures them that their weapons are useless against the "ministers of fate," and explains to them their present fate through a reminder of their deed against Prospero:

> But remember
> (For that's my business to you) that you three
> From Milan did supplant good Prospero,
> Expos'd unto the sea (which hath requit it)
> Him, and his innocent child; for which foul deed
> The pow'rs, delaying (not forgetting), have
> Incens'd the seas and shores—yea, all the creatures,

Against your peace. Thee of thy son, Alonso,
They have bereft; and do pronounce by me
Ling'ring perdition (worse than any death
Can be at once) shall step by step attend
You and your ways, whose wraths to guard you from—
Which here, in this most desolate isle, else falls
Upon your heads—is nothing but heart's sorrow,
And a clear life ensuing. (3.3.68–82)

The tempest has been a delayed, divine vengeance for the foul deed against
Prospero and his daughter, and they will continue to suffer horribly unless
they have remorse ("heart's sorrow") and reform their ways.

The pious Gonzalo does not see the apparition, and is baffled by
Alonso's reaction: "I' the name of something holy, sir, why stand you / In
this strange stare?" Alonso is in anguish over what he has heard and over
the fate of Ferdinand and himself: "That deep and dreadful organ-pipe,
pronounc'd / The name of Prosper; it did base my trespass" (3.3.98–99).
Sebastian and Antonio, on the other hand, are resolved to fight the "legion"
of fiends, "one fiend at a time" (3.3.103–104). Gonzalo guesses about all
of them that "their great guilt" is behind their desperation, but in this he
is only partly right. To feel guilt, one needs a conscience, and as Antonio
had said, "I feel not / This deity in my bosom." He and Sebastian could
be brought, by the initial apparition of the feast, to a renewed faith in the
stories of unicorns and other creatures told by travelers, but that is not a
religious faith; lacking consciences as they do, they are moved by the threat
of divine vengeance from the second apparition *not* to remorse but to careful defiance. The conscience is the seat of humans faith in divine beings.
Prospero will accordingly have to use threats of a more mundane nature
against them.

Act IV

Prospero now undertakes another educative performance, not with enemies
but with his daughter and future son-in-law. Having "punish'd" Ferdinand,
if too severely, he claims, he will now provide compensation with the offer
of the hand in marriage of Miranda, "a third of mine own life / Or that
for which I live" (4.1.3–4). But Prospero then makes clear that his deeds
in fact lacked any intent to punish at all. "All thy vexations / Were but
my trials of thy love, and thou hast strangely stood the test" (4.1.5–7). His
intention, now disclosed, had to be kept hidden in order to be accomplished; had Ferdinand known of it, his desire to overcome the artificial
challenge may well have flagged, since the base service would then have
been to satisfy Prospero, not the result of an injustice that could be borne

for Miranda's sake. What Prospero has done with Ferdinand resembles in this respect what he has just attempted with the royal party, who had to remain unaware that he was behind the apparition if it were to succeed in its intended moral effect. In what Prospero is about to attempt, by contrast, the couple's awareness that Prospero will be producing the effect through his art is not only known but is even needed for what is (allegedly) the very purpose of the apparition: to manifest "vanity of mine art" (4.1.40–42).

Prospero first vows before heaven to give Miranda to Ferdinand, with an important proviso and warning, made for the sake of their happiness together:

> But
> if thou dost break her virgin-knot before
> All sanctimonious ceremonies may
> With full and holy rite be minist'red,
> No sweet aspersion shall the heavens let fall
> To make this contract grow; but barren hate,
> Sour-ey'd disdain, and discord shall bestrew
> The union of your bed with weeds so loathly
> That you shall hate it both. Therefore take heed,
> As Hymen's lamps shall light you. (4.1.13–23)

Prospero had called on heaven to ratify his gift, and he here appeals to the heavens and their actions, following the mention of a "full and holy rite" of marriage, to punish terribly any premarital sex. It is sufficiently clear from the previous scene that Prospero does not regard the appeal to heaven as effective without human artifice that presents itself as divine. Prospero's speech here has, however, the intended effect on Ferdinand:

> As I hope
> For quiet days, fair issue, and long life,
> With such love as 'tis now, the murkiest den,
> The most opportune place, the strong'st suggestion
> One worser genius can, shall never melt
> Mine honor into lust, to take away
> The edge of that day's celebration,
> When I shall think or Pheobus' steeds are founder'd
> Or Night kept chain'd below. (4.1.23–31)

Ferdinand provides a very strong affirmation of his intent to remain chaste until the wedding day. But if he should not? Will all the horrible consequences that Prospero has called for come about? That is still the question. Before we consider it further, we might well ask: why prohibit premarital sex?

With modern medical technologies, we are inclined to forget or put out of our minds that children are conceived through sexual relations. It may even be worth noting that our relatively lax sexual mores did not come into being before reliable and widely available birth control, which vastly increased the confidence of human beings that sex would be without issue, a confidence further bolstered by the legality of abortion on demand. One of the concerns directing the injunction to chastity is, or was, prospective children. As with modesty, so a fortiori with chastity, the guiding thought was that children ought to be conceived in marriage in order to ensure the successful rearing of offspring. The public institution of marriage could provide some guarantee of the genuine identity of the father, and hence of his assuming the burdens of rearing his offspring, since human beings tend to prefer their own children as a continuation of themselves and of their beloved in posterity. Finally—and this is clearly part of Prospero's design—prenuptial chastity was a means of learning self-control, so that the mind directed the passions and not vice versa. As with other passions, so with erotic passions, and perhaps the more so, their rule over reason spells trouble. We would, if passions directed us, fear the flies buzzing about our heads, become drunkards, angry avengers of every slight, gluttons for laughter or attention, and so on. We wouldn't be very admirable, self-respecting, or just. Others would have to spend their time and energy cleaning up the messes that we would make, small and large, material and spiritual. We would, in short, be oppressing others. Even the passion that often appears most noble, pity, which moves us to help others, must—as we have seen in the case of Miranda—be regulated by our reasoning if it is to be, as it wishes, genuinely helpful to others. We see Prospero so regulating his passions, and demanding it of his future son-in-law.

How, though, is such regulation to be brought about? For reason is, in truth, a rather weak part of us. Prospero's response to Ferdinand's vow to remain chaste offers the beginning of an answer: "Fairly spoke," he states (4.1.31). Though this is praise, it is fairly weak praise; it could carry the implication "but talk is cheap." The sequel suggests that in fact it does. Prospero asks Ferdinand to speak with Miranda as he speaks with Ariel, in preparation of the spectacle of the "vanity of mine art" that he has promised the couple (4.1.40–41). But as his conversation with Ariel concludes, he turns his eyes back to the young couple:

> Look thou be true; do not give dalliance
> Too much the rein. The strongest oaths are straw
> To th' fire i' th' blood. Be more abstemious,
> Or else good night your vow! (4.1.51–54)

Already the couple's amorous embraces are moving in a sexual direction. Talk is indeed cheap; even vows are weak against sexual passion. And so something more than vows is needed. "No tongue! All eyes! Be silent!" (4.1.59). What Prospero is about to present is better than any exhortation or reasoning could be in bringing about the end, chastity, of which reason approves. Through his monarchic rule of spirits (cf. 4.1.36–41) Prospero will now use them for "such another trick" as the one so well executed with the royal party, in which the heavens or fates were presented as just, repentance called the means to salvation. The couple's own erotic experiences will be re-presented to them within a vision of a larger (imaginative) whole, one that includes divine beings, a vision in which those experiences will be reinterpreted and guided through the exploitation of the poeticizing to which, as we have seen, love naturally inclines.

Prospero had warned that a lack of chastity would result in an unprosperous life, one of "barren hate, sour-ey'd distain, and discord" (cf. 4.1.17–20). To this fearful counsel is now added, not through reason but through art, the more hopeful, golden results of chastity; Prospero will tap into the great and powerful promise of love and all that it causes us to imagine, including the relation of it and ourselves to the world around us. Iris, messenger of Juno (Hera), wife of Jupiter (Zeus), calls on Ceres (Demeter), the goddess of grain or agriculture, to come celebrate a contract of true love and to bring a devotion to the blessed lovers. Ceres isn't sure she wants to come: Venus (Aphrodite) and her son Cupid (Eros) *must be absent*. The reason can perhaps be best appreciated by recollecting a tale told about Aphrodite in the *Odyssey*. So attractive is she, according to that tale, that, when she is caught in flagrante delicto with Ares in a web spun by her cuckolded husband Hephaistos, and made thereby a laughingstock to all the gods who witnessed it, Hermes is moved to remark to Apollo that he would gladly endure such shame to be together with her (*Odyssey* 8.266–369). Aphrodite and her inducements incline one to shamelessness and to deeds that should be the object of just laughter. Here, Ceres reports merely that Venus (Aphrodite) and her creepy son Cupid (Eros) plotted to get her daughter Persephone down into Dis (Hades), succeeding in the end in doing so for half the year. It was all their fault (4.1.60–91).

Iris answers Ceres that the shameless mother and son are not here; they had wanted to be here, and were here earlier (i.e., when Prospero had to warn the amorous couple of passion's strength against vows), but they rode away, in failure (4.1.91–100). The couple's recent chaste victory over their passions is thus incorporated into the apparition they behold. Induced to be engrossed in this manner in the tale, the couple is then shown the entry of Juno (Hera), who has come to offer her blessing of prosperity and honored issue. She and Ceres sing a song about the harvest, the autumn, and the lack of winter, singing of the planting in the spring and the harvest in the fall. Nymphs and Niades are called, as well as harvesters (sicklemen). The whole golden scene is one of nature reproducing things that human beings plant. The moral is that the couple's premarital chastity, their resistance to Eros and

Aphrodite, their true love, will allow them eventually to produce this rich, golden scene. This is the unspoken but clearly intended effect of Prospero's display of his "vanity."

The spectacle is suddenly interrupted, however, by Prospero's remembrance of the minor conspiracy of Caliban. "I had forgot," he exclaims: Caliban and company are plotting against his life. Because of this disconcerting remembrance, and the need to attend to the conspiracy, Ferdinand receives a glimpse of Prospero that the latter never intended, in a state in which Miranda has never before seen him, distempered (4.1.139–162). Prospero, still shaken, explains himself and attempts to reassure Ferdinand, in the most memorable speech of the play:

> You do look, my son, in a mov'd sort,
> As if you were dismay'd; be cheerful, sir.
> Our revels now are ended. These our actors
> (As I foretold you) were all spirits, and
> Are melted into air, into thin air,
> And like the baseless fabric of this vision,
> The cloud-capp'd tow'rs, the gorgeous palaces,
> The solemn temples, the great globe itself,
> Yea, all which it inherit, shall dissolve,
> And like this insubstantial pageant faded
> Leave not a rack behind. We are such stuff
> As dreams are made on; and our little life
> Is rounded with a sleep. Sir, I am vex'd;
> Bear with my weakness, my old brain is troubled.
> Be not disturb'd with my infirmity.
> If you be pleas'd, retire into my cell,
> And there repose. A turn or two I'll walk
> To still my beating mind. (4.1.146–164)

Prospero's injunction to Ferdinand ("Be cheerful") suggests that the cause of Ferdinand's dismay is the loss of the apparition he had created. And it is—but also dismay over Prospero, its creator. Prospero's attempt to comfort Ferdinand is, however, in his agitated state, soon turned into the statement of a truth that he would otherwise have kept to himself. Rather than limit himself to stating that the actors are melted into thin air, he compares the fate of the world to theirs, to the "baseless fabric of this vision." All things, he blurts out, will perish; we are very little, destined in our "little life" to perish like "this insubstantial pageant," and leave "not a rack behind." We invest our lives with a significance that they do not have (and one that visions such as he has conjured sustain). Religion—temples, gods, and so on—will perish, as will political things (towers, palaces, etc.), which hopeful human beings believe to be permanent. Prospero briefly speaks what the focus of his mind's eye ever tells him to be the ultimate end of all things, in their unredeemed and irredeemable nature. He blurts out the sad truth that nothing is to remain.

Catching himself, Prospero is moved immediately to take back or "clarify," as we now say—that is, to explain away—what he has just said. But its truth abides. Prospero has been startled. He had in his grand project not anticipated the conspiracy of Caliban, and having been told of it, had forgotten it. A wise man has forgotten a fortuitous but important development. Startled by the remembrance of it, he has blurted out a truth that he ever remembers but never speaks: the order we perceive in things is by accident, lacking even a design like his own, a mere dream. We die; we did not exist before, and we will return to nothing. So too will all things, however grand and glorious they now seem. The matter of the universe, one might say, is impervious to any human design or hope. And the matter in his "old brain" caused him to forget; his mind could not encompass all things at once. And so, in the middle of his display of his art, he was reminded of the perishability of all things.

★   ★   ★

Prospero now turns his attention to Caliban and company, whom Ariel, as he now reports, has led on a nasty walk through briars and thorns and finally through a filthy pool of stagnant water. "Well done," replies Prospero to the report (4.1.184). His plan now is to catch the conspirators through the allurement of fine clothing on their way to his cell. Before Ariel returns with the clothing Prospero delivers his harshest judgment of the conspirator Caliban:

> A devil, a born devil, on whose nature
> Nurture can never stick; on whom my pains,
> Humanely taken, all, all lost, quite lost;
> And as with age his body uglier grows,
> So his mind cankers. (4.1.188–192)

Caliban seems hopeless, an embodiment of the vain character of all human endeavors. Yet when the three conspirators enter, under the secret watch of Prospero and Ariel, a Caliban cleverer and far greater than Prospero had thought appears. To the threats of a disgruntled and resentful Stephano and Trinculo, Caliban answers with prudent imprecation:

> Good my lord, give me thy favor still.
> Be patient, for the prize I'll bring thee to
> Shall hoodwink this mischance; therefore speak softly,
> All's hush'd as midnight yet. (4.1.204–207)

Stephano is for his part intent upon drinking more liquor and on possessing the clothes, after Trinculo calls them to his attention (4.1.217–223). Caliban exhorts them away from the clothes as "but trash," but Trinculo mocks him as a monster who knows not trash from treasure. Caliban persists: do the murder first. And he fears that with the other two distracted by the clothes, all his planning will be for naught (4.1.2.224–249). Ariel and his spirits, as hunting dogs, then set upon the three, driving them away, but not before Caliban has in this manner unexpectedly passed an unexpected test. As his enemies lie finally at his mercy, Prospero reiterates to Ariel his promise of imminent freedom (4.1.264–266), and will soon manifest a similar disposition toward a repentant Caliban.

Act V

Prospero prepares now for the denouement of his "project," three hours after he raised the tempest (5.1.1–6 with 186). Ariel reports to him that the royal party's members remain prisoners of a strong spell, with Alonso, Sebastian, and Antonio "distracted," and the rest full of sorrow and dismay at them. He singles out Gonzalo, "Him that you term'd, sir, 'the good old Lord Gonzalo,' / His tears runs down his beard like winter's drops / From eaves of reeds" (5.1.15–17). Ariel suspects Prospero's affections would "become tender toward them," were he to behold them, prompting a remarkable exchange.

> *Pros.*   Dost thou think so, spirit?
> *Ari.* Mine would, sir, were I human.
> *Pros.*   And mine shall.
> Hast thou, which art but air, a touch, a feeling
> Of their afflictions, and shall not myself,
> One of their kind, that relish all as sharply
> Passion as they, be kindlier mov'd than thou art?
> Though with their high wrongs I am strook to th' quick,
> Yet, with my nobler reason, 'gainst my fury
> Do I take part. The rarer action is
> In virtue than in vengeance. They being penitent,
> The sole drift of my purpose doth extend
> Not a frown further. Go, release them, Ariel. (5.1.19–30)

As with Ferdinand, so with the royal party, Prospero's pretense to punishment—the pretense spoken by Ariel-as-harpy, the pretense that the Fates had brought vengeance—hid his true purpose. With Ferdinand that purpose had been to make trial of his love, that is, to see if Ferdinand would wish to prove himself deserving of Miranda by acts of self-sacrifice. With the royal party, the purpose had been to induce penitence, that is, a sense of deserving punishment and a wish to correct by self-sacrifice wrongs done to others, in order to right their lives. Prospero professes to feel the offense of their "high wrongs," which have left him for many years on the island with Miranda and Caliban. But he does *not* wish to punish them for their wrongs; his "reason" argues against it, and being directed by what accords with reason is, to Prospero, "virtue." His reason counsels *against* fitting punishment, a giving to them what they deserve; it will stop as soon as they are penitent, that is, just. Yet this means that Prospero would have the royal party guided by the very sense of desert that he himself does not understand to be in accord with reason. In other words, he himself is not guided by the belief in divine justice that he has affirmed in them—a belief affirmed not by any appeal to reason but by the captivation of their imagination. And even the wish to affirm this belief in them is part of his overall "project" that is guided by the good of Miranda (cf. 1.2.16), who is to Prospero, to repeat, "a third of mine self, or that for which I live." So while he, unlike Ariel (and, it would seem, unlike any god or spirit), can feel pity for the royal party, his actions are directed not by it but by his reason, and are therefore of a "rare" virtue.

Prospero now vows to abjure the godlike powers that have permitted him to achieve his ends, powers that he calls his "potent art" and "rough magic." From his description of what he has done with it, the magic appears most potent indeed. He has not only brought about all the parts of the tempest, and "rifted Jove's stout oak / With his own bolt" (5.1.45–46; cf. *King Lear* 3.2.5) just as he liberated Ariel from a pine tree, but has even raised the dead: "Graves at my command / Have wak'd their sleepers, op'd, and let 'em forth / By my so potent art" (5.1.48–50). The pagan magic has permitted him to do what Christianity promises God will do at the last judgment, or what Shakespeare can be said to do when bringing ghosts, or perhaps even characters from the past, upon the stage. But he will break his staff, "Bury it certain fadoms in the earth, / And deeper than did ever plummet sound / I'll drown my book" (5.1.55–57). It is unclear whether he considers the overcoming of death (in others) to be a bad thing—he doesn't tell us what the awakened dead are like, after all—but it is clear that he thinks his potent art must be kept out of the reach of other, lesser men, with which the world abounds (cf. 3.3.32–35). Nature is not to be conquered but, as he is about to indicate, taken as a guide.

The members of the royal party enter the enchanted circle Prospero has drawn on the ground, and are then slowly released from the spell under which they suffer. Addressing each still dazed member of the party in turn, Prospero first weeps tears as he beholds the tears of "Holy Gonzalo, honorable man," whom he promises to reward as his "true preserver, and a loyal

sir / To him thou follow'st" (5.1.62–70). The two parts of Gonzalo's worthy
service—the preserving of Prospero and loyal deed on behalf of Alonso—are
of course at odds with each other, but Prospero clearly could not and does
not expect any more of this "holy" man than what he was in his weakness
able to accomplish on Prospero's behalf. Gonzalo may speak of an imaginary commonwealth, but he was no one to stand up and oppose Alonso's
exile of Prospero. And when assessing Gonzalo's worth in Prospero's eyes,
we must recall in particular that Gonzalo furnished Prospero with beloved
books from his library—that Gonzalo is a friend of, supports, Prospero's
philosophizing.

To Alonso Prospero simply declares that he used Prospero and his daughter "most cruelly." To Alonso's brother Sebastian, "a furtherer in the act," he
states "thou art pinched for it now." Turning to his own brother Antonio,
Prospero cites "nature" against him:

> Flesh and blood,
> You, brother mine, that [entertain'd] ambition,
> Expell'd remorse and nature, whom, with Sebastian
> (Whose inward pinches therefore are most strong),
> Would here have kill'd your king, I do forgive thee,
> Unnatural though thou art. (5.1.75–79)

Prospero distinguishes the affection one naturally has for a brother from
remorse, the activity of one's conscience. He charges Antonio with expel-
ling both and, after forgiving him for what he has done to him, repeats
the charge of his unnaturalness. As we have seen, Prospero realizes that the
activity of the conscience is sustained not by reason's attention to nature
but by the work of the imagination. He finds, on the other hand, that the
natural affections of a man toward a brother as a brother, as one's "own flesh
and blood," provide an inclination that it is reasonable to follow—as is the
affection for one's own children.

Dressing now as the Duke of Milan, Prospero sends Ariel to retrieve the
ship's master and the boatswain, who have been, along with the mariners
and the king's ship itself, magically kept safe and sound. Ariel is gleefully
anticipating his imminent freedom, singing "merrily" of the carefree life he
will have. He thus serves gladly. "Why, that's my dainty Ariel! I shall miss
thee," declares Prospero. "But yet thou shalt have freedom" (5.1.95–96). The
fully harmonious relation between master and slave requires the promise of
freedom to the slave and thus the master's loss of his services. Nature does
not support slavery.

Gonzalo is the first of the men to have his understanding awakened, and
we see that the ordeal he has undergone has dispelled his opinion that the

island is perfect for human habitation. "Some heavenly power guide us / Out of this fearful country" (5.1.105–106). We have seen how dear this old faithful servant is to Prospero. It is therefore a bit surprising that Prospero does not embrace him immediately; he first attends instead to the great business of retrieving his title. He announces himself ("Behold, sir King, / The wronged Duke of Milan, Prospero") and embraces Alonso, not out of affection but so that Alonso can feel that Prospero is real. Alonso, recovering, renounces the Dukedom of Milan and entreats Prospero's pardon (5.1.119). The education of the king has been successful, with the result that Prospero's rule of Milan is restored. He then, and only then, embraces Gonzalo, "noble friend, / ...whose honor cannot / Be measur'd or confin'd" (5.1.120–122). The reason for this procedure becomes clear in the sequel. For after welcoming all as "friends," Prospero warns Sebastian and Antonio in an aside that he could "pluck his Highness' frown upon you / And justify you traitors. At this time / I will tell no tales" (5.1.127–129). And when Sebastian exclaims, expectedly, that "[t]he devil speaks in him," Prospero responds with a simple "No," and then turns to Antonio:

> For you, most wicked sir, whom to call brother
> Would even infect my mouth, I do forgive
> Thy rankest fault—all of them; and require
> My dukedom of thee, which perforce, I know
> Thou must restore. (5.1.130–134)

The dukedom has already been restored to Prospero by Alonso (see also 5.1.168), upon whom the imaginative education in justice has worked. Given the reaction of Sebastian and Antonio to the speech of Ariel-as-Harpy—their manifest lack of remorse—Prospero could not reasonably anticipate (though he may have still hoped for) such success in their cases. He clearly thinks this mundane fear of having their conspiracy disclosed is still needed if they are to be held in check. Whether it will be sufficient to deter future machinations by them is doubtful; Antonio speaks not a word of repentance.

With the first part of his plan thus accomplished, as best it can be, Prospero turns to the second. Alonso announces the death of his son, and Prospero, coyly, the loss of his daughter, speaking in a manner that at first suggests to the desolate Alonso a need to seek in his disconsolate state the help of a goddess (cf. 5.1.187), or (were he a Christian) of Mary Comforter of the Afflicted.

> I rather think
> You have not sought her help, of whose soft grace
> For the like loss I have her sovereign aid,
> And rest myself content. (5.1.141–144)

When Prospero explains the "like loss" as the loss of his daughter, the news moves the reeducated Alonso to wish the couple could have been married and become the future king and queen of Naples. Prospero can then doubly restore his joy by disclosing—after reassuring them that he is indeed Prospero—Ferdinand and Miranda lovingly playing chess in his cell. Alonso fears that this is another "vision of the island," and Sebastian—upon whom the education appears now to have had some effect—proclaims it "a most high miracle." Ferdinand, regretting his curses of what he now calls the "merciful" seas, kneels to the father whom he had thought lost. Alonso wonders if Miranda is the "goddess" who has led them there, but Ferdinand corrects him: she is mortal, but mine by "immortal Providence" (5.1.45–189). Ferdinand's own initial deification of her has been corrected into a faith in divine providence.

After Ferdinand speaks warmly of Prospero, Duke of Milan, his new "second father," Alonso happily calls himself the same to Miranda. "But O, how oddly will it sound that I / Must ask my child forgiveness." Prospero graciously forbids it. "There, sir, stop. / Let us not burthen our remembrances with / A heaviness that's gone" (5.1.197–199). Prospero has no desire to mortify the king, to exploit Alonso's remorse in order to gratify a sense of vengeance. And Gonzalo, too choked with inner tears to speak hitherto, now prays:

Look down, you gods,
And on this couple drop a blessed crown!
For it is you that have chalk'd forth the way
Which brought us hither.

Alonso answers "amen," and to Alonso's call for grief upon those who do not wish the young couple joy, Gonzalo answers "amen" (5.1.201–215). The steadfast piety of Gonzalo, the "holy" Gonzalo, is now also the piety of the king. Prospero's education of him has fully succeeded.

The union of piety and governance for which Gonzalo stands, and which Prospero has now made regnant in the royal party, is made the clearer when Ariel leads in the ship's master and boatswain. Gonzalo reminds everyone of his prophecy of the gallows for the boatswain's "blasphemy" during the tempest—of his hope for punishment of the boatswain for his manifest lack of respect for the king and his men. But there is to be no capital punishment for this capital crime. It is not that words of forgiveness are spoken to the boatswain, by Gonzalo or anyone else. Rather, the boatswain's relating of the wondrous fate of the king's ship and its crew, both safe and sound, moves them all to such amazement that the business of punishment is overlooked or forgotten. "These are not natural events," declares Alonso, and as he hears still more from the boatswain, he declares that "there is in this business more than nature / was ever conduct of" (5.1.227, 243). Throughout the boatswain's speech, Prospero's asides of praise to Ariel—who is eager to hear them—provide the final, strong reminder that the true being to whose providential care thanks are due is Prospero. That in his generosity he does not demand those thanks makes him, of course, a most attractive character. But it should not blind us to the fact that he has committed a blasphemy far more serious than that of the Boatswain, becoming indeed a providential being, though the others reverently pray to the gods. It is true that when Alonso opines that an oracle is needed to "rectify our knowledge" of the events that nature cannot have brought about, Prospero offers himself as a substitute:

> At pick'd leisure,
> Which shall be shortly, single I'll resolve you
> (Which to you shall seem probable) of every
> These happen'd accidents. (5.1.247–250)

But this promise falls considerably short of a pledge to tell the whole truth and nothing but the truth. What will "seem probable" to Alonso will, we must think, accord with the pious education in divine providence that Prospero has given him. The explanation will be given at "pick'd leisure," and Prospero, as we have seen, blurts out the truth only when his mind is distracted by the urgent need to attend to a mortal peril.

★ ★ ★

At Prospero's order Ariel sets out to free Caliban and his two companions from the spell that confines them (5.1.252–253), and the three enter, comically attired in Prospero's clothing, smelling of the swamp, Stephano and Trinculo still drunk. Caliban freely speaks his fear that his master will chastise him, or that he will be "pinched to death," but Prospero, ordering him to go with his two companions to trim his cell, indicates that he will instead pardon him (5.1.262–263, 276, 292–294). Caliban leaves with an expression of remorse for his foolishness:

> Ay, that I will; and I'll be wise hereafter,
> And seek for grace. What a thrice-double ass
> Was I to take this drunkard for a god,
> And worship this dull fool! (5.1.295–298)

He thus departs on friendlier terms with his master than will Ariel, who in the final lines of the play is promised yet again his freedom but told that he will receive it only on the next day, after he has seen to the business of creating perfect weather for their sailing to Naples; doubtless disappointed to have his freedom delayed yet again, he makes no reply. (Given what is said in the Epilogue [4–11] it is even unclear whether Ariel carried out the final order.) A forgiven Caliban will, by contrast, either sail back with the company to Naples, or become king of the island when the rest depart. While Prospero does not speak highly of him, neither does he speak harshly to him, nor with the resignation to his nature that he had previously expressed. Prospero's disposition is best gauged by contrast to that of Antonio, who—in his only lines in Act V—speaks cynically of the marketability of Caliban as a fish (5.1.265–266). Prospero had, we recall, taken pains to educate Caliban, and turned harsh toward him only with the attempted rape of Miranda, and the persistent absence of remorse for it. He had considered him uneducable. He had not allowed for the fact that what he could not teach Caliban directly—deference to his wisdom, and the need for self-control—Caliban might learn from another experience, if he had sufficient freedom and alternative masters for comparison. Prospero seems now to have realized this mistake, and is disposed therefore to forgive Caliban, who for his part now shows remorse. The conspiracy of Caliban against Prospero's life has resulted in the education of both.

Prospero promises the whole company a restful evening that will include

> such discourse as, I not doubt, shall make it
> Go quick away—the story of my life,
> And the particular accidents gone by
> Since I came to this isle. (5.1.304–307)

The company will as it were be treated to the enchanting gospel of Prospero. But however much they will associate the apparently miraculous events with him, he has no intention of becoming a god in their eyes. The political authority that he looks to resume in Milan—a third of his life—will be now a substitute for the magic he has abjured. He hopes first to see the marriage at Naples of Ferdinand and Miranda—another third of his life. And at Milan, "every third thought shall be of my grave" (5.1.312). If, as we have seen, Prospero keeps ever in the back of his mind awareness of the eventual annihilation of not only himself but of the whole world, and if, as Plato's Socrates says, for one who philosophizes truly philosophy is nothing other than the practice of dying and being dead (*Phaedo* 64a), then we may say that Prospero will continue to devote a third of his life to philosophy.

★   ★   ★

The Epilogue to *The Tempest*, spoken by Prospero to the audience in a manner that bends (without breaking) the dramatic illusion, appears to present the poet himself, and so provides a fitting conclusion not only to this play but to the five we have examined. "Now my charms are all o'erthrown, / And what strength I have's mine own, / Which is most faint." (Ep. 1–3) As an aged Prospero has given up his magic, so an aged Shakespeare declares his strength weak (though he wrote two subsequent plays). But after thus announcing the overthrow of his magic, he immediately, and charmingly, alleges magic to be in the possession of the audience:

> Now 'tis true
> I must be here confin'd by you,
> Or sent to Naples. Let me not,
> Since I have my dukedom got,
> And pardon'd the deceiver, dwell
> In this bare island by your spell. (Ep. 3–8)

No longer is the island a dream, or a creation of the poet; as much as Naples it has become real to the audience, whose prisoner the speaker is. But is then the speaker Prospero, or Shakespeare—seeking like Prospero the means to his retirement? The next lines make clear that it is the poet:

> But release me from my bands
> With the help of your good hands.
> Gentle breath of yours my sails
> Must fill, or else my project fails,
> Which was to please. (Ep. 9–13)

The wind of applause will fill his sails for Naples, or rather, it will show that his "project" has been a success, his end met. This means, however, that in truth Shakespeare has the audience in his spell; they have their power to release him only because he has pleased them by enchanting them. His entire purpose, he alleges, was "to please." His capacity to do so is a great power, as great as his understanding of the human soul and its deepest hopes and fears.

But his power is necessarily limited, at the same time, by the opinions and tastes of his audience, and this is a limit that threatens to make him (or any poet who needs applause) a slave of his time, the valet of its morality. That Shakespeare has overcome that threat is suggested by what he says next.

Since he will have failed if he fails to win applause, he must (to guarantee the applause) ask their forgiveness for his crimes:

> Now I want
> Spirits to enforce, art to enchant,
> And my ending is despair,
> Unless I be reliev'd by prayer,
> Which pierces so, that it assaults
> Mercy itself, and frees all faults.
> As you from crimes would pardon'd be,
> Let your indulgence set me free. (Ep. 13–20)

The echo of the Lord's Prayer is unmistakable, but what crimes has Shakespeare committed?

There are at least three possibilities. The first possibility is obvious: drama critics may find this or that conceit of the playwright less than it might have been, this or that line improvable; making a plea for their indulgence cannot hurt his standing with them. The second possibility is only slightly less obvious: Prospero has tampered with nature, and in such a way as to usurp the place of a providential God—though the polytheistic, pagan speeches of the play's characters tend to make this crime more palatable than it would otherwise be to a Christian audience. This points to a third and less obvious possibility: Shakespeare has given some philosophic instruction to some viewers of the play, in an effort to people the world with a few Shakespeares, but at the risk of displeasing the rest of the audience.

We may approach this third possibility by recalling that Prospero's education of the royal party, achieved above all in the Ariel-as-Harpy apparition, was (like Edgar's education of Gloucester in *King Lear*) attempted through a deceit, and that its effectiveness required that it remain a deceit. The royal party did not know that Prospero was, from above, the apparition's creator, nor that it was an apparition. But of Miranda and Ferdinand, the education was achieved through the known or manifest practice of Prospero's art, in the theatrical spectacle of divinities who bless marriage. The latter spectacle was in this respect much more like a play put on by Shakespeare himself than was the former. And while it too was presented as a mere pleasing display for its audience, a "vanity" of Prospero's art (4.1.41), and its immediate effect was indeed an increase in Ferdinand's admiration for Prospero (1.4.118–123), its intention clearly went beyond this. It captivated the minds of its young audience members with the presence of divine beings who could help to explain their desires, affections, thoughts, and actions, and direct their hopes in a salutary way. So has Shakespeare clearly done with his plays; the claim to wish merely to please the audience is false.

But he has also shown us, in the character of Prospero, that what the two young audience members were seeing was *not* the truth, however salutary it may have been for them. And he has gone even beyond this; he has allowed us to hear from a temporarily unmasked Prospero, at the abrupt ending to his performance, the unpleasant truth, which Prospero, in an effort to maintain in his audience salutary but untrue teachings, then attempts to discount ("Sir, I am vex'd; bear with my weakness.").

By this third possibility, Shakespeare's crime is to have openly stated the truth, in some of the most memorable lines in all of his poetry. He is not content to be a slave to the opinions of the majority of his time, a subordinate of its opinions and tastes. He desires something more than simply to please it or even to give it a salutary direction by flattering its deepest but untrue opinions. And so he has rather openly conveyed the truth that runs the risk of rankling the majority—a truth that, as we have seen, caused a tempest in the mind of so impressive a man as King Lear. He does, to be sure, and as we have seen, convey from time to time in his other plays truths that are as unpopular as they are most necessary for the wise direction of our lives. But he usually conveys these truths between the lines. In this play, a most important truth has been conveyed rather clearly to a majority that stands to be repulsed by it, however gratified that majority may be by the rest of the play. He asks forgiveness, then, for having conveyed too clearly the true vision of eternity that he, like his Prospero, never allowed himself to forget. We, however, living in a time characterized by a nature-conquering science and a political life that tends to make us oblivious to that true vision of eternity, cannot but be grateful for this crime.

NOTES

Introduction

1. *Leviathan*, Chapter 15, on the ninth Law of Nature. Emphasis added.
2. See *Leviathan*, Chapter 17, "Why Certain Creatures without Reason, or Speech, Do Nevertheless Live in Society, without Any Coercive Power" (MacPherson, ed., 225–26) with Chapter 13 (185), and Chapter 14, "The End of an Oath" (200).
3. *Leviathan*, Chapter 18 (Macpherson ed., 234) with Chapter 13 (184–85).
4. Richard Kraut, "Are There Natural Rights in Aristotle?" *Review of Metaphysics* XLIX.4 (June 1996), 763. On the difference between ruling and governing, see Harvey C. Mansfield, Jr., "Hobbes and the Science of Indirect Government," *APSR* 65 (March, 1971) 97–110; Clifford Orwin, "On the Sovereign Authorization," *Political Theory* III.1 (February 1975), 26–52; Francis Slade, "Rule as Sovereignty: The Universal and Homogeneous State," *The Truthful and the Good. Essays in Honor of Robert Sokolowski*, John J. Drummond and James G. Hart, eds. (Dordrecht: Kluwer Academic Publishers, 1995), 159–80.
5. *Leviathan*, Chapter 10, "Worth" (MacPherson ed., 151–52).
6. Consider the opinion of the majority in *Casey vs. Planned Parenthood*: "At the heart of liberty is the right to define one's own concept of existence, of meaning, the universe, and of the mystery of human life. Belief about these matters could not define the attributes of personhood were they formed under the compulsion of the State." Compare the opinion of Judge Reinhardt, of the Ninth Circuit Court of Appeals, in *Compassion in Dying v. Washington* (March 6, 1996), and of Judge Minor of the Second Circuit Court of Appeals in *Quill v. Vacco* (April 2, 1996).
7. Allan Bloom, *Shakespeare's Politics*, with Harry V. Jaffa (New York: Basic Books, 1964).
8. John Alvis, *Shakespeare as Political Thinker*, coedited with Thomas G. West (Durham: Carolina Academic Press, 1981). Enlarged second edition published by Intercollegiate Studies Institute (2000).
9. Paul Cantor, *Shakespeare's Rome: Republic and Empire* (Ithaca: Cornell University Press, 1976).
10. Mary Nichols, "Tragedy and Comedy in Shakespeare's Poetic Vision in *The Winter's Tale*," in *Shakespeare's Last Plays*, Travis Curtright and Stephen

Smith, eds. (Lanham, MD: Lexington Press, 2002); and "*The Winter's Tale*: The Triumph of Comedy over Tragedy," *Interpretation: A Journal of Political Philosophy* 9.2–3 (September 1981), 169–90.

11. David Lowenthal, *Shakespeare and the Good Life: Ethics and Politics in Dramatic Form* (Lanham, MD: Rowman and Littlefield, 1997).

12. Leon Craig, *Of Philosophers and Kings: Political Philosophy in Shakespeare's* Macbeth *and* King Lear (Toronto: University of Toronto Press, 2001).

13. Jan H. Blits, *The End of the Ancient Republic: Shakespeare's* Julius Caesar (Lanham, MD: Rowman and Littlefield, 1993); and *The Soul of Athens: Shakespeare's* A Midsummer Night's Dream (Lanham, MD: Lexington Books, 2009).

14. Nasser Behnegar, "The Political and Theological Psychology of Shakespeare's *Measure For Measure*," *Interpretation: A Journal of Political Philosophy* 29.2 (2001–2002), 153–69.

15. Dustin A. Gish and Bernard J. Dobski, *Souls with Longing: Representations of Honor and Love in Shakespeare* (Lanham, MD: Lexington Books, 2011).

1 *Julius Caesar*: The Problem of Classical Republicanism

1. See Aristotle, *Politics*, Book Three, Chapters 12–18.

2. Jan Blits calls attention to Murellus's "non-republican" and even "anti-republican" disposition, but traces it to a subpolitical understanding of Rome and the impending triumph of personal loyalty over political deliberation. *The End of the Ancient Republic: Shakespeare's* Julius Caesar (Lanham, MD: Rowman and Littlefield, 1993), 26–28.

3. For a very helpful examination of the tension between devotional love (of Rome or or of other human beings) and the manly desire for honor (or desire to be the object of devotional love), see Blits, *The End of the Ancient Republic*, 14–19. The present study differs from that of Blits in presenting this conflict as two contradictory sides of justice, incapable of ever being resolved, as Blits suggests they can be, in a tempered or mixed version that is coherent.

4. For an interpretation of the significance and the irony of the allusion to Vergil's poem, see Robert S. Miola, "*Julius Caesar*: Rome Divided," in *Shakespeare's Rome* (Cambridge: Cambridge University Press, 1983), 82–85.

5. A. D. Nuttall argues, convincingly, that the soliloquy is not a "rationalization" in the usual sense of the term, and that the Brutus we see here remains a fundamentally sympathetic, honorable character. *Shakespeare the Thinker* (New Haven: Yale University Press, 2007), 179–84. What I argue is that the speech's reasoning for a preemptive strike is a way for Brutus to hide from himself the deep problem that monarchy (as opposed to tyranny) poses for an honorable man like Brutus.

6. On the stand against oaths, and the two subsequent positions of Brutus in this scene, see the helpful discussion of Blits, *The End of the Ancient Republic*, 44–61. Blits seems to me mistaken, however, to conclude that Brutus's

conception of the general good "lacks a public or republican spirit" (52). Blits arrives at this conclusion by ignoring the public-spirited nature of Brutus's opposition to tyranny in the "It must be by his death" soliloquy, by mistaking Brutus's concern with the conspirator's public reputation as not public-spirited, and by overlooking the fact that there is no "public good" higher than the cultivation of virtue.

7. See Allan Bloom, *Shakespeare's Politics* (New York: Basic Books, 1964). "The plot should have been led by one man who had the qualities of both Brutus and Cassius" (92) and "the failure of the plot can be traced directly to the victory of Brutus's principles over Cassius' prudence" (92, 96; cf. 98). See also Miola, "*Julius Caesar*," 107: "Noble but foolish, [Brutus] admits of no compromise with political necessity."

8. See Bloom, *Shakespeare's Politics*, 96, and the alternative interpretation of Blits, *The End of the Ancient Republic*, 50. The latter, in presenting Brutus's efforts here as aimed at "moral transparency" or as showing the disinterested motive of the deed, must overlook the stated impossibility of killing Caesar's spirit without killing his body, and the persistence of the central problem that this impossibility represents. Blits's argument in fact repeats the play's central problem: he articulates very well that for Brutus virtue must be exercised "for its own sake" or must be "the only good or perhaps even the highest good" (48), but he also argues that for Brutus the "sacrifice of what he holds most dear" is the loss of his beloved Caesar (51), i.e., *not* the loss of virtue. Finally, Blits faults Brutus for failing to recognize that "the necessary" can be "just" (59), but in truth, the necessary *cannot* be just. Brutus is not peculiar in holding that "virtue is voluntary" (47); anyone who distinguishes the just from the unjust must hold this, and deny necessity's sway.

9. For a brief but unusually perspicacious appraisal of Shakespeare's positive presentation of Caesar and his greatness, see Harold Bloom, *Shakespeare: The Invention of the Human* (New York: Riverhead Books, 1998), 106–12. David Lowenthal, taking a markedly different path, nonetheless notes that Shakespeare chose "to keep Caesar's immoralities, illegalities and injustices almost completely out of sight…omitting the whole ugly undercarriage of Caesar's career." *Shakespeare and the Good Life* (Lanham, MD: Rowman and Littlefield, 1997), 133.

10. Lowenthal must dismiss this remarkable difference between Plutarch's and Shakespeare's accounts, and must rely upon what he admits is an "improbable" thesis concerning Caesar's contemplation of a "prolonged period of civil war leading to the ultimate victory of Caesarism," in order to arrive at his conclusion that Caesar is "lacking in justice—that is, in fairness and concern for the common good." This conclusion also requires Lowenthal to accord Caesar an impossible ability to foresee events that took place hundreds of years later, so that Caesar can be seen as "sacrificing all for a regime that would…permit…some of the most corrupt and barbarous rulers the world has ever seen." *Shakespeare and the Good Life*, 145–46 with 120.

11. Miola mistakes Caesar as condemning "*all* attempts to influence his judgment" (*Shakespeare's Rome*, 98; emphasis added).

12. Miola's claim that Caesar, "[i]instead of remaining constant as the northern star,...dies at the hands of his friends" (*Shakespeare's Rome*, 78) misses what this constancy means—that it is in no way affected by what the conspirators do to him. Blits, similarly, finds a contradiction where there is none between this constancy concerning justice and Caesar's indecisiveness about whether to attend the Senate (*The End of the Ancient Republic*, 63). Blits's subsequent claim that Caesar planned all along to go to the Senate and to be assassinated presents this indecisiveness as part of a ruse. Both this subsequent claim—that Caesar arranged his own assassination as part of a plan of deification—and almost all of the particulars adduced to support it, were spelled out 11 years earlier in David Lowenthal's "Shakespeare's Caesar's Plan," *Interpretation, A Journal of Political Philosophy*, vol. 10, no. 2 & 3 (May & September 1982), 223–50.

13. This success is well brought out by T. S. Dorsch, *The Arden* Julius Caesar (London: Cambridge University Press, 1947), lii. Contrast Lowenthal, who calls Brutus's speech "a stiff and weak oration" in *Shakespeare and the Good Life*, 141.

14 A. D. Nuttall calls these four words "the most telling political moment in the history of drama." But like most critics he finds that the words show the plebians to be "witlessly" cheering for Brutus, "babbling mindlessly." *Shakespeare the Thinker*, 174.

15. Bloom, *Shakespeare's Politics*, 100.

16. On the absence in Octavius of the virtues or nobility displayed by republican Romans, see Paul Cantor, *Shakespeare's Rome: Republic and Empire* (Ithaca: Cornell University Press, 1976), 28–30.

2 *Macbeth*: Ambition Driven into Darkness

1 See Raphael Holinshed, *Holinshed's Chronicles of England, Scotland, and Ireland,* 5 (London: J. Johnson, et al., 1808), 268.

2. See ibid.:

Duncan was so soft and gentle of nature, that the people wished the inclinations and manners of these two cousins to have been so tempered and interchangeably bestowed betwixt them, that where the one had too much of clemency, and the other of cruelty, the mean virtue betwixt these two extremities might have reigned by indifferent partition in them both, so should Duncan have proved a worthy king, and Macbeth an excellent captain. The beginning of Duncan's reign was very quiet and peaceable, without any notable trouble; but after it was perceived how negligent he was in punishing offenders, many misruled person took occasion thereof to trouble the peace and quiet state of the common-wealth, by seditious commotions which first had their beginnings in this wise. (265)

Macbeth...set his whole intention to maintain justice, and to punish all enormities and abuses, which had chanced through the feeble and slothful administration of Duncan...Macbeth showing himself thus a most diligent punisher of all injuries and wrongs attempted by any disordered persons within his realm, was accounted the sure defense and buckler of innocent people. (269)

In the beginning of his reign he [Macbeth] accomplished many worthy acts, very profitable to the common-wealth (as ye have heard). (277)

3 The Merchant of Venice: Roman Virtue in a Christian Commercial Republic

1. See, e.g., Allan Bloom, "On Christian and Jew: *The Merchant of Venice*," in *Shakespeare's Politics* (New York: Basic Books, 1964), Chapter 2 (13–34).
2. 3.2.292–296. I wish to thank Thomas Pangle for drawing my attention to this important passage.
3. See *Julius Caesar* 2.1.267–302.
4. Compare Aristotle, *Politics* 1258a1.
5. See Genesis 27.
6. See Genesis 34:30–31, 35:22.
7. Contrast Augustine, Letter 138.
8. 1.3.133–34 with 83–84 and 94–95; and see Aristotle, *Politics* 1258b1–20.
9. Contrast Desdemona's disposition in *Othello* 1.3.252.
10. "Thus conscience does make cowards of us all." *Hamlet* 3.1.318–319.
11. Compare Genesis 27. Launcelot demands to be called "master," but the blind father refuses; Launcelot tries to reveal who he is by asking his father's blessing, rather than hiding who he is in order to receive it; the father expresses mistaken doubt when he feels what he takes to be the son's hairy beard, rather than gaining mistaken confidence through feeling a hairy disguise; and the father comes to believe when the son correctly names his mother, rather than being misled through the mother's deceit of having the son misname himself.
12. See Matthew 10:34–36; Luke 12:51–52.
13. Compare again *Julius Caesar* 2.1.267–302, esp. 274.
14. Contrast again Augustine, Letter 138.
15. Consider, e.g., the parallel words of Brutus in *Julius Caesar* 5.1.59–60.
16. See *Julius Caesar* 4.3.7–8.
17. See *Julius Caesar* 4.3.1–28, 5.5.45–48, and 3.1.33–73.
18. "Daniel" means "God is my judge," and in the Babylonian court Daniel was known as Balthazar. See Daniel 1:7.
19. See Daniel 12:1–3.
20. See *Julius Caesar* 5.5.36–42, 50–52.
21. See ibid., 4.3.30–35. Cf. *Macbeth* 4.3.91–103.

4 King Lear: The Question of Divine Justice

1. On this plan, and its wisdom, see Harry Jaffa, "The Limits of Politics: *King Lear*, Act I, scene i," in *Shakespeare's Politics*, by Allan Bloom, with Harry Jaffa (New York: Basic Books, 1964), 113–145.

2. See Aristophanes, *Plutus* 507–534, and consider Aristotle, *Politics* 1253a30–37, 1253b33–1254a1, 1255b13–15, 1256a30–1256b9, and 1257a33–38; Plato, *Republic* 341c4–c42d7, 369b-372e, and 373d1–2; Plato, *Laws* 676a1–682d1, esp. 680d4–7; *Protagoras* 320c-322b; Lucretius, *De Rerum Natura* V.805–1447; Cicero, *De Republica* I.24–25. And see Leo Strauss, *Socrates and Aristophanes* (Chicago: University of Chicago Press, 1966), 297 and note 98, p. 319; and Wayne Ambler, "Aristotle on Acquisition," *Canadian Journal of Political Science* 17.3 (September 1984), 487–502.

INDEX

Printed and bound by CPI Group (UK) Ltd, Croydon, CR0 4YY